D0730167

Israel FIRST!

The Key to Understanding the BLOOD MOONS, SHEMITAH, Promises to ISRAEL, and the Coming JUBILEE

Gidon ARIEL and Bob O'DELL

Published by
ROOT SOURCE PRESS

ROOT
SOURCE

PRESS

First Edition

Israel FIRST! A Key to Understanding the Blood Moons, Shemitah, Promises to Israel and the Coming Jubilee

Copyright © 2015 by Gidon Ariel and Bob O'Dell

Numerous English translations of the Bible were used in preparing this work. More often than not, the translation was modified by the authors to better reflect the meaning of the original text, the passage's readability, and/or its context in this work. We encourage readers to look up the verses quoted herein in their favorite translation and consider the differences to more deeply appreciate the Word of God.

All rights reserved. No part of this publication may be reproduced, distributed, or transmitted in any form or by any means, including photocopying, recording, or other electronic or mechanical methods, without the prior written permission of the publisher, except in the case of brief quotations embodied in critical reviews and certain other noncommercial uses permitted by copyright law.
Graphs on pages 125 and 126 courtesy of www.ObservationsAndNotes.blogspot.com.

For permission requests, write to the publisher, with the subject
"Attention: Permissions Coordinator," and send to the below address.
Root Source Press
Love of the Land Street #1
Maale Hever, DN Har Hebron 90420 ISRAEL
rspress@root-source.com
www.root-source.com
www.IsraelFIRSTBook.com

Special discounts are available for churches, book clubs, corporations, associations, resellers, trade bookstores, and wholesalers. For details contact the publisher at the above address.

Gidon Ariel and Bob O'Dell are available to speak at your church, fundraiser or special event.

Printed in the United States of America
Cover design, illustrations and layout by Arnulfo and Bituin Aquino
arn.aquino@gmail.com
Publishing Consulting by Mel Cohen of Inspired Authors Press
www.inspiredauthorspress.com

Paperback: 978-965-7738-00-9
eBook   978-965-7738-01-6
ePDF: 978-965-7738-02-3
Hardcover: 978-965-7738-03-0
Audiobook: 978-965-7738-04-7

This publication is designed to provide accurate and authoritative information in regard to the subject matter covered. It is sold with the understanding that the authors or the publisher are not engaged in rendering any type of professional services. If assistance is required, the services of a competent professional should be sought. Effort has been made to verify accurate Internet addresses. The authors and the publisher assume no responsibility for Internet address errors.

1. Judaism 2. Christianity 3. Bible Study 4. Bible Commentary 5. Blood Moons
6. Shemitah 7. Prophecy 8. Israel 9. Current Issues

I. Ariel, Gidon and O'Dell, Bob
II. Israel FIRST! A Key to Understanding the Blood Moons, Shemitah,
Promises to Israel and the Coming Jubilee

To two special people in my life
A woman of faith who believed in me
A man, a believer, who put his faith in me
Thank you, Devra and Bob

G. Ariel

To my father.

B. O'Dell

Acknowledgements

When we set out to write this book together, like with so many projects taken on by two partners, we naturally divided up responsibilities, including writing of the chapters. Every chapter was written by one of us and reviewed by the other (in addition to a small army of others!). And so it happened that I, Gidon, pulled the task of drafting this section of acknowledgements.

This was no chore for me! Saying thank you is one of my favorite pastimes; I guess the day we learned that in kindergarten made a strong impression on me. And recognizing the people who contributed to the book you hold in your hands (or are viewing on your Kindle; or are listening to on your player) is especially enjoyable, because just thinking about these wonderful, helpful people always puts a smile on my face. As I wrote in an email to Bob close to the beginning of our partnership: I am honored to meet people, all are God's representatives on this earth, veritable prophets of a message to me if I can find it, and a possible part of important works when God deems it the proper time.

The harder part of writing acknowledgements is finding a comprehensive list of deserving people and figuring out the best way to present them. The solution I came up with was to review my emails labeled "Bob." The earliest of these was way back in January 2014, not long after Bob and I met. Except that I personally feel that I need to thank some people who helped me way before this book was even dreamed of, laying the foundation for this achievement.

Certainly I must start with my parents, my mother (may she live and be well) and my father (of blessed memory). Their allowing and even encouraging me to search out my own way even if it goes against the stream unquestionably set the foundations of what my life is today and will be until its end.

I think the next category of people I must thank are my friends and leaders from Bnei Akiva of North America, who introduced me to the values of Torah, Israel, Zionism and liberty. More often than not, while I was playing a game with my grade school buddies.

Afterwards chronologically, I remember fondly my years in Netiv Meir high school in Jerusalem and in the Birkat Moshe Hesder yeshiva in Maale Adumim, where those Religious Zionism values were reinforced for nearly a decade. Most impactful were my rabbis Nachum Rabinovitch, Yitzchak Sheilat, Haim Sabato, and Elchanan Samet.

Skipping forward to my "Christian education," I thank my friends for our relationship and in many cases their mentoring: David Decker, Merv and Merla Watson, Christine and Peter Darg, Cheryl Hauer, Becky and Tom Brimmer, Jürgen Bühler, Tim King, Ray and Sharon Sanders, Jim MacKenzie, Wayne Hilsden, David Nekrutman, Josh Reinstein, Rivka Kidron, Faydra Shapiro, Dumisani Washington, David Zwebner, Irene Levy, Victor Styrsky, Doug and Kimra Steckbeck, Tommy Waller, Laurie Cardoza-Moore, Dr. Marvin Wilson, all the people who wrote endorsements for this book, and the hundreds of people who I have just insulted by not mentioning them by name.

Since Bob and I began the journey that is Root Source, we have benefit from the friendship, advice and services of many, including Pam Conners, Avraham Norin, Elisheva Ariel, Gal Hoffman and Tal Ben Moshe, Simon Jackson, Rodan Gordon, Gilad Sugarman and Oshrat Lasry, Reuven Karasik, Ben Fitts and Chris Swann, our first twenty customers, Elana Horwitz, Ken Quinn, Moshe Rothchild, Frank Costenbader, Rita Adams, Steve Hoelscher, Stacey and Kevin Howard, Hank Allen, Eli Lizorkin-Eyzenberg, and the rest of you—you know who you are.

This is the point to mention our wonderful Root Source teachers who are world class innovators with regards to the Jewish mandate to spread the Word of God to the nations. Thanks to all: Rabbi Elan Adler, Dr. Rivkah Adler, Rabbi Yehudah Glick, David Haivri, Rabbi Aryeh Leifert, Avi Lipkin, Rabbi Gedalia Meyer, Rabbi Ken Spiro, and Shimshon Young. I am grateful to the English alphabet too, as otherwise I would not have been able to decide what order to list these phenomenal teachers in!

Our Root Source journey turned into a turbo marathon just as we met Rabbi Tuly Weisz of Israel365.com, and we cannot thank him and his team enough for bringing us to the next level. May God bless you all!

Now we finally come to the present. Our deepest gratitude goes out to the wonderful people without whom this book would not have happened: Mel Cohen, Agnes Hilario, Bituin and Arnulfo Aquino (and Jaron Hezekiah!), Mark Biltz, John Hagee, Mark Hitchcock, Jonathan Cahn (discoverers of and evangelists about Blood Moons and Shemitah), John Bibee, Anne Severance, Eliza Enriquez, Sheenah Freitas, and the authors of our forewords, Mark Biltz and Nena C. Benigno.

We now come almost full circle. I have dedicated this book to my wife Devra, and my friend and partner Bob. They also are, hands down, the two people without whom I would still probably be sweeping the floors somewhere (I still do that, but not for a salary). To paraphrase Rabbi Akiva who wrote about his wife Rachel to his students: Yours and mine—is theirs.

I said almost full circle, because I must thank you, dear reader, for believing in us. We created this book for you, and we hope that the ideas herein will spread worldwide.

And finally, we thank God, who powers us and empowers us. Thank you and bless You, Lord our God, King of the universe, who has kept us alive, and sustained us, and enabled us to reach this glorious time.

Gidon Ariel   **Bob O'Dell**
Hebron, Judea, Israel   Austin, Texas

August 2015

Jerusalem, 12 August, 2015
27 Av, 5775

Mr. Gidon Ariel
Founder and CEO of Root Source

Dear friend,

I was glad to hear about the publishing of your new book, "Israel First!" co-written with Bob O'Dell, that offers a thorough examination of the Tanakh and its continued relevance in our time.

Your dedicated efforts throughout the years to deepen the ties with the Christian community around the world through the establishment of an international joint learning site as well as through this book are worthy of the highest esteem. The support that Christian communities lend to the state of Israel is vital to Israel's public diplomacy in particular and to the future of the country in general. An in-depth Tanakh-based study strengthens these relations.

I wish you many more years of fruitful and fulfilling work.

Sincerely,

M.K. Yuli Yoel Edelstein
Speaker of the Knesset

9

Minister of Science, Technology & Space

August 10, 2015
sar103

Dear Friends,

The State of Israel is proud to advance values and technological innovations that serve as a light unto the nations in a variety of ways. As the Minister of Science, Technology and Space I find it to be a great honor to oversee so many of these initiatives.

I know that millions of our Christian friends watch the news from our region with a Bible in their hand, as they follow the amazing rebirth of the Jewish people in our historic homeland.

My friend Gidon Ariel, who is a long-time activist in the field of Christian Zionism, has shared with me his latest endeavor: his book explaining Biblical prophecy and how important it is to support Israel in our days. I found this book makes an important contribution to the study of this topic. One might not agree with all of Gideon's conclusions, but we can all agree that the Jewish people are extremely fortunate – and even blessed – to have such good friends around the world.

Blessings from Jerusalem,

MK Danny Danon
Minister of Science, Technology and Space

Endorsements

"The discussion of Israel is always highly complex, theologically, religiously, and politically. It can promote feelings of love–and feelings of hatred. I write as one who spends his life in the Middle East working in Iraq, Jordan and Israel. I see that the Middle East is at the heart of God's plans and purposes. Unlike most people, I ardently love both the Jews and the Arabs and refuse to see that just one side is right.

Amidst this entire dilemma is the Land of The Holy One, that has such a profound effect on Jewish, Christian and Muslim communities. *Israel FIRST!* covers top-of-mind points of discussion amongst much of the evangelical Christian community. It deals in depth with so many of the issues which challenge the church today: the Blood Moons, the Shemitah year, and the Messianic age. Here is a unique book written by two unique people, an Orthodox Israeli Jew and an American Evangelical Christian. From them you will get answers to your many questions. Enjoy this outstanding book!"

THE REVEREND CANON DR. ANDREW WHITE
President of the Foundation for Relief and
Reconciliation in the Middle East
www.frrme.org

"Bob O'Dell and Gidon Ariel raise critical questions and give solid answers on topics long hidden, but recently brought to light. I hope the biblical viewpoints presented in *Israel FIRST!* will garner greater support for their Root Source work in educating all who pick it up to read. This book stimulates areas of concern for all of us, and provokes us to deeper thoughts. Everyone owes it to themselves to read *Israel FIRST!* What makes it so special is that it is a joint effort by an evangelical Christian and an Orthodox Israeli Jew. Every lover of the Scriptures interested in the future of man should have this information and can do no better than to begin with this book."

SHARON K. SANDERS
Co-Founder & Director, Christian Friends of Israel-Jerusalem
www.cfijerusalem.org

"Having been privileged to introduce my good friends Gidon Ariel and Bob O'Dell to one another on our annual Jewish-Christian prayer walk on the Old City walls, now their new book takes reconciliation between Christians and Jews to a whole new level! I believe we are living in days prophesied in the Book of Daniel that "words are rolled up and sealed until the time of the end." Besides the meaty content, *Israel FIRST!* truly breaks new ground as a prophecy book written jointly by an

Orthodox Israeli and an evangelical Christian. Now that's truly prophetic within itself! Hallelu-Yah!"

CHRISTINE DARG
Founder, The Jerusalem Channel
www.jerusalemchannel.tv

"This is a very welcomed, scholarly project that will no doubt strengthen Jewish-Christian relations, in times when both respective groups are being marginalized. It is of no surprise that such an initiative is birthed out of Israel and brought into the world by those who love God's Land and His People. I cannot recommend this work highly enough. I too look forward to times of spiritual enrichment through the study of this material."

FATHER GABRIEL NADDAF
Spiritual leader, Israeli Christian Recruitment Forum
and Head of the Christian Empowerment Council
www.goo.gl/va8Pbg

"The book by Gidon Ariel and Bob O'Dell "Israel First" is an adventurous nonfiction attempt at explaining current events in light of Biblical prophecy. This book is about our world and our days, but it goes from news broadcasts to ancient Scriptures, giving hope and education to Christians who want to discern the times. I like this book because it has elements of Judaism, the Bible, action and adventure in it. A book which makes the Bible relevant by connecting Jewish and Christian beliefs is to be lauded."

DR. SUSANNA KOKKONEN
Director, Christian Friends of Yad Vashem
Christian.friends@yadvashem.org.il

"We are facing tumultuous times globally. Those whose faith rests in the G-d of Israel, and in His promises to us, are taking note of the unprecedented events converging in Jerusalem this year; namely, the occasion of the Fall Feasts - with their deep and significant themes of Repentance, Redemption and Rejoicing, the culmination of the astonishing tetrad sequence of Red or Blood Moons, the 7 year cycle of the Shemitah year and the 50 year Jubilee celebration. Does this mean anything?

My husband, Dr. Dwight A. Pryor (z"l, of blessed memory), used to point out that G-d is a covenantal and "coming down" G-d. He seeks intimate relationship and active participation with His people and with all of Creation. G-d has challenged us, Bible-believing Jews and Christians together, with the task of carrying forward His vision for human history.

This requires that we be aware of "the signs of the times."

Gidon Ariel and Bob O'Dell, in their book *Israel FIRST!* have provided an excellent tool to help one acquire a clear, balanced, and grounded understanding of key and relevant issues. Read the book and be informed regarding the scientific, historic and biblically prophetic aspects of this pivotal season of history."

KEREN HANNAH PRYOR
Author, A Taste of Torah; A Dash of Drash
www.His-Israel.com

"If Christians desire to truly understand the Scriptures, then a paradigm shift must take place. True Biblical understanding can only be found from the perspective of *Israel FIRST!* Many Christians are suddenly enthralled by the Blood Moons, the Shemitah year, covenant promises to Israel and the Year of Jubilee. Yet without a Hebraic insight and perspective, published information regarding these events is rife with misinterpretation and speculation. This is the very reason Gidon Ariel and Bob O'Dell's teachings are a must for any and all truth seekers."

REV. GARY CRISTOFARO
Director of Development
Ezra International, www.ezrainternational.org

"Gidon Ariel is a man driven by a vision – to ignite relationships between Jews and Christians, and to lead a dynamic partnership into the coming period of redemption. He is a man committed to the land of Israel, and one who believes with all his heart that the key to the future lies in an unbreakable partnership between Jews and Christians. With incurable optimism, unquenchable enthusiasm and determined faith he has followed this dream, at much personal cost. We admire Gidon for his passion and his persistence in this task he feels laid upon him by the Almighty. We pray that this prophetic new partnership will lead to healing of old wounds, strengthening of ties between Jews and Christians, and blessing for Israel and the church."

DAVID AND LESLEY RICHARDSON
Mount Zion Fellowship Jerusalem
Co-authors, The Hand That Writes the Love Song
(Also Holds a Gun)

"If you love the God of Israel, sit down with Gidon and Bob to experience the insights of *Israel FIRST!* As a Bible teacher and frequent traveler to the Holy Land, my great privilege is helping Christians better understand the Jewish roots of their faith. As a radio host, I strive to share the powerful truth of today's Holy Land with American listeners.

Israel FIRST! helps me do both of those things. Followers of Jesus who join Gidon and Bob on this journey will better understand their Savior and their Bible. If you need to be encouraged, educated, or enlightened, read Israel FIRST!"

TREY GRAHAM
Pastor, Author, Radio Host, www.TreyGraham.com

"Bob O'Dell's research and insights are refreshing and unique. Rather than connecting the dots between the Shemitah year, Blood Moons, and other phenomena, and laying claim to a particular outcome as some have done, Bob educates, raises questions, and offers understandings that are thoughtful and valuable. Working together with Gidon Ariel, they bring something unique to the table as far as understanding these and other issues that are important to us all: as Jews, Christians, and certainly Israelis and those who care about Israel, and the rest of the world.

"I have had the privilege to get to know both Bob and Gidon and discuss these and other issues with them in person. For those who haven't had that opportunity, Israel FIRST! ought to be a required read to experience their insights as close to first hand as possible."

JONATHAN FELDSTEIN
Director, Heart to Heart
www.saving-lives-in-israel.org
firstpersonisrael@gmail.com

"This is a crucial book for these times—times when Israel is being ostracized not just by western governments but also by many Christians. For hundreds of years, to the detriment of Western civilization, the Hebrew Bible has been neglected and viewed by many as only a precursor, a story, irrelevant or passé. These studies will prove that the treasures found in our Bible are as vital and relevant today as they were thousands of years ago. This scrupulously researched material is not only fascinating—it will also advocate for the timeless necessity of the Bible in a changing world."

KAY WILSON
Israeli tour guide (specialization in Jesus of Nazareth and Second Temple Judaism) and terror survivor
www.letmypeoplegiggle.com

"We are entering into a dynamic revolution, and this book is part of it.
"As the prophecy of Isaiah 2 states: "His Teaching will go out from Zion, the Word of the Lord from Jerusalem..." This is becoming the reality of our generation.

"We are entering into a new era, where Jews and Christians are studying and searching the Scriptures together.

"Our Jewish brothers have been studying the Torah for more than three millennia and have a deeper understanding of the mind of our Father.

"Bob and Gidon are a perfect example of these phenomena. You will never think the same way after reading this book."

MARTIN AND NATHALIE BLACKHAM
Presenters of In The Last Days TV Programme
www.inthelastdays.com

"In a ground-breaking effort, Gidon Ariel and Bob O'Dell have literally bridged the Testaments to build a framework upon which to build wisdom for the coming years. They have pulled together both Judaic and Christian sources to intelligently bring the messages together in a coherent and timely report for our generation."

J. DAVID PITCHER, JR., MD
Author, After the Rapture and the Oldest Midrash.
The Identity of the Messiah
www.amazon.com/After-Rapture-J-David-
Pitcher/dp/088270916X

"As the guardians of the Judeo-Christian ethic, Christians and Jews must be encouraged to strengthen their alliance. Gidon Ariel's work in this arena has been most impactful. Through the launching of www.Root-Source.com and the publication of Israel FIRST!, Gidon & Bob O'Dell have added valuable tools to help all people of faith combat the negative elements within our culture. Get involved, become their student and read this book."

ELIE PIEPRZ
Director of International Affairs for the YESHA Council

"How good it is for brothers to dwell together in unity!

It is wonderful to see a book written by a Christian and a Jew together.

We have so much in common, and as a Christian, I am so thankful to the Jewish community for keeping the Scriptures pure.

We owe so much to the Jews! It is great that in this time of trial in the world today, Christians and Jews can stand side by side guarding each others backs."

This book will be an insight and a blessing to everyone who reads it."

PAUL CALVERT, *Focus on Israel Radio*
www.facebook.com/focusonisrael.radio

"I grew up in a Christian family in Germany and read the Bible every day. My greatest desire was to understand the real meaning of the Bible. I tried to compare different German and English translations. But it didn't help to understand better; it just confused me even more. Only when I started to study Hebrew and read the Jewish commentaries did I finally learn the deeper meaning of the Bible. I thank Gidon Ariel for teaching me Hebrew and giving me deep insight into the Jewish traditions of the Bible.

If you want to finally understand your Bible the way it was meant to be understood when it was written, I highly recommend this book."

ANDREAS BOLDT, Israel advocate
boasinfo.wordpress.com, www.facebook.com/Freunde.Israels

"As the founders of Root Source, Gidon Ariel and Bob O'Dell are making history as a Jew and Christian who have teamed up to provide Christians around the world with access to top notch Israeli teachers. Their new book Israel FIRST! outlines their exciting vision through a fascinating discussion of the Blood Moons, Shemitah, the Jubilee Year and Genesis 12:3. If you really want to understand how each and every one of us can play a part in God's plan, I highly recommend reading Israel FIRST!"

RABBI TULY WEISZ
Founder and Director, Israel365.com

Foreword

Thank you Root Source for bringing awareness to God's signs in the heavens, emphasizing the need to be on God's calendar, and highlighting Israel as the focal point of history.

From the beginning, when I originally made the discovery of the four Blood Moons and their related solar eclipses with their historical significance of falling on the Biblical holy days, I prayed and asked that others would bring more things to light on the subject. Bob and Gidon are bringing out their perspective, which is always greatly appreciated as we are all searching for truth. None of us have all the answers and we all need each other's insight.

While we may not totally agree on all the details, we totally agree that when it comes to global events, Israel is the apple of God's eye and Jerusalem is becoming the cup of trembling for all nations. There is no way prophecy can be properly understood without seeing the importance of the Jewish Roots of Christianity and the role it still plays today.

Thank you Root Source for being at the forefront with other organizations that are building bridges between the Jewish and Christian communities that respect each others' faiths without trying to change them.

Blessings!

~ PASTOR MARK BILTZ
*Author of Blood Moons: Decoding
the Imminent Heavenly Signs
Founder, El Shaddai Ministries*

✡ ✡ ✡

Whenever God does great, amazing things on planet Earth, he sometimes calls on the most unlikely people from the farthest places to witness the event. He drew forth Abraham from Ur (modern day Iraq) to watch as He marked out the scope and boundaries of the Promised Land he was to inherit. He called three Magi from the East to come and discover the Christ child under the Bethlehem star. Now, as the end of the age looms, the Blood Moons rise and the Jubilee Shemitah unfolds, many witnesses from many nations are rising up to behold and ponder the signs of the times in the distant horizon.

No two witnesses could be more unlikely, yet more fitting, more astride the times and more deeply insightful than the co-authors of this book, Israel FIRST! They are Gidon Ariel, an Orthodox Jew from Israel, and Bob O'Dell, an evangelical Christian engineer from the United States. Gidon draws from deep wells of wisdom from the Root Source, the God-ordained family line of Abraham, Isaac, and Jacob and the Bible that chronicles their history and faith. Bob drinks from the overflowing waters of that Source as one grafted into the Jewish heritage through Yeshua HaMashiach, Jesus Christ, the Christian Messiah.

Gidon and Bob's rare, combined insights are culled from the prophecies in the Torah; the hidden and accurate meanings of Hebrew words; the history of Israel and the Jewish people; and the revelations that come from the whisperings of the Spirit within. Most significantly, the moving power behind this whole work is hope, love, and prayer—love for the God of Israel, hope for this final generation of humankind so desperate to understand the signs of the times, and prayer for the direction in which the world is going.

It is therefore with great excitement that we look forward to the success of Israel FIRST!, a landmark project that is both historic and prophetic. It is the fruit of the labors of Gidon Ariel, a Jewish brother who has graciously and effectively bridged the gap between Christians and Jews for many years; and Bob O'Dell, a Christian author who has original and arresting insights into the Blood Moons, the Jubilee Shemitah and other signs of the end of our age that uniquely draw from the timeline of Jewish history and the wisdom of the Torah. It is probably the most significant and insightful book on these apocalyptic times that one will find anywhere. And the most reassuring.

This is a book whose perfect time has come. Christians refer to this authorship tandem as one new man, Jew and Gentile together preparing the nations for the coming of Messiah. For its Jewish author, this partly fulfills the call to the people of Israel to be a Light to the Nations, especially in this time of deep, gathering darkness.

These are also opportune, apocalyptic times for the Philippines, the United States, and Israel. As kindred Bible believers, we now look to the skies together in anticipation of the arrival of the Messiah; we pray for the peace of Jerusalem; and we stand as Watchmen on the Wall as Jerusalem begins to take its place as the Center of the Nations, the City of the Great King, the eternal capital of the living God. We are the cord of three strands that twine more tightly together as the world spins seemingly out of control.

Filipinos have long felt a deep kinship with Israel and the Jewish people. The Jews gave us the Bible that set us apart as the first Christian nation in Asia more than four centuries ago. Our nations are both tiny islands of faith, People of the Book, in regions dominated by Islam and other religions. We have long looked towards Israel, the Jewish people and the Scriptures to define our destiny, our identity, and our past. Now we look towards them once again, for a glimpse of the future.

The fact that I, a Filipina, am writing this foreword speaks even more about the heart and purpose of this book. I, too, am an unlikely witness from a distant land. I work with the Christian Broadcasting Network Asia (CBN Asia) and The 700 Club Asia TV show, established in the Philippines by two passionate American evangelical Christian supporters of Israel—CBN founders Pat Robertson and his son Gordon. Our country, the Philippines, has a long history of providing refuge for the Jews. We took in Jewish voyagers fleeing the Spanish Inquisition; we were the only nation that opened its doors to Jewish refugees fleeing the Holocaust from 1938 to 1941; and we were the only Asian nation to vote for the rebirth of the state of Israel at the United Nations plebiscite in Flushing Meadows, New York in 1947.

We have long loved, revered, and sought to bless our Root Source, the God of Israel, the nation he calls his Firstborn, his Treasure, the Apple of His Eye. We have been recipients of Israel's legacy of freedom and faith as the People of the Book. We were the first Bible-believing Christian nation in Asia and its first democracy. As a people, we have also been scattered among the nations, but are now returning as the times of restoration have come.

What Israel FIRST! provides is the fulcrum, the focus, the Alpha and Omega of all that is happening around us. All roads lead to Israel. It is where history begins and ends. And begins again, forevermore. Do read this to the last page. And look to the skies with expectation.

This book will be a beacon of light in the chaos, hatred and fear that mark our age, and point us to that great light in the horizon, the Desire of Nations, the coming of the one that the prophet Isaiah called "Wonderful Counselor, Mighty God, Eternal Father, Prince of Peace. Of the greatness of His government and peace, there will be no end." (Isaiah 9:6-7). As a mass media practitioner, I highly recommend that we not just get a copy of Israel FIRST! but conscientiously proclaim its message to a confused and fearful world. The best is yet to come. It all begins and ends in Israel.

~ **NENA C. BENIGNO**
Watchman, Jerusalem East Gate
Prayer Watch; Author
and Senior Writer - CBN Asia,
The 700 Club Asia, and
Asian Center for Missions

Table of CONTENTS

CHAPTER 1

Introduction

Never before have so many Christians felt so much foreboding about the future. And if you ask them about what time period they are most concerned, the consensus of opinion is: "Right now!"

Why? Consider the following signs and issues we face:

Signs in the Heavens
- o The fourth and final Blood Moon, appearing on September 28, 2015
- o The *Shemitah*, or Sabbath Rest Year, that ends on September 13, 2015

Concerns about Islamic Conflict
- o The rise of the Islamic State (ISIS/ISIL) in Iraq and Syria
- o The escalation of militant Islam and random jihadist attacks in Western nations
- o The Iran Nuclear Agreement, which was signed on July 14, 2015, and could lead to an arms race, and even war, in the Middle East

Issues concerning Israel
- o The rise in anti-Semitism and anti-Israel sentiment, including the Boycott, Divest and Sanction (BDS) movement
- o The tense relationship between President Barack Obama and Israeli Prime Minister Benjamin Netanyahu
- o The concern among Christians that the United States may turn against Israel and bring upon it the curses described in Genesis 12:3: "I will bless those that bless thee, and the one who curses you I will curse."

Degrading Morals
- o Rampant materialism
- o Prevailing sexual sin in all its various forms
- o The passage of same-sex marriage laws in twenty-one countries, including the United States on June 26, 2015

Economic Issues
- o The weakest economic recovery in the modern era, averaging

only 2 percent yearly growth in most modern nations
- o Slowing growth in China with a major drop in its stock market
- o Lack of wage growth among workers in most modern nations
- o The long U.S. stock market rally of almost seven years, with many feeling that a correction is overdue

Social Issues
- o Sharp divide between social groups within communities along the lines of race, economic status, or political agenda

In this book we will present our findings, based on biblical viewpoints, regarding four related phenomena: the Blood Moons, the Shemitah (Sabbath Rest Year), Promises to Israel, and the Year of Jubilee. Some of this material is not pleasant to read, but know this:

While we expect God to intercede in history, and difficult days are coming, this is not simply a book that predicts bad news. As a matter of fact, the good news we cover is much more than a silver lining beneath the dark cloud.

God works in and through the events of history to bring about His redemptive process on earth. The news is not all bad, because Almighty God is in control. As you learn to distinguish the various ways in which God intervenes in history, we hope you will find yourself walking more confidently than ever, without fear, and that you will find new ways to be a blessing to others in the days ahead.

What is the basis of our insights? They derive from this one fundamental idea:

To truly understand the history and the future of mankind, you have to first view everything through the lens of Israel and the Jewish people.

That is why we entitled this book:

ISRAEL FIRST!
The Key to Understanding the Blood Moons, Shemitah, Promises to Israel, and the Coming Jubilee

It is not that we believe in emphasizing the importance of any one nation over another. God loves all people, all nations, and He is intimately and lovingly concerned with the affairs of all mankind.

However, we believe the key to understanding—and therefore predicting—His plans on earth starts with a perspective that puts Israel at the center of all nations.

In the years since Constantine and the formalization of the Christian Church, a belief began to seep in, and then set in, that the Scriptures of the Old Testament referring to Israel should be understood allegorically rather than literally, since God had forsaken the Jews because of their role in the death of Jesus Christ. However, starting in the 1600s, and then accelerating in the 1800s and 1900s, there was a growing realization that the Old and New Testaments both affirm God's promises to Israel as a People, Land, and Nation— and God's promises are irrevocable. The re-emergence of Israel as a nation in 1948 swung opinion even more in that direction. Yet even today, "Replacement Theology" continues to be firmly entrenched in some Christian quarters. Israeli Jews are broadly thankful for these Christians who stand against Replacement Theology, and this book would not be possible without the softening of hearts of both Jews and Christians alike. This is good news.

We would add that if Christians would take one more step forward—not just stand against Replacement Theology, allowing Israel the right to exist—but humble their perspective enough to recognize Israel to be at the center of God's plans, then suddenly many more prophetic pieces will start to fall into place more naturally and easily than ever before.

We invite you to join us on this fascinating journey!

WHAT TO EXPECT

In this book we will weave together for you a complete and comprehensive view of:

- **Blood Moons**
  - o The current Blood Moon Tetrad began in 2014 and concludes on September 28, 2015.
  - o The importance of this tetrad and of Blood Moons in general is immense. Their impact can be instantaneous—or can take many years to unfold.
  - o History shows the Blood Moons to be extremely beneficial to Israel, but not so good for the most powerful nations of the day such as the United States.

- **Shemitah**
  - o Also called the Sabbath Rest Year, the Shemitah ends on September 13, 2015.
  - o Shemitah teachings to date indicate when God might act but not exactly what He will do.
  - o We introduce a new Biblical model that predicts the what—passages which accurately predicted the seven year cycle that began in 2001, the seven year cycle beginning 2008, and the surprising predictions for the next seven years beginning in 2015, and more.
  - o We will explain why the Shemitah is so powerful worldwide, and why abortion and gay marriage were enacted during the Shemitah, and how and when God might respond.

- **Promises to Israel from Genesis 12:3: "I will bless them that bless thee, and the one who curses you I will curse."**
  - o The blessings and curses God spoke over Abraham (and Israel) are still in full force today.
  - o These blessings and curses can occur anytime.
  - o We will show that God levied a Genesis 12:3 curse upon the U.S. in 1929, ushering in the Great Depression, and how that very same curse was later broken.
  - o We will explain how a U.S. President could trigger another Genesis 12:3 curse today.

- **The Coming Jubilee**
  - o We will explain why a new Jubilee year begins in the fall of 2015 through fall of 2016.
  - o Jubilee years are extremely important for the Land of Israel, and we will tell you what powerful changes to watch for during the next 12 months.
  - o We will reveal that Christians have an amazing, once-in-a-lifetime opportunity to join in God's Jubilee year, not only by supporting Israel, but by proclaiming freedom in their own nations as well.

In each case, as we explain how the Blood Moons, Shemitah, Genesis 12:3, and Jubilee all work, you will see the following common themes:

- Each of the four effects works very differently from the others.

- Each of the four effects can be understood best by looking at its Jewish roots.

- Each of the four effects should be examined through the lens of Israel first, and then to see what patterns ripple out to encompass the entire world.

- Each of the four effects can yield both blessings and troubles.

WHO ARE THE AUTHORS?

This book is quite unusual in that it is a cooperative effort of Gidon Ariel (an Orthodox Jew) and Bob O'Dell (an evangelical Christian). In the process of developing and revealing their Blood Moons perspective to tens of thousands of Christians worldwide, what fascinated them was the striking alignment of the Jewish and Christian conclusions reached in this book concerning Israel

Bob O'Dell (left) and Gidon Ariel at the National Religious Broadcasters Conference in 2014, prior to the founding of Root Source.

and the rest of the world. Regarding the future, the concept of Messiah is central to Jewish belief. While Jews and Christians may not agree on the Messiah's identity, they are in full agreement that the Messiah is coming and worthy of eager anticipation.

Because this book is written for Christians, Gidon has given Bob complete freedom to write his chapters in a way that fully proclaims Jesus as the Messiah, so no Christian teaching was watered down. Naturally, such passages are Bob's work and not Gidon's. Similarly, passages that describe the traditional Jewish perspective which are not in line with Christian theology are Gidon's alone. So, while this book might ruffle some feathers on both sides of the religious aisle, it advances the building of bridges between these two related faiths.

GIDON ARIEL

Gidon Ariel is the co-founder and CEO of Root Source. Gidon made Aliyah (return to the Holy Land) to Israel in 1978 at age 14, and spent close to a decade in advanced Jewish studies institutes (*Yeshivas*) and the Israel Defense Forces (IDF). Raised as an Orthodox Jew and still an observant Jew, Gidon has kept Jewish traditions his entire life. Quite unexpectedly, in 2005, he felt a personal call from *Hashem* (God) to begin to reach out to Christians in friendship and to bless and educate them about Jewish life, thought, and insights about Hebrew Scriptures. After spending a lot of time working with Christian individuals and organizations in Israel and around the world, Gidon came to see that the Jewish concern about getting "too friendly with Christians" is largely unfounded. He sees God calling upon Jews and Christians to come together in relationships, and to find ways to work together based on the truth of the Bible. Gidon still serves in the IDF reserves as a Captain in the Military Spokesperson's Office after spending over 20 years in the Armored Tank Corps. Besides being CEO of Root Source, Gidon teaches Jewish Prayer and the Leadership of Moses on Root Source. He can be reached at **gidon@root-source.com** or through **www.root-source.com.**

BOB O'DELL

Bob O'Dell is a non-Jewish Christian, former high-tech executive with Motorola and Wintegra. He has worked with Israeli Jews for over 25 years, visiting Israel frequently since 1990. Bob founded Root Source with Gidon Ariel to promote Gidon's vision of Israeli Jews teaching Christians worldwide. Bob has been changed—and his perspective of his Jewish roots has changed—through direct contact with Israeli Jews such as Gidon and other Root Source teachers and their study of the Hebrew Scriptures. An astronomy enthusiast for more than 35 years, Bob was the first to reveal that the March 20, 2015 Total Solar Eclipse shadow would cross the North Pole for two minutes at sunrise on the first day of spring for the first time in 100,000 years. Gidon and Bob jointly called for a worldwide two minutes of prayer that "the earth would be full of the knowledge of the Lord as the waters cover the sea" (Isa.11:9). Bob attends an evangelical church in Austin, Texas. He sees Jewish teaching as a way of enriching his understanding of his own Christianity. He can be reached at **bob@root-source.com** or through **www.root-source.com.**

✡ ✡ ✡

I made the decision a long time ago that I, Bob, did not want any proceeds from the selling of any Blood Moons media—books, videos, and the like. However, there is an Israeli organization that you blessed when you purchased this book: Root Source. I care deeply about the Israeli Jewish teachers who are doing something ground-breaking, exciting, and unique, and my Christian faith has been enriched from this experience.

Gidon, my partner in Root Source, said to me in early 2015, "I think you should teach the Blood Moons on Root Source."

"But wait," I argued, "this is a Jewish teaching website—Jews teaching

Christians."

"You're a Christian; teach Christians," he replied. "Do ̣
thing; teach it in your way."

I was encouraged that he trusted me enough to position my Christia ̣.
teachings side-by-side with Jewish teachings. In the end we made that
lesson series a bonus channel, to distinguish it from the regular Jewish
channels. Similarly, you would not be reading this book today without a
decision Gidon made in the summer of 2015, surprising me again—that we
write this book together as part of Root Source.

WHAT IS ROOT SOURCE?

Today, more and more Christians and Jews are hearing a divine
wake-up call to engage with each other.

Root Source is answering that call. In an informal and loving manner,
scholarly Orthodox Israeli Jews teach Christians around the world
online about Jewish concepts, ideas, and thought, to help Christians
understand the roots of their faith.

Root Source enables and encourages dialogue and relationships
between Christians and Jews, and empowers Christians to learn like
Jews have been learning for centuries. Our Israeli Jewish teachers
respect the identity and faith of their Christian students.

Root Source gives Christians access to world-class Jewish biblical
teaching online, helping you learn deeper truths and reach higher in
your Christian faith, with the opportunity to ask any question openly.

Our members are often surprised at how quickly they can learn
deeper biblical truths from Orthodox Jewish teachings and practically
apply those teachings to their own Christian faith.

Current courses cover topics such as:
  o Jewish Prayer
  o Jewish History and Future
  o Biblical Hebrew
  o Women of the Bible
  o Leadership of Moses
  o Solomon's Proverbs
  o Jewish Ethics
  o Land of Israel
  o The Deceptions of Islam
  o The Holy Temple
  o Names and Images of God
  o Blood Moons, and more

Learn more at
www.root-source.com

Section ONE:

BLOOD MOONS

CHAPTER 2

Blood Moons Basics

The discussion of Blood Moons is one of the most interesting and controversial topics that have ever taken hold of the Christian community. Our goal in discussing Blood Moons is not to convince you of our view, but to give you enough knowledge and information so you can decide for yourself—or, at least, ask the right questions.

Jews often say, "A good question can be far more valuable than a good answer."

I (Bob) live in Austin, Texas. When people ask me, "Where is Austin?" I often reply, "Four hours south of Dallas," or "Three hours west of Houston, depending on how fast you drive." That is a Texas-centric answer. But it's possible to answer this question from a different perspective: "Go to the geographic center of the Continental United States, turn south, and you will run right into Austin."

I don't think I've ever answered that question in that way, and I don't think I've ever heard anyone else answer it that way. But that answer is a larger view of where I live. Is a larger view useful? That's my point here. This book will surely give you a different perspective on the Blood Moons. It will be larger. But will it be useful? That's for you to decide, and we will offer you that chance in Chapter 7.

We will sometimes propose questions, but may or may not immediately give you our opinion. For example, was I correct when I said that Austin is due south of the geographic center of the United States? It turns out that Austin is close to but not precisely on the center line of the United States. Does it matter? Was I inaccurate when I told you that I live due south of the center line? The right answer depends on the context. If I'm talking to somebody in France about where I live within the United States, then my description is just fine. But if you own a helicopter and you're coming to rescue me, and I tell you to go to the geographic center of the United States, turn south, fly exactly four hundred miles and then land your helicopter, I'd be dead, because you'd miss me by a few miles. Correctness depends on context.

And this example leads us to our first big point. That even in the area of science, which we think of as being exact, there is some wiggle room; information is not always precise to the last decimal point. The Blood Moons deal inherently with **science,** of course. But more than being a scientific phenomenon, the Blood Moons recall **history.** And more than history, the Blood Moons are referenced in the **Bible,** which we consider to be the ultimate authority.

So within each of these three areas—science, history and the Bible—some key questions need to be asked.

For our purposes, the key question in science is: **When is a fact accurate enough?** Facts can be used as data, to target and weaken opposing views. That is not our purpose. We don't wish to take aim at anybody—we want you to have enough information to be able to think for yourself.

The key question in history is: **How do we really see history through God's eyes?**

In fact, we can even ask a question about this question. Is it arrogant to even hope to see history through God's eyes, given that His ways are so much higher than our ways? Yet this question is relevant to our topic.

For the Bible, we could ask so many questions, but this one is key: **How many verses does it take to corroborate a theory when it comes to Blood Moons and what they might mean?**

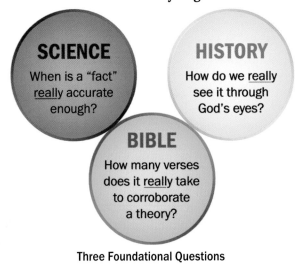

Three Foundational Questions

These are our three foundational questions. We will be coming back to them as we go along. Again, we want to give you tools to help you think for yourself.

Nobody has a full picture of the Blood Moons. I've read all the books and articles I could find on the subject. Every book I've read makes some valid points. Even the books that argue that the Blood Moons mean nothing have some validity.

When it comes to a perspective on the Blood Moons, there is also the dimension of time. Information tends to become clearer in hindsight, and it may be that six months or a year after the end of all of the Blood Moons, we can look back and say, "Oh, so that was the meaning of the Blood Moons." Then again, it may not be so easy.

In addition, this book will discuss four different topics, of which the Blood Moons is only one. We believe they all work differently, and we will teach you how we think they can be distinguished from one another.

Because the Blood Moons is the most complex of the four, we will grapple with it first. This section will do much more than offer information about the Blood Moons. It is the means by which we will attempt to teach you how to think for yourself when some new idea is presented. You will find that our topics weave together hard facts, history, people, and exploring the nature of God. In fact, you will see a "story" develop behind the scenes, which we hope will encourage you in your own journey with God.

So, stick with us. Don't give up. A rich reward is coming. Something beautiful awaits.

And once we finish with the Blood Moons, it will take us far less time to explain the other three topics. Thinking about them will flow naturally out of the learning you will experience in our discussion of the Blood Moons.

Are you ready to begin?

✡ ✡ ✡

Most people know the definition of a solar or lunar eclipse. If you need a refresher, you can find some good diagrams on Wikipedia.

The largest number of total lunar eclipses that can ever occur in succession in nature is four. "Succession" in this context means that there are no partial eclipses between the total eclipses. It is, of course, possible to have two or three total lunar eclipses in a row, but never more than four. When four occur in a row, scientists refer to this as a "tetrad," which derives from the Latin word for "four." Tetrads can occur anywhere from zero to eight or so times in a century.

But a Blood Moon Tetrad is much rarer. A Blood Moon Tetrad (often simply called Blood Moons) occurs when those four lunar eclipses fall on the Jewish Feast Days of Passover and Sukkot for two successive years, which has occurred in both 2014 and 2015.

The diagram below shows the dates of these Blood Moons.

2014	2014	2015	2015	2015
April 15	**October 8**	**March 20**	**April 4**	**September 28**
PASSOVER	SUKKOT	RELIGIOUS	PASSOVER	SUKKOT
Nissan 15	Tishri 15	NEW YEAR	Nissan 15	Tishri 15
		Nissan 1		

In addition to the four Blood Moons, we observed an interesting total solar eclipse on March 20, 2015. The total solar eclipse on March 20 fell on the very first day of the biblical New Year of the Jewish calendar. It is Nissan 1, the day when God said to Moses "This shall be the beginning of the year for you." Notice that the solar eclipse occurred on the first day of the biblical month, while the total lunar eclipse always falls in the middle of the month, the 15th of the month of the Jewish calendar.

One beautiful aspect of the Jewish calendar is that its months are always aligned with the moon. Every Jewish month begins with a new moon, and the middle of every month is always a full moon.

Passover is the first major feast of the biblical calendar year and always occurs on the night of a full moon. The second of the major feasts is Shavuot (literally, the Feast of Weeks, also called Pentecost by Christians) fifty days later, which always occurs when the moon is a crescent moon. The third major feast is Sukkot (the Feast of Tabernacles or Booths), which occurs in the middle of the month of

2: BLOOD MOONS BASICS

Tishri with a full moon.

God instituted these feasts. He determined the timing of them. God decided that the Passover and Sukkot feasts would be exactly six months apart, which is the ONLY way we can ever have a Blood Moons tetrad. This is an alignment. When tetrads occur, they occur six months apart—every time. Passover and Sukkot are six months apart—every time. So, for an ordinary tetrad to become a Blood Moons tetrad, the first lunar eclipse of the four needs to fall on Passover eve, usually in mid-April. Once that happens, everything falls into place just as it did in 2014 and 2015. How frequently do Blood Moons tetrads occur? Not very—it has only happened nine times over the last 2000 years.

Probably the biggest difference between a solar eclipse and a lunar eclipse is how many people can see the actual event.

Who can see a total lunar eclipse?

The answer is about one-half of the earth's residents. Anyone who is on the dark side of the earth while the eclipse is happening can go outside, find the moon in the sky, and see it (assuming it's not cloudy). Then, on the next lunar eclipse, half of the earth's residents again will be able to see it—but not necessarily the same half. Why? Because the earth is spinning, these

Total Lunar Eclipse

eclipses don't occur at exactly the same time of day in each case.

Partial Solar Eclipse

And who could see the March 20, 2015 solar eclipse?

There are two answers to that. The first answer is that some people can only see a partial phase—when the moon covers the sun only partially, covering only about 15 percent of the earth's surface. On March 20, people in Africa, Europe, Western Russia and the Middle East, including Israel, could see this partial solar eclipse. But since the moon is only covering a fraction of the sun, the sun is still extremely bright, and unless you have proper filtering, you might not even know something special is happening.

But a total solar eclipse is something completely different. The totality is gorgeous, but it touches only 0.1 percent of the earth's surface! Imagine a path on the earth that is fifty miles wide and a few thousand miles long. It may start in America and end in Africa. Or it may begin in Europe and end in Southeast Asia. Whoever is standing underneath the sun as it travels along this path will see the total solar eclipse. But only a very small percentage of the people on earth can see this.

Who got to see the totality on March 20, 2015? Its path, shown below, was almost completely and exclusively over the Atlantic Ocean.

Black curve: Total Solar Eclipse Path of March 20, 2015

The path of the Total Solar Eclipse began south of Greenland and curved up between Europe and Iceland. North of Scotland are the Faroe Islands, home to fifty thousand people. It was cloudy that day over the Faroe Islands. Farther along its path, the sun passed over an island series called Svalbard, located off the coast of Norway, home to less than three thousand people. Those people were blessed with beautifully clear skies and, together with dozens of astronomy buffs from all over the world who made the special trip, got to see the totality for two minutes.

Did you notice the most interesting part? Look at the path carefully: Can you see where it ends? Doesn't it look like it ends at the top of the world? The North Pole?

That is the picture that caused my jaw to drop to the floor in 2013, and started a series of curious events that would have more profound implications than I'd ever thought possible, including the reason you are reading this book. It was that picture that I found buried in a NASA website that started it all.

That story—my story—will come later, but for now we will focus on this amazing solar eclipse.

In the chart below, you can see that the path of the shadow of the sun reached the North Pole on March 20 at 10:19 a.m. Universal Time

(UTC), which is also the time in Greenwich, London (GMT). But other special events happened on that day. The biblical New Year began on Nissan 1, at sunset in Jerusalem, which on that day was 5 1/2 hours later at 3:50 p.m. UTC. That day, March 20, also marked the first day of spring, called the vernal equinox, which was about seven hours later, 10:45 p.m. UTC. This was the day that the North Pole began its six-month-long daytime, the day the sun rises at the North Pole.

These three events occurring together on the same day—as far as I've been able to research—have never occurred before in human history!

SUMMARY

Total Eclipse at North Pole: 10:19 a.m. UTC March 20
Nissan 1 Biblical New Year Begins: 3:50 p.m. UTC March 20
Spring Begins for Northern Hemisphere: 10:45 p.m. UTC March 20

Unique in Recorded Human History

Why is this so rare?

Pick any spot on the earth at random. On average, that location should see a total solar eclipse about once every 300 years. So the North Pole should get a solar eclipse every 300 years. That is not so rare. But for that event to occur on the first day of spring would be a one-in-365 chance. Multiply those two numbers and you see that you would have a total solar eclipse on the first day of spring at the North Pole only once every 100,000 years. This is actually much, much rarer than the Blood Moons!

Why was this amazing event never noticed before? Because the eclipse tables estimated the path of totality stopping short of the actual North Pole by a few miles. But they forgot to include the impact of the earth's atmosphere, which bends the light near the horizon. My years of experience told me to look deeper. What I discovered was that although "on paper" the computers' calculations determined that there was no eclipse at the North Pole, in reality there was! And what a sight it was, on what turned out to be a very clear North Pole day of March 20! No, I wasn't there. Nobody was there except God. But if you had been there, standing on the polar ice cap at the top of the world, you and God would have seen the sun rise above the horizon after six long months of darkness. Then, while skimming along the horizon, moving from left to right, the sun would be fully eclipsed by the shadow of the moon for two wonderful minutes! It would have looked something like this.

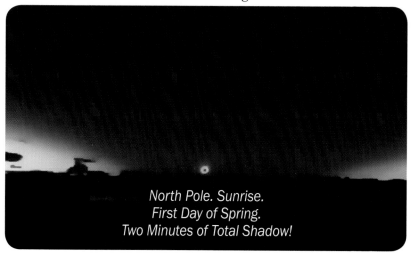

North Pole. Sunrise.
First Day of Spring.
Two Minutes of Total Shadow!

So what we have then, on this earth, at the North Pole, is a total solar eclipse skimming the horizon for two minutes on March 20, the first day of spring, for probably the first time in 100,000 years, on the very day Israel began its religious New Year at sundown—all these events combined for the first time in human history.

Now, for the question you've been waiting for: What does all this mean? I was personally very concerned that if this news got out, Christians and others might predict the end of the world. I shared this concern with my colleague at Root Source, Gidon Ariel. We both know that the Messiah will come soon, but had no desire to fuel claims that the end of the world was nigh. But did this historical event mean nothing at all? Or could it have extraordinary meaning?

I'd like to draw your attention to something that Jewish sages have said about lunar and solar eclipses:

Lunar eclipses bear upon the Nation of Israel, and solar eclipses bear upon the rest of the world.

This seemed especially significant with regard to our solar eclipse: The eclipse occurred at the North Pole, an international site nobody owns. If you put a flag there in the ice, it will drift away from the North Pole within a few minutes.

We started thinking about all of this: The solar eclipse's special timing... in an international, ownerless location... its path that never left the water at any time... and the end of its route on a polar ice cap at the top of the world.

So Gidon and I came up with an idea: What if we were to pray? What if we were to take this opportunity to turn to God?

We thought about some verses that would have to do with the ocean and the world. I kept thinking about Habakkuk 2:14: "For the earth will be filled with the knowledge of the glory of the Lord, as the waters cover the sea." But something in my spirit told me this was not right. And when the right answer didn't come, I felt the Lord saying, "Gidon will choose."

Gidon ended up selecting Isaiah 11:9. "They shall not hurt nor destroy in all my holy mountain, for the earth shall be full of the knowledge of the Lord, as the waters cover the sea." This was a passage that had Messianic implications, and he was calling both Jews and Christians around the world to pray it! I would not have dared be so bold as Gidon!

For how long should we pray? The answer was obvious—two minutes, of course!

When should we pray? During the exact two minutes that the shadow would be over the North Pole.

Where? I was in Austin, and it would be dark here in the USA, but the time would be just after noon in Jerusalem. Indeed, God provided a nice clear day for a group of Christians and Jews to come together at the southwestern corner of the Temple Mount. We live-streamed the event, and tens of thousands of Christians worldwide from many countries participated. The Temple Mount was the perfect place to be the center of all the prayers given, as the Scripture directly mentioned "my holy mountain."

We also asked Steve Hawthorne from Waymakers to write a prayer around Isaiah 11:9 for the event. His beautiful prayer can be found at **www.root-source.com/blog/special-prayer-for-nissan-1-eclipse.**

We will talk further about the events of that day in Chapter 7, but before we close, I'd like to share a story of something that happened the very last Saturday before the eclipse.

A day or so after we issued the call to prayer, our Israeli friend

Rabbi Tuly Weisz was in a synagogue, listening to the weekly Torah portion being read. That Sabbath, Exodus 31 was read in synagogues all over the world. During the reading of that passage, Tuly said he started feeling goosebumps rise all over his body. Exodus 31 begins with the world's first great craftsman, Bezalel, from the tribe of Judah, and echoes the Messianic language from Isaiah 11 that Gidon had selected. The Lord speaks over Bezalel "a spirit of wisdom and understanding," just as the Lord speaks over the Messiah in Isaiah 11. Interesting, but that's not all. Bezalel's skill as a craftsman was to be used for the construction of the Tabernacle. When might you guess that the Tabernacle was to be dedicated at Mount Sinai? God told Moses to officiate the dedication on Nissan 1, the very date of this historically unique solar eclipse!

But even *that's* not all. Tuly knows Hebrew, so he realized these connections, but he also saw something deeper. He realized that the name Bezalel, in Hebrew, means: "in the shadow or protection of God." Without realizing it, we had stumbled upon a Scripture that tied the solar eclipse of Nissan 1 to a heartfelt prayer to bring forth the Messianic Age!

As soon as we released news of the eclipse, many publications began predicting severe judgment for the world. We are not saying that judgment is not part of the mix. Indeed, this book will have plenty to say about judgment. But we found in this passage a message of great joy, a message we now see right through this scary event to God and His purposes for the earth! This event needs to be seen as something **good**, not bad. This is an opportunity for all of us to come together and call for the knowledge of God and the Messianic Age to be brought in around the world! It is a good thing to be in the shadow or protection of God, don't you think?

Go ahead and pray Isaiah 11:9 with us right now. Our God, who is outside of time, is completely capable of considering your prayer, prayed this very moment, as having also been part of that special event on March 20, 2015, when the shadow of God fell for two minutes upon the very top of the world.

Pray out loud as we did that day: "*For they shall not hurt nor destroy in all my holy mountain: for the earth shall be full of the knowledge of the Lord, as the waters cover the sea.*" (Isa. 11:9 KJV) ✡

CHAPTER 3
Origins

In the previous chapter, we explained that the Blood Moons combines science, history, and the Bible. In this chapter, we are going to focus on *history*.

How do we see history through God's eyes? And what kind of history do you expect we are going to discuss? Do you think perhaps the history of Israel as recorded in 1967, 1948, or even the expulsion of the Jews in 1492? No, not quite yet.

There's another kind of history we need to explore first. Would you agree that the Bible is God's story? Would you also agree, that God speaks through people in the Bible? He not only sends His writings to us as if they were mysteriously inscribed on the side of a mountain; they were penned by people. And would you agree that those people who have penned the Scriptures—both the Old Testament and the New Testament—also have a story? And would you then agree that the Bible usually covers those stories in intricate detail? Major historical figures, like Moses, effect great change in the world. But we don't just hear about Moses bringing the tablets down from Mount Sinai, we get the backstory, too. We get the whole story—how the Children of Israel went into Egypt, for hundreds of years became slaves, and how God freed them from their slavery in Egypt. As they traveled toward the Promised Land, God met with Moses on Mount Sinai. Backstory and context make all the difference.

So before we unravel the history of the Blood Moons, we need to address the origins of their discovery. I will introduce you to some significant contributors to the backstory, such as Mark Biltz, John Hagee and others. I will also say a few words about my astronomy background. This will help provide you with context for the facts, impressions, and perspectives that I've come to regarding the Blood Moons and the other topics in this book.

I have been an astronomy enthusiast since I was young. The first constellation I found in the sky was by looking at a star chart. I found Cygnus, often called the Northern Cross. Did I think a "spiritual connection" was significant at the time? No. I was fifteen years old, and was simply interested in science.

I acquired an interest in photography at an early age and started photographing the moon. I was fascinated, for some reason, by thin moons, also known as Young Moons. I was fascinated to discover how thin a crescent you could possibly see.

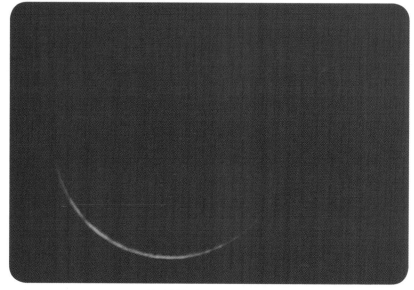

Very Thin Crescent Moon

In this photo, the moon is only about 24 hours old. That means that 24 hours before this photo was taken, the moon was a "new moon," completely hidden within the glare of the sun. Very few people have ever seen a crescent this thin. You have to make an effort: know exactly where to look for the crescent moon, find it through binoculars, and only then can you try to make it out with the unaided eye.

One of my more serious projects was to assist in the mapping of the north and south poles of the moon by observing grazing occultations. These occur when the very edge of the moon passes over a star. The star disappears from view when it goes behind a mountain on the moon, and pops back into view when it comes into a valley, on and off many times. Below is a photograph I took of the moon "grazing" the planet Venus.

The Moon Grazes Venus

One of the most awe-inspiring sights I have ever seen was the view through the 107-inch telescope at McDonald Observatory in West Texas. Today almost no one looks through a giant telescope; they take photographs. Below (left) is the observatory and its mirror; on the right is a photograph that shows what it looked like when they pointed that huge telescope at the Whirlpool Galaxy on a clear, moonless night.

The McDonald Observatory and the Galaxy I Saw

I was not following the Lord back then as closely as I am now, but when I saw the galaxy through the 107-inch telescope, I actually had to shout, "Praise the Lord!" The wonder of His creation! Incredible!

Over the years, I drifted away from observational astronomy because I was bothered by the godless nature of the astronomical community. I even wrote a letter to a few of my astronomy associates, saying, "I'm tired of the constant assertion that life sprang into existence on the earth, evolved into higher and higher forms of life on its own, and that anyone who considers another possibility is a science-hater."

In that letter of September 3, 2012, after 30 years of study and observation, I was moving on to a more fascinating field of exploration: the Bible. My point was that the Bible was a treasure trove of beauty and mystery and wonder. I had fallen in love with God's Word some years before, and now it was time to cut the cord with astronomy.

Two months later, in November 2012, my sister called and said, "I visited Cornerstone Church today in San Antonio, and I heard a teaching by John Hagee on something called 'Blood Moons.' You'd better check it out."

I wasn't interested! Christmas came, and my sister handed me the DVDs from John Hagee's talk.

Still not interested.

Finally, on January 21, 2013, I got around to dropping one of those DVDs into our player. The next day, I went to the eclipse tables on the NASA website—and realized:

The March 20, 2015 solar eclipse, in the "middle of the Blood Moons," was going to reach the North Pole for two minutes on the first day of spring on the Jewish calendar.

I knew this was a rare occurrence, and for the eclipse to fall on the day that Israel begins its biblical new year would be *extremely* rare.

When I look back at those DVDs and John Hagee's tagline, *Blood Moons: Something Is About to Change*, I have to agree. Yes, something was about to change—me!

I realized that I had handed astronomy over to the atheists and walked away. Now it was time for me to repent and give astronomy back to its rightful owner, God. My thoughts began turning to the Blood Moons. Would this new theory be able to withstand my kind of scrutiny? I decided I would not make up my mind in advance. I would let the evidence lead and then draw conclusions from the evidence.

We will pick up that story later, but right now it is time to switch gears and talk about the real stars: the people who discovered the Blood Moons in the first place. So...what is the backstory? What are the origins of the initial discovery? Who? What? When? Where? How?

What should we be looking for in a discoverer's story? I suggest that we should be looking for a few principles.

The first principle is something I have noticed both in the Bible and also in contemporary life:

God relishes using the unlikely person.

Moses is an example. He grew up in privilege, but ended up running from the law. His story is unlikely, but God used him. Then we have the story of the boy who became king–David. That choice was certainly not obvious to his family. The same thing with Paul, a Pharisee of Pharisees, but God used him in an unlikely way.

Second, we need to look for a period in a person's life that is marked by struggle and testing. For instance, Abraham waited more than 25 years to receive the promise of an heir. Jacob spent 20 years under the authority of his uncle Laban. Joseph served time as a slave or prisoner in Egypt. Moses spent 40 years in the desert of Midian, not knowing the plan God had for him.

Third, there should be something in this person's heart that God really likes. David is called a man after God's own heart. Moses was known as the most humble man on the face of the earth; Job, the most righteous man.

And finally, the overall arc of the story must bring glory to God's Name more than anything else. This explains why God enjoys using the unlikely. Notice I did not say He *only* uses the unlikely; rather, that He *relishes* in it.

So with these principles in mind, let's take a look at the origins of the Blood Moons.

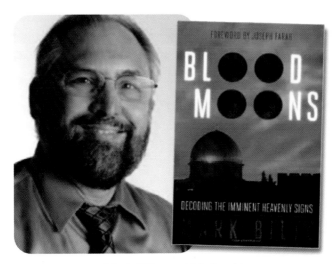

Mark Biltz and his book

The pattern of Blood Moons was discovered by **Mark Biltz.** While on his computer, Mark saw a total lunar eclipse from a live-feed over the Temple Mount in Israel. This was February 21, 2008. In March, he started wondering how often an eclipse like this occurs. One thing led to another, and Mark discovered that four Blood Moons were expected to occur in 2014 and 2015. He began wondering if that had ever happened before. Further research revealed a distinct correlation and pattern of the Blood Moons in other significant historical time frames: 1967-1968; 1949-1950; 1493-1494.

So God began using Mark Biltz to unlock some of the mystery of the Blood Moons. Is Mark an "unlikely person"? I'll let him speak for himself. In his book *Blood Moons: Decoding the Imminent Heavenly Signs*, he writes: "In 1975, at the age of 19, I got saved. And for the next 18 years I did as much volunteer work for God as I could possibly do." For a while, he held a roofing manufacturing job, then worked with Brinks Home Security in Sales. Time passed—lots of it—then came a moment when he "was totally burned out on the church." He became interested in Jewish things after his wife bought him a book written by a rabbi. He calls that a turning point for him. He now pastors a church in Tacoma, Washington. Hmm, I'd say he's a pretty unlikely candidate for discovering God's purposes for the Blood Moons, the first principle on our list. In addition, this part of his story suggests the second principle: 18 years of faithful service, struggling to the point of burnout, but without giving up.

Next, I see Mark's huge excitement for God's creation, and I believe God loves that about him. When you view Mark's videos from 2008 to 2010, where he explains these moons and what is becoming clear to him, there is no doubt about his love for God. He has an uncommon openness to sharing his discoveries with others. He didn't try to hide or keep this discovery to himself. He began talking about it openly to anyone who would listen. Why? Probably because of his great love for God and God's amazing creation!

Finally, the overall arc of the story must bring glory to God's Name more than anything else. We will revisit this one in Chapter 7, so I won't shock you with my proposed answer just yet. We have more background to cover first! Ultimately, any answer will still only be a partial answer because Mark's story is not finished. But I'll give you a hint: Mark Biltz has Jewish heritage on his father's side.

Do these facts about Mark prove the Blood Moons are a message from God? No! It doesn't prove anything, but there are no red flags in his storyline. His story seems consistent with the principles of how God uses people.

As I have mentioned, God uses the unique gifts of people in different ways. For example, **Bill Koenig** deserves an honorable mention at the very least. The Blood Moons were discovered in March 2008, but as late as January 2013, there was very little on the Internet about them. Bill Koenig's website told the story of Mark Biltz and was an important resource in those early days.

✧ ✧ ✧

Pastor **John Hagee** heard about the Blood Moons in early 2012, directly from Mark Biltz. John was attending a *Night to Honor Israel* event in Mark's church in Tacoma, Washington. A *Night to Honor Israel* is the premier event of CUFI (Christians United for Israel), of which Hagee is the Founder and National Chairman.

New York Times and USA Today Bestseller

FOUR BLOOD MOONS

SOMETHING IS ABOUT TO CHANGE

JOHN HAGEE

John Hagee and his book

With John Hagee's influence, including his nationwide and worldwide resources, he was able to expand awareness about the Blood Moons. Probably most of the people who heard about Blood Moons initially heard about them through the efforts of John Hagee. My own story stems from seeing the DVDs of John's talks.

These fine men, Mark Biltz and John Hagee, have invested much of their time and effort in supporting the nation of Israel and encouraging others to do so. There's a Jewish story that goes like this:

A man comes to a rabbi and says, *"Rabbi, let me to tell you what I believe."* The rabbi replies, *"There's no need for that. Let me follow you for thirty days. Then we'll sit down together and I'll tell you what you believe."*

It's one thing to believe in something; it's another to act on it as these men have done.

I have an opinion about the respective callings of these men. I would say that John Hagee's calling is reminiscent of Paul, and Mark Biltz's calling is more like Peter's. Peter, the former fisherman, was there from the very beginning, and preached the very first Christian sermon to the world. The highly credentialed Paul came along later, but with his writings and extensive travels, he expanded Christianity to reach so many more people. In that sense, both Mark and John deserve respect, and we can appreciate them in these different lights.

There's also another player in this story: **Mark Hitchcock,** a well-known prophetic writer.

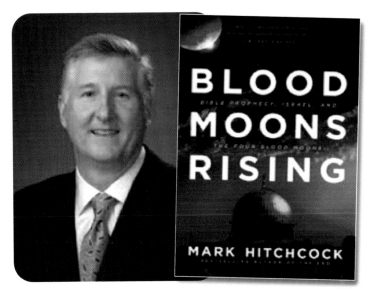

Mark Hitchcock and his book

He wrote the first book that disagrees with John and Mark's conclusion about the Blood Moons. Hitchcock believes that the others don't make their case for tying the Blood Moons to the Second Coming or other prophetic, end-time events. Hitchcock is not alone in that view, and quotes others who support his opinion.

I'd like to make a couple of comments about this: First of all, Mark's book is respectful, and he should be commended for that. We will reference some of the points Mark Hitchcock makes in Chapter 5, because ultimately, given all the facts, you will decide for yourself. This is not a matter of who's right and who's wrong. In fact, there's a whole different way to look at these kinds of conflicts.

We do a great injustice to our Christian brothers and sisters when we focus on picking winners and losers rather than trying to look for God's heart in each point of view. In fact, the Jews say that when two Scriptures contradict one another, there must be a larger principle in play. Is there such a principle behind the theories of these three leaders?

We don't have enough information to answer it yet, but whenever solid, respectable people disagree with each other, we should be asking ourselves: Is there a larger principle in play?

Furthermore, people's callings are different. God empowers some to push ahead and take more risks. He empowers others to validate, correct, or codify. We need all kinds of giftings in the Body of Christ.

We have mentioned a number of people. Are YOU part of this story? Have you considered the topic of the Blood Moons? Have you had a thought or idea on the subject, something that you had not previously read? If so, YOU are part of this story also!

My list here is woefully incomplete, but God's list isn't. Anyone who serves Him will be rewarded. If you know someone who serves God through Blood Moons, fill in the blank in this prayer: *We thank You, Lord, for the insights You gave to* _____ *who is one among Your list of servants who thoughtfully considered the topic of the Blood Moons.*

Are we covered now? Have we missed thanking God for anyone? How about rabbis or Jewish teachers from Israel? There is only one mention of eclipses in the Talmud. But don't you imagine that there might have been many Jewish rabbis and scholars who could have looked up, seen an eclipse on the night of Passover or Sukkot, and considered its spiritual significance? Jewish navigators used the stars to guide their ships and were predicting the phases of the moon and eclipses all the way back to the days of Columbus.

That is exactly where our next chapter begins. In Chapter Four, you will discover new surprises about some very special eclipses in the year 1492. ✿

CHAPTER 4

1492

In Chapter 2, we posed some significant questions that need to be answered regarding the three main areas of the Blood Moons: science, history, and the Bible. Then we revealed the amazing coincidence of the March 20 solar eclipse that reached the North Pole on the first day of spring, which also was the first day of the biblical New Year.

In Chapter 3, we proposed some ways to evaluate whether a person's story was consistent with the way God uses people to proclaim His truth. We took a look at Mark Biltz, who discovered the Blood Moons, and saw that there was no inconsistency between Mark's story and how God uses people for His purposes. However, we emphasized that this does not confirm Mark's interpretation of the Blood Moons' meaning. In fact, we pointed out the controversy swirling around the subject.

We can summarize this controversy with a question raised by this verse from the Bible (Psalm 19:1-2):

"The heavens tell the story of the glory of God; and the horizon tells of his handiwork. Day to day the declaration is spoken; and night to night wisdom is opined."

A reasonable question would be: With the discovery of the Blood Moons, is this verse being fulfilled in a general sense, or more specifically?

If you agree that one can see the stars, the moon, the sun, and other celestial bodies as the glory of God, marvel at this amazing Creator, and praise Him, then this verse is being fulfilled in a general sense. Most believing people would concur with the truth of this statement. The real controversy is whether natural events in the heavens can speak specifically to us? Blood Moons are not random; they are "pre-programmed." They are set to happen at certain times in certain ways. So can something fixed be used as a sign of something that is not fixed, for example, a move of God?

Let's take this idea to the opposite extreme: Let's take the movements of the planets, the moon, and the sun, and tie them to earth events, without any consideration of God. You know what that's called? Astrology. That's wrong! If we try to separate the sun, the moon, and the stars from God and use them in any way not connected with Him, we're off base. In fact, in the Torah, Deuteronomy 17 declares that we must not worship the stars, the moon or the sun, because if we do, there will be a severe penalty:

> If there is found among you, within any of your gates which the LORD your God gives you, a man or woman who does that which is evil in the LORD your God's sight, in transgressing His covenant, and has gone and served other gods, and worshiped them, or the sun, or the moon, or any of the stars of the sky, which I have not commanded; and you are told, and you have heard of it, then you shall inquire diligently. Behold, if it is true, and the thing certain, that such abomination is done in Israel, then you shall bring out that man or that woman, who has done this evil thing, to your gates, even that same man or woman; and you shall stone them to death with stones.
>
> **Deuteronomy 17:2-5**

If we place nature above God or interact with it independently from God, we have created an idol. Granted, in Western nations, few people would admit to overtly worshiping the sun, moon and stars.

But there is also the danger of people merely dismissing the possible significance of the Blood Moons. Perhaps there is a middle ground. If so, what might it be?

To help us explore this middle ground, we are going to examine two interesting eclipses from the past, both occurring in the pivotal year 1492.

On March 31, 1492, Queen Isabella and King Ferdinand issued the Alhambra Decree. In this decree, they ordered all Jews to leave Spain, and believed that the emigration could be completed in three months. Ultimately, it took longer, so they extended the deadline to August 1. August 2 was the 9th day of Av in the Jewish calendar, the traditional day of mourning for the Jews; on that day, they lost the Holy Temple. That date is significant, too, because of the many other trials and tragedies that have beset the Jewish people on the 9th of Av. These events can be verified by history. The next day, August 3, 1492, Christopher Columbus began sailing to what he thought was the Far East, but instead, discovered the "New World"–North and South America.

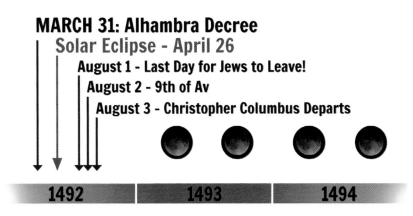

MARCH 31: Alhambra Decree
Solar Eclipse - April 26
August 1 - Last Day for Jews to Leave!
August 2 - 9th of Av
August 3 - Christopher Columbus Departs

1492 **1493** **1494**

Timeline of Key Events

The Blood Moons did not occur in 1492. They were observed in 1493 and 1494. So, Christopher Columbus departed for the New World on August 3, 1492 and returned before the first of the Blood Moons took place! Are the Blood Moons significant if they did not actually occur in 1492?

I made a surprising discovery when I was studying the eclipses in and around 1492. I found a solar eclipse that occurred on April 26, 1492–during the Alhambra Decree, when all Jews were commanded to leave Spain. That solar eclipse had been overlooked because it was not in the middle of a Blood Moon series.

I learned two exciting facts about that solar eclipse.

First, it is a direct ancestor of the amazing solar eclipse of March 20, 2015 that reached the North Pole. It turns out that all eclipses are part of a family of eclipses called a Saros, which is a family of eclipses that appear eighteen years apart. So you can think of it like this: Every eighteen years a new eclipse child is "born"; eighteen years later, that eclipse grows up and has a child of its own. By this analogy, if the eclipse of April 26, 1492 were to be called "Generation 1," then the March 20, 2015 eclipse would be "Generation 30."

The second exciting fact is the path of the 1492 solar eclipse. Where did its shadow fall on the earth?

Path of the April 26, 1492 Solar Eclipse

The path falls between North America and South America, splitting the continents. It begins in the South Pacific, south of the Equator, then veers north of the Equator, and finally ends at the Equator itself. What a beautifully symmetrical path!

Now let's zoom in for a closer look and see a place where the path of the eclipse touches land. It goes right through Panama—where the exit of the Panama Canal would be built in the early twentieth century—into the Atlantic Ocean.

What is the meaning? Is there a meaning?

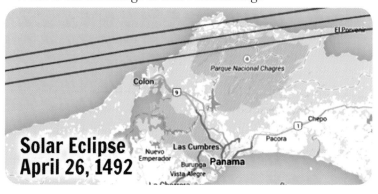

I want you to have an opportunity to look at both sides of this debate, and decide for yourself whether this particular eclipse has a meaning. So I am going to first propose a meaning—and then I am going to try to speak against that proposal.

Here's a possible interpretation: God knew before the foundation of the world that Spain would expel the Jews in 1492, and He wanted to make a statement: "Yes, I have given you free will. You can expel the Jews. But if you decide to do that, then I'll do this: I will open up the New World and I will provide a place for Jews to be safe in the years to come. They will come to South America first, and then to North America later, as it develops. I will mark this with a sign on the earth after your decision, but before the Jews leave. And as soon as they leave, I will send Columbus to discover this new land."

Now I will speak against that proposed meaning by making this observation: No body of water more clearly signifies the separation between North and South America than the Panama Canal. The Panama Canal was built in the early 1900s. If God wanted to hint at North and South America, why wouldn't He have caused the path of this eclipse to go right through the very center of the canal, rather than at its entrance? That's a valid question. God is perfect, right? He can do anything, right? So if He wanted to signify a meaning, why not put the shadow's path over the exact middle of the Panama Canal?

Let me switch sides again and give one counterpoint to that argument: If the 1492 eclipse was on the future spot of the Panama Canal's exact middle, then on March 20, 2015, that eclipse would have never reached the North Pole because if you move one eclipse path, you move them all. All of these eclipses are connected to each other in a grand pattern. Maybe the important thought here is to see the North Pole eclipse and the Panama Canal eclipse as a combined message!

I promised we would examine a second eclipse in this chapter, and this eclipse is connected to the Blood Moon lunar eclipse of April 4, 2015.

2014	2014	2015	2015	2015
April 15	**October 8**	**March 20**	**April 4**	**September 28**
PASSOVER	SUKKOT	RELIGIOUS	PASSOVER	SUKKOT
Nissan 15	Tishri 15	NEW YEAR	Nissan 15	Tishri 15
		Nissan 1		

These Two Eclipses are Siblings!

But before I show you the surprise connected to this eclipse, you need to know one more thing about science. Did you know that solar and lunar eclipses always come in pairs? You can't have one without the other! This may be news to you, but every time the earth has a solar eclipse, a lunar eclipse occurs two weeks before or two weeks after. You can think of the solar/lunar pair as a pair of eclipse siblings.

So if there were a pair of eclipses in 2015, should there not have been a pair of eclipses in 1492 as well? You now know the answer must be yes! The date of the lunar eclipse was May 12, 1492. It is the sibling of the solar eclipse we just discussed, occurring two weeks after the one whose path crossed near the site of the Panama Canal.

Every lunar eclipse draws a unique line on the earth, an imaginary north-south 'center line' that indicates the exact middle of that lunar eclipse. The center line for the May 12, 1492 lunar eclipse was in a very special location, a location that would never have been discovered without the help of computers! Let me show you that line.

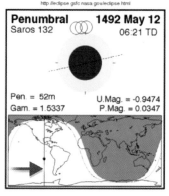

That center line of the eclipse, indicated by the red arrows, and represented by the purple line, passes nearly over the geographical center of the continental United States, represented by the red star. It is another case, like Panama, where an eclipse path comes very close to something that would have a lot of significance later!

Now you know why I told you, back in Chapter 2, that my town of Austin, Texas was pretty much due south of the center of the United States. It prepared the way for this moment. But wait, there's more! John Hagee lives in San Antonio, which is also very close to that center line. And Mark Biltz, who now lives in Tacoma, Washington, grew up in Kansas, right next to the purple line as well.

As this book progresses, you will see other hints that God uses the center line of the United States as a way to speak to the entire country!

But before we leave this topic, I would like to make one more connection to Mark Biltz. Remember that we said the Saros family of eclipses occur eighteen years apart? In studying Mark's story, he mentioned that he had experienced many struggles and much testing in his life. That period of struggle lasted eighteen years!

Mark is an amateur astronomer like I am, so he knows about the Saros series and that it lasts eighteen years. But I wonder if he ever made the connection to the idea that God was making him wait the same amount of time as a Saros eclipse? Do you catch the beauty of the symbolism here? After eighteen years, God gives Mark an understanding of the Blood Moons–that they are completely interconnected with an eighteen-year pattern. My personal belief and experience is that God loves to weave things together in our lives in surprising ways, and enjoys seeing our reaction when we reach that aha moment!

I can't be positive that God is giving us a clue about Mark's life using these eighteen years as a pattern, but I do know this: Eighteen years is a recurring theme in Scripture. For example, there is the story of Jesus healing the woman who was bent over with a kind of physical deformity (see Luke 13:10-17). She had been crippled for eighteen long years before Jesus released her from her infirmity. So, there is a scriptural basis for an eighteen-year period of being in some kind of holding pattern. Similarly, one of our Root Source students pointed out that Jesus waited eighteen years from age twelve before beginning His ministry at age thirty.

Is God throwing in a hint here by setting that same time period in Mark's life? It is something to think about.

But here is something that is so obvious we don't even have to think about it. Whether or not the 1492 solar eclipse path over the future country of Panama and the 1492 lunar eclipse path over the center of the future United States were planned by God from the beginning, we can say this for certain: God is worthy of praise! Let us praise Him in reading the verses below:

Who is like unto thee, O Lord, among the gods? Who is like thee, glorious in holiness, fearful in praises, doing wonders?

Exodus 15:11

Remember the former things of old: for I am God, and there is none else; I am God, and there is none like me. Declaring the end from the beginning, and from ancient times things that are not yet done, saying, "My counsel shall stand, and I will do all my pleasure."

Isaiah 46:9-10

We can't be 100 percent certain that a solar eclipse means anything. But we can be 100 percent certain that this verse from Scripture is real, and it is alive. Whatever God says, He will do. When He says, "My counsel shall stand, and I will do all my pleasure," we can take it to the bank!

There is no question that God had His eye on the Jewish people. There is no question that when they were being expelled from Spain, He cared. And there is no question that He knew He was going to make a way for them to have a place in South and North America. He knew, of course, that the United States would ultimately be the place where the greatest number of Jews in the entire world would live after their numbers were decimated in World War II. The United States has harbored more Jews than any other nation until a few years ago, when Israel surpassed the United States in total Jewish population. God knew that He was going to make that happen—and He did. For that, we can certainly praise Him!

I hope you're beginning to have a good time with the Blood Moons. It's fun to attempt to see what God might be up to. He Himself says, "It is the glory of God to conceal a thing: but the honour of kings is to search out a matter." (Prov. 25:2)

We get to be kings! We have the honor of trying to find God at work in one of His natural phenomena and search out His treasure.

There is only one problem with being a "king." Kings often find themselves coming face to face with problems they have no possible way of solving... and that brings us to a discussion of "valleys and shadows" in the next chapter. ✡

CHAPTER 5

Valleys and Shadows

Teacher types are big on review, so stick with me. What did we learn in the last chapter? We began by quoting Psalm 19:1-2:

The heavens tell the story of the glory of God; and the horizon tells of his handiwork. Day to day the declaration is spoken; and night to night wisdom is opined."

Then we asked the question: Is Psalm 19 fulfilled specifically or generally when considering the Blood Moons and other natural phenomena?

We have talked about the three foundational questions of science, history, and the Bible.

Let us look at the question again.

In science: When is a fact really accurate enough?

Facts are accurate enough when you allow them to challenge the weaknesses of your own arguments. Otherwise, you are not teaching, you are selling. Ouch!

In my high-tech career, I had a sales team reporting to me. So you cannot accuse me of being anti-sales. But when you are selling, conventional wisdom dictates that you are not compelled to reveal every weakness of your product unless you are asked. When you are teaching, the opposite is true: the idea is to bring as much truth as possible to bear on the situation.

Does this mean that you cannot make a case for a given argument? Of course not! Building an argument is like building a structure.

When you have a thesis, you supply facts and supporting evidence to help prove your thesis. The best teaching in uncertain areas requires the teacher to reveal the facts that do not support the argument, facts that may actually refute that argument. Sometimes, your supporting arguments may have cracks in them, cracks that–if they were discussed–could weaken the entire structure.

The greatest teaching, in my view, exposes everything that allows the students to come to a possibly different conclusion from the teacher. This is what I love about Jewish teachers who have been Yeshiva-trained. In a Yeshiva (a Jewish school of learning), students are encouraged, even required, to debate respectfully with others, to have an open mind so that their arguments can be improved upon by others. This openness is the seed truth behind the common quote about Jewish debate: Two Jews, three opinions!

And when it comes to the Blood Moons and the End Times, there is plenty of room for debate.

End-Time Dilemma

Since the Book of Joel refers to "the great and terrible day of the Lord"–associated with what Christians call the "End Times"–we will delve into that period in this chapter. But before we do, I would like to help you understand two Jewish perspectives on this controversial subject.

Did you know that, in general, Jews find Christians' fascination with the End Times distasteful, even painful? That is because they see us as treating the matter involving Israel like a cosmic scorecard of prophecies to check off, prophecies that are yet to be fulfilled before the Messiah's return.

OUR COSMIC SCORECARD

☑ Psalm 83 Israel War
☑ Ez 38-39 Israel War
☑ Armageddon
☐ Messianic Age

While we are thinking about the glorious, expected arrival of the Messiah, they are thinking about this list and seeing the death of many Jews. You can now understand why Jews are less than enthusiastic about the Christian fascination with the End Times. I am not saying that we are wrong to speak about this forthcoming event; I am just saying this kind of talk can bring up justifiably painful feelings for our Jewish friends.

Secondly, did you know that most Jews are not very interested in the End Times—that they are not very aware of these prophecies? Rabbi Ken Spiro from Root Source explains it to Christians this way: "Jews are interested in the present because they feel called to engage in *tikkun olam*, to repair the world." More than just a Jewish concept, this gives us an insight into the difference between Western culture and Hebrew culture. Jews do not just think—they act. Jews believe that good thoughts, whether they are about the future or other people, are not worth much unless they are accompanied by action. The Greeks were known for thoughts, but the Hebrews were known for deeds."

The Blood Moons—The Big Picture

We have explained before that a tetrad is a series of four total lunar eclipses in a two-year period. These tetrads have fallen on biblical Feast Days (Passover and Tabernacles) only about nine times since the birth of Christ. Here is a diagram of the appearance of the last of these Blood Moons:

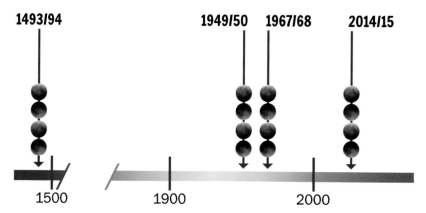

These are the occurrences of the Blood Moons that are getting the most attention in current popular literature. These are the Blood Moon Tetrads of 1967-1968, 1949-1950, 1493-1494, and of 2014-2015.

The premier Scripture that is used with respect to the Blood Moons comes from Joel 3:4 in the Hebrew Bible, or Joel 2:31 in the English versions:

The sun shall be turned into darkness and the moon into blood
before the great and the terrible day of the LORD'S *coming.*

When Mark Biltz discovered this phenomenon, he was the originator of the term "*Blood Moon.*" But what was the origin of this Scripture being applied to the Blood Moons? Let us hear from Mark in his own words, in his book "*Blood Moons: Decoding the Imminent Heavenly Signs*":

> *In March that year, I saw on the Internet an incredible lunar eclipse over the Temple Mount in Jerusalem. I had read all the Bible verses in Isaiah, Joel, the Gospels, and Revelation where the text talks about the moon turning into blood and the sun to sackcloth. I began to ponder the possibilities of tying the eclipses mentioned in the Bible to the possible coming of the Messiah.*

This was Mark's first reaction when he saw the eclipse over the Temple Mount in Jerusalem. That early connection between Mark's initial thought about the Blood Moons and the Messiah has shaped the attitude of many Christians toward this celestial phenomenon ever since.

Although he mentions this line of thinking in the preface, Mark does not emphasize that belief. Neither does John Hagee in his book *Four Blood Moons: Something Is About to Change*. And yet *this initial connection of the Blood Moons with the return of the Messiah* seeded the entire Christian community with this idea. Regardless of what Mark and John actually said in their books, a wide perception soon developed that the Blood Moons are connected with the arrival of the Messiah.

Is this your belief as well?

If so, after having journeyed with me to this point, my next statement may jolt your worldview: **I do not think the Blood Moons is signaling the Messiah in any special way.** May I explain why? Will you hear me out on this?

Three Big Problems

It all starts with this key verse used for the Blood Moons in all the books written on the subject:

The sun shall be turned into darkness and the moon into blood before the great and the terrible day of the Lord *come."* (Joel 2:31)

I have three big problems with the use of this verse as evidence for the Blood Moons.

• Problem #1 – Use of the Word *Before*

Before **indicates that something will happen regarding the moon before "the great and the terrible day of the Lord." Does history show this kind of pattern with the Blood Moons?**

Let us take a look at the timing, beginning with 1492, when Jews were expelled from Spain. Certainly, that was a terrible day for the Jewish people. In that year, Christopher Columbus sailed to America and returned home safely. That journey heralded great days, although nobody really knew at the time how great they would be. But all those things happened before the occurrence of the Blood Moons. The Joel 2:31 Scripture quoted above says it will be the other way around!

Now let us look at 1947 and 1948. In 1947, the UN voted in a homeland for the Jewish people. In 1948, Israel declared her independence, and the surrounding Arab states declared war immediately. Once again, these historic events happened before the Blood Moons.

Third, in 1967, we do have the great events of the reunification of Jerusalem and the amazing miracles of the Six-Day War between the first and second Blood Moons.

Since one of the four Blood Moons occurs before that event, we can say that there is a bit of support for the Joel verse in that year. But three of the Blood Moons still occur after, so there is a crack in the theory.

Today, many people cite the current Blood Moons cycle of 2014/2015 as an indication of some kind of serious judgment in the fall of 2015. But that could be mixing apples and oranges. By now, many people have read Jonathan Cahn's book, *The Mystery of the Shemitah*. If something terrible does happen in terms of judgment after the Blood Moons, then how do we know that the event was not a result of the Shemitah (Sabbath year) effect that he has written about, rather than the Blood Moons? Just because two things are coincident in time does not mean that they have the same meaning. What if their meanings were different, but complementary?

Please hear me out: I am not trying to be difficult, or burst anyone's bubble. You do not have to agree with me, and we will still be friends.

• Problem #2 – The Crucifixion Darkness Does Not Fit The Pattern

Acts 2 tells us that during Peter's sermon, Yeshua's (Jesus) fiery disciple claims that those who looked on were witnessing the fulfillment of Joel 2. If this is the fulfillment, then where are the solar and lunar eclipses?

Peter lists all of the main elements of the Joel prophecy in his Acts 2 speech, including the appearance of the sun and moon. Peter repeats that the sun darkening and the moon turning to blood would happen **before,** not after the day of the Lord. How, then, could the prophecy of the darkening of the sun and the moon have been fulfilled in 33 AD by solar and lunar eclipses?

Let us examine this detail more closely. Scripture is very clear that the sun was darkened for three hours on the day Christ died. Christ died on the eve of Passover, which is always when the moon is full. During this phase, the moon is on the opposite side of the earth from the sun. So darkness on the earth on that day could not possibly have been caused by a solar eclipse. Furthermore, solar eclipses do not fully darken the sun for more than about eight minutes. The darkness must have come from some other source, most likely supernatural.

Interestingly, the moon is not mentioned anywhere in the crucifixion story. This does not prove that the moon did not somehow turn blood red that night–it might well have–but we can know for certain that there was no total lunar eclipse that night, and there was no Blood Moon Tetrad anytime even close to the year 33 AD. (Yes, in 32 AD there were two Blood Moons that fell on feast days, but the Blood Moons theory proposed in Biltz and Hagee's books are built around four Blood Moons, not just two. I have studied the many historical cases of two consecutive Blood Moons to see if any historical pattern emerges, and I could not find any connection.)

All this leads to the conclusion that without a doubt, whatever caused the sun to turn dark for three hours was unique. And if something happened to the moon to make it particularly red, that was unique as well, not some pre-programmed event like Blood Moons or solar eclipses.

• Problem #3—Tossing Out Data

Half of the Blood Moon tetrads in history have been virtually ignored and were not considered in the development of the theory.

The Blood Moon tetrads have occurred nine times since the birth of Christ:

- 162/163
- 795/796
- 842/843
- 860/861
- 1428/1429
- 1493/1494
- 1949/1950
- 1967/1968
- 2014/2015

No writer on the subject has ever found a strong historical meaning for the first five of these nine Blood Moon tetrads:

- 162/163
- 795/796
- 842/843
- 860/861
- 1428/1429

So, all five of the earlier Blood Moon tetrads are "tossed out," using the reasoning that the important dates around the latter four Blood Moons seemed to be clearer.

But we just explained that the more recent cases do not fit the Joel Scripture very well either. It does not fit at all in 1492 or 1948, nor does it fit perfectly in 1967. Frankly, I am just not comfortable with tossing out data. In the scientific field, you are not allowed to throw out half the data, *ever!*

So when I considered these issues, I said to myself: There are three big problems, and I have reached a point in my research when I am just not satisfied with the conventional answers.

A Diving Catch for the Three Big Problems

Now, there is one last way we could rationalize all the Blood Moon tetrads and connect them to the Joel verses. That would be to treat all of them as one big group before "the great and terrible day of the Lord" in Joel 2. If we created a graph, it would look like this:

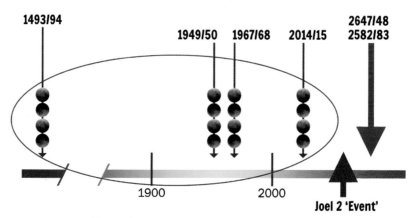

How to force Blood Moons to Occur before Joel 2

But this argument is missing a fact that may surprise many of you.

The Blood Moons of 2014/2015 are likely NOT the last Blood Moons. There are two more Blood Moon tetrads coming in about 600 years. So, the day of the Lord would occur during the Millennium. Does that not seem awkward to explain away?

Some people would argue back that the Millennium is a special period of time, so the Blood Moons of that era could have a different meaning as well. But by that reasoning, the "Joel 2 Day of the Lord" could happen anytime at all, before or after any Blood Moon tetrad– with no restrictions! In that case, the Blood Moons mean nothing. This kind of reasoning feels too much like forcing a square peg into a round hole. These explanations do not satisfy me, neither as a student of the Bible nor as a scientist.

Respect for Pioneer Mark Biltz

At Root Source, we believe our relationships with Christian leaders are important, so let me follow these critiques with the strongest positive statement yet about Mark Biltz. I think he is a great man. I think he was chosen by God to reveal these signs to the world.

Yet I am concerned that some will be angry with Mark if the Messiah does not come soon after the next Blood Moon, in spite of his never having made that claim in his writing. For those who might be angry if some amazing event does not happen soon after the last 2015 Blood Moon, I would like to say something on Mark's behalf. Even Christopher Columbus did not know what continent he had found when he discovered America, and he is still a hero today. Even Abraham, who knew he was on a great journey with God, could not possibly have known all that God had in mind for his great-great-grandchildren in the Promised Land.

Therefore, with all that we have discussed, we will begin to lay the groundwork for a different theory of the Blood Moons.

The Making of a Brand New Theory

The next chapter will offer a theory that fits all nine of the Blood Moon tetrads that have occurred since the birth of Christ, not just the recent Blood Moons. Then in Chapter 7, you will see what that new theory predicts about the future beyond 2015. To lay the groundwork for the theory, though, we need to discuss its story—its origins.

Everyone, including myself, has biases. The question you will need to decide for yourself as you listen to my story is whether my biases were given to me by God, or whether my theory results from my biases. I will provide enough facts so you can decide for yourself.

You may remember that I was quite excited in January 2013 when I watched the John Hagee Blood Moons DVDs, and the very next day, realized that an incredible solar eclipse would reach the North Pole on March 20, 2015. Over the next three months, I put in many hundreds of hours, studying everything I could find on the subject. But by May 2013, after wrestling for months through the issues just explained, I had come to the conclusion that I was not satisfied with this Blood Moons theory; I was not convinced that it was correct. I even began wondering about the significance of my North Pole eclipse discovery. It was frustrating to have invested so much time in investigating the history surrounding the Blood Moon tetrads, the science of eclipses, and Bible passages for the End Times, and then to feel that I was knocking on a closed door.

Eventually, I paused to re-evaluate. It was then that my study took an entirely different direction: I began to study Jewish and Christian history.

I had worked with Israeli Jews for a while, but had never before studied Jewish history. Within this study, one topic kept coming up again and again—the persecution of the Jews throughout history. I read around fifty books on the subject from various viewpoints. While reading, I started an Excel spreadsheet, and every time I ran across an event describing the persecution of Christians or Jews, I documented it in that sheet. As I kept reading, it became clear that the incidents of Jewish persecution would far outpace the rest. When I added them up one day, I counted 500 incidents of the persecution of Jews—and I am sure the list is not nearly complete! The sheer size and scope of this persecution caught me completely off guard.

On the 9th of Av that year, 2013, the customary day of Jewish mourning for the loss of the First and Second Temples, I decided to read through the items in my spreadsheet, one by one. If I spent one minute considering each item, I could complete it in one full day, albeit in 8 hours! I would spend a minute of time considering each item, whether a pogrom, a lynching, a riot against Jewish homes, forcing Jews to wear special clothing, an expulsion of Jews from a town or region, special laws going into effect to restrict Jewish life, a piece of anti-Semitic writing from a Christian forefather, humiliation, or a violent demonstration of Jewish hatred. I would think about each one, trying to imagine what it must have been like to have been there. And then I would move on to the next. They just kept coming and coming... there were so many. I kept thinking not only about how much the Jewish people had endured, but also about the fact that this disgrace had not been talked about. **I had worked with Jews for 25 years and had no idea what I did not know!**

As I read of hundreds of these events in chronological order, one after the other, from the second century up through about the 1200s, the vile acts just continued to get worse and worse. Sometime in the early afternoon, I became physically ill and had to stop. I was overwhelmed by the atrocities committed against the Jews by my Christian forefathers...

Then I noticed something unusual: There was no record of a systematic repaying of evil for evil by the Jews for all that they had suffered. Something broke in me that day, something I sense I may carry for the rest of my life. And in the weeks that followed, I would reflect on it often as an experience of Psalm 23:4. In coming to terms with the awful truth, I felt as if I had walked through "the valley of the shadow of death." It was a valley full of deep, dark shadows. And I learned this, of all days, on the 9th of Av.

Two months later, on September 14, 2013–Yom Kippur that year–I decided to write some prayers of repentance. I would take the information I had read, turn them back to God, and ask for forgiveness for the things my Christian forefathers had done, for the fact that I had never really cared to know these things before in 25 years of working with Jews, and for the overall silence within the Christian world to admit the scope and depth of the hatred toward Jews.

After that day, Yom Kippur, the Blood Moons just did not seem to be so important to me anymore. **So I let the study of the Blood Moons go.** There were other more important things on my mind now–thoughts of Israel and of what a proper response could possibly be for me, concerning the terrible things I had learned over the summer.

My Blood Moons story had come to a full stop right there in September 2013. But every once in a while, when you lay something down, it comes back. About six weeks later, when I least expected it, I got a surprise–a new idea popped into my head out of nowhere, a new perspective on the Blood Moons: Perhaps I was looking at them from the *wrong direction.*

Until then, I had been looking up at a Blood Moon from the ground, thinking as a man: *These four Blood Moons must be special. They are a sign of the future because they appeared on four successive feast days.* But what if I were to take the opposite perspective? What if I were to imagine myself high above the earth, looking down? From that perspective, I might say, "Hey, Earth, your next four Feast Days are special because of those Blood Moons!"

That new perspective changed everything, as you will see in the next chapter.

In the meantime, please consider for yourself how a change in perspective might affect the way *you* view the Blood Moons, or some closed door you are struggling with in your life. This is your chance to jump into the story with me! But let me give you a hint: What was changing within me was a perspective on *history.*

And this brings us to our second foundational question.

History: How do we really see history through God's eyes?

Israel! You see world history through the lens of Israel's history!

It is likely that your reading those words does not connect you with the enormity of that idea immediately. So, to help you take this idea from your mind to your heart, to understand how God feels about Israel, I want to ask you a question about Jesus.

We Christians see Jesus in the Old Testament, right? Of course, we do. But when you read the Old Testament, the Hebrew Scriptures, do you see Jesus a little or a lot? Many Christians think about Jesus when they read Isaiah 53 and Psalm 22, and in Genesis when Abraham was about to sacrifice his beloved son Isaac. But others can hardly open the Old Testament without seeing Jesus in almost every paragraph they read!

So how often do you see Jesus in the Old Testament? I believe that God the Father would say this to you: **As often as you see Jesus in the Old Testament, to that same degree you need to see Israel in the historical events of the world.**

In other words, the way to see all of history is to see it through God's eyes, from His heart, through the nation which He chose to be formed, exiled, returned, exiled again, and then regathered. That everything that happens historically is not independent of, but rather is *fully integrated* with God's overall goal and plan for Israel.

Israel is God's number-one priority when it comes to world history. It has always been that way—even for the 1878 years between 70 AD and 1948, when Israel was reborn. Israel is the nation God cares about the very most. No world event, no matter how dramatic or potentially prophetic, supersedes it in the heart of God.

Do you want to understand an event's meaning, its significance? Look at it in terms of how it helps or hinders God's plan for Israel, and you will suddenly be light years closer to understanding His heart. This applies to whether it is an event that occurs between Arabs and Jews in Israel, or an event between two rural tribes deep in the jungles of Laos. Somehow, that skirmish between two tribes in the jungles fits into God's master plan for the People and Nation of Israel.

Does God care for other nations and love them as much as Israel? Yes, of course! He loves us all, but He assigns different roles in world history to different nations, and Israel is chosen to be the centerpiece. Chuck Missler often reminds his students that there is more prophesy in the Bible about Israel than any other subject.

In summary, I believe that the *only* way to make sense of history is to put Israel at its center, and place every other nation as a satellite around that nation. And the cyclical pattern of the Blood Moons covered in the next chapter begins to make a lot more sense once they are viewed through the lens of God's heart for Israel.

The Blood Moons, in our view, are a repeating pattern of God's love for the people of Israel. They are not so much about predicting the coming of the King of Israel; rather, they essentially reveal God's covenant love for the people of Israel. We believe the Blood Moons are nothing more and nothing less than a wonderful gift directly from the hand of God to the Jews, to Israel, and ultimately to all of us. ✡

CHAPTER 6
Waves of History

Several times now we have asked if you believe Psalm 19:1-2 is being fulfilled specifically or generally by the Blood Moons:

> *"The heavens tell the story of the glory of God; and the horizon tells of his handiwork. Day to day the declaration is spoken; and night to night wisdom is opined."*

Here is what we have concluded: I believe that God has designed His heavenly systems so that they *can* speak specifically, but *He* controls the message and the timing of that message, *not man.* In other words, the heavens do not serve us or our interests; we serve God and His interests. When we are faithful to do that, He may choose to reveal Himself through the heavens or show us other things about His plans. God's plans can be summed up in one word: *glory.* If the message we think we are hearing does not result in more glory for God, I guarantee you, we did not hear correctly!

We further proposed that the Blood Moons demonstrate that God is a covenant-keeping God, that the appearance of these moons is a gift from God to Israel, and that we Christians are privileged to be spiritually grafted into the Root that is Israel.

We have also raised three foundational questions and answered two of them:

When is a fact accurate enough? A fact is accurate enough when we are willing to use it to refute our own arguments.

How do we see history through God's eyes? The way to see world history through God's eyes is to look through the lens of Israel–the Jewish people, the Land of Israel, and the modern-day State of Israel.

How many Bible verses does it take to corroborate a theory? We will attempt to answer this third question now.

The first answer is simple: the more biblical backup, the better.

But there is a second answer: *Greater theories require more scriptural corroboration than lesser theories.*

We are cautious about new theories, especially if they are based on a small number of verses from the Bible. Every verse is valuable, but if the context is small, it's easy to miss an emphasis in the application.

The theory in this chapter is well supported. In addition, this theory makes no claim at all about the timing of the Messiah's arrival. My view is that the Blood Moons do not specifically address the coming of the Messiah. If the moon suddenly and, for *no apparent reason*, started turning blood red, and the sun also darkened, I would certainly think that the "great and terrible Day of the LORD" was at hand and the Messiah would be arriving at any minute!

So let's discuss the details of this theory so you can decide for yourself.

Our Theory of Blood Moons—and Why

Simply stated, the theory is that Blood Moons highlight certain feast days and point out their significance.

In the book of Exodus, we read about the very first Passover in Egypt, followed by the very first Sukkot in the desert. The first feast days ever instituted by God were celebrated just after the Exodus. These days are obviously very special. Many Scriptures describe the events that occurred before, during, and after the Exodus. What can we learn?

First, we learn from Scripture that the period before these first feast days was a time of great difficulty. The children of Israel were enslaved in Egypt under the wicked Pharaoh and had been crying out to God for deliverance for four hundred years. In answer to their cries, an unexpected benefactor arrived on the scene—Moses. After ten dreadful plagues sent by God and many broken promises of Pharaoh, the evil ruler finally agreed to let them go. But where? Into the wilderness. Not to die there, rather, to prepare for the eventual move into their promised homeland.

Furthermore, between Passover and Sukkot of that first year, after their miraculous deliverance at the Red Sea, the children of Israel experienced struggles of various kinds, including military conflicts. Soon after their escape from Egypt, they were attacked by the Amalekites. The Bible says Moses needed help from Aaron and Hur to hold up his hands to guarantee that Israel would prevail in this battle. They won, but God warned that they would be at war with Amalek continually. In time, they received a spiritual treasure that would bless the entire world–the Torah itself, written by the finger of God on Mt. Sinai.

Watch this: After the Israelites celebrated their very first Sukkot in the desert, they were no longer attacked there! I want to apply this to Blood Moons and make a special note of this important pattern: **All the Blood Moon tetrads signal a time of *shalom*, peace for the Jews.** After the second of four Blood Moons, the immediate conflicts for the Jewish people cease for a while, and this period of *shalom* continues until well after the fourth Blood Moon.

Trouble and Tragedy

What about the difficulties that occur *before* the Blood Moon Tetrads? How does that line up with more recent history?

1492 and 1948 – Everything fits perfectly in 1492, because all the hardship for the Jewish people happened beforehand. It also fits well in 1948, because most of the conflict occurred before the Blood Moons were detected in 1949.

Let's look at this 1948 case in more detail:

All the elements of great conflict were present leading up to 1948. Most obvious was the Holocaust of World War II–the death of six million Jews and utter destruction throughout Europe, devastating the continent. There were broken promises to the Jews regarding their homeland and declarations prohibiting Jewish immigration to the Land. Then, there was the unexpected benefactor, Harry Truman, who assumed the presidency of the United States after the death of President Roosevelt, who passed away while in office. As soon as the war was over, many Jews began making Aliyah to Israel from all over the world.

Do you know what happened in the fledgling nation of Israel in

1949 and 1950? They celebrated as never before, with dancing in the streets! At no time in the history of the Jewish people would Passover and Sukkot have been observed with greater joy than in those years!

1967 and 2014 – When we look back at 1967 and 2014, we see something quite interesting. Both of those tetrads appeared before times of war. Let's look at those wars and compare them with the historic period of the Exodus.

- **Miraculous victory (Red Sea)**
  6-Day War in 1967 **1967/68**

- **Nagging conflict (Amalekites)**
  Operation Protective Edge 2014
  2014/15

Both the Six-Day War of 1967 and Operation Protective Edge of 2014 occurred between the first and second Blood Moons of the cycle. The Six-Day War reminds me of the miraculous victory of the Red Sea in that it was brief, and nothing short of miraculous.

In 2014, Israel had to defend herself from attacks from Gaza. This war was not a definitive victory for Israel, but merely a push back until the attacks stopped. This is exactly what happened in the Amalekite war after the Red Sea crossing. In fact, several rabbis made this very connection in the summer of 2014, noting that the way the Amalekites targeted Israel's women and children was identical to what Hamas had shamelessly done—firing rockets into the civilian centers of Israel.

But while there are some key similarities between these recent tetrads and the ancient patterns, there are some missing pieces. For instance, in 1967-1968, where is the slavery? Where are the plagues? And in what way did the Jews leave home after the Six-Day War? You could make the case—and it is true—that this is when they started to settle in the West Bank, but that answer is still not as definitive as the influx of new arrivals after 1948.

As I looked into this theory more thoroughly, I could see the problem: No single tetrad combines everything seen in the tetrads surrounding the original Exodus. So do we throw out the theory? Or is there a solution? Is there a larger view?

Tetrads Come in Waves

Any surfer will tell you that big waves come in "sets." Actually, what you hear most commonly is that a set consists of three big waves.

The Tetrads come in waves, also. There will be 500 years of quiet, followed by a set of either one, two, or three Blood Moon tetrads, occurring over a much shorter period. No random coincidence here. There is scientific proof!

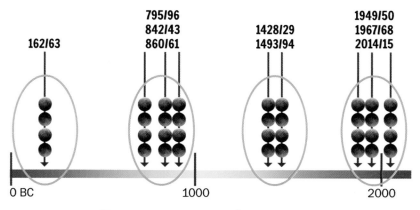

Tetrads come in Waves

So if that is true in science, is it true of history? When God makes a move, does His move also come in waves? Consider these facts:

- The Northern Kingdom saw more than one wave of its people being exiled, even though the main date is considered to be 721 BC.

- Same thing with the Southern Kingdom in 586 BC.

- Several hundred years later, the Jews suffered two waves of destruction. The Second Temple fell in 70 AD, and sixty-five years after that, all Jews were banished from Jerusalem in 135 AD after the Bar Kokba Revolt.

If you study the Blood Moons, you will often see a pattern of sixty-five years between them!

Are there counter examples in history? What about the Exodus? We think of the Exodus as one major event, but even this event could be viewed as taking place in multiple waves. Moses was a foreshadowing of all of Israel when he ran from Pharaoh at age forty into the desert and remained for forty years. The children of Israel did the same thing forty years later. So you can view the Exodus in either one step, or two steps.

Now the key question: Does Jewish migration from place to place during the last 2000 years of exile come in waves as well? And if so, do those migrations match the years of the tetrads?

YES! They match quite well.

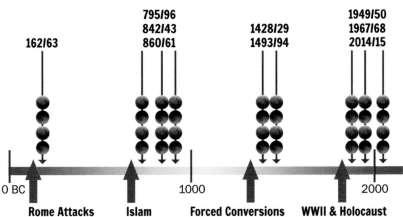

We have the attacks by **Rome** before the first set, the upheaval of **Islam** before the second set, the **forced conversions and the Inquisition** before the third set, and the **Holocaust** before the fourth set.

And after each one of these times of upheaval, we had a great migration—to Babylon (once again as had happened in the past), to Spain, to the Americas, and finally into Israel.

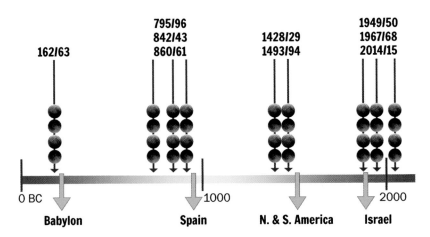

Let's follow the trail in more detail to see if this theory fits.

The Roman and the Rabbi

After Rome attacked in 135 AD, Jews started leaving Israel in large numbers, but not everyone left. Some stayed in the Land.

What good thing, what celebration of the feasts might have occurred by 162-163 AD that could have given Jews hope for the future in such trying times?

Marcus Aurelius came to power in 161 AD and ruled until 180 AD. He was known as the last "good" emperor; he ruled for the good of the Roman people rather than for his own pleasure. His rule happens to mark the peak of the Roman Empire in land and influence. Marcus Aurelius had a curious behavior, though. He persecuted only Christians, but not when Jews and Christians were together. Here is something you won't find in any Roman literature, but you will discover in many Jewish writings: Marcus Aurelius was a close personal friend of a Jew—not just any Jew, but the leading rabbi of the time, Rabbi Yehudah HaNasi, known as Judah the Prince, who was buried in the Galilee.

So Jews had an inside track with the leader of the Roman Empire! Marcus Aurelius sought this rabbi's advice continually. Some say that the emperor eventually even practiced Judaism secretly. According to Jewish historian Rabbi Berel Wein in his teaching series "Great Non-Jews of Jewish History," the emperor eventually even practiced Judaism secretly! The Jews knew this. It was a special time in the life of the post-exilic Jews, and offered rays of hope for the future.

Yehudah HaNasi went on to revolutionize Jewish history forever by being the first person to write down the oral law on paper! Jews had been passing down additional knowledge and tradition for centuries. He knew that difficult times could lie ahead, and their people could not afford to depend upon oral repetition alone. The great treasure he released to the world in that period was called the Mishnah.

But the future was not in the Land of Israel; it was in the region of Babylonia. Once Rabbi Yehudah HaNasi rescinded the prohibition of writing things down, the Talmud would soon follow the Mishnah; most of these documents were written in Babylonia as that region became the center of Jewish life for well over 500 years.

We need to give an honorable mention to the empire that received these Jews, the greatest empire you never studied in school—Parthia.

The Empire of Parthia

To the east of the Euphrates, east of the Roman Empire, was the great empire of Parthia. Parthia ruled for 500 years in the same period as the Roman Empire, from about 250 BC to 226 AD.

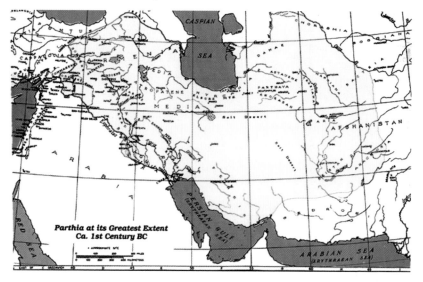

The Empire of Parthia

More was written about Parthia in Rome than any of its other foes. The Romans hated them, probably because Parthia was the only empire the Romans never conquered.

But if Parthia was so big and important, why was it not recorded in Scripture? Well, it is.

In Acts 2:9-10, listing all the nations from which Jews had come to Jerusalem, Parthia is mentioned. In fact, it's first on the list, possibly because it had the largest contingent of immigrants, and because the next three nations listed were under Parthian control.

What was so attractive about Parthia that caused Jews to flock there? Parthia offered *freedom of religion.* Different regions in Parthia, different people groups, including the Jews, could worship whatever gods they wished, as long as they paid taxes faithfully to the central government and supported the national defense. This was a "live-and-let-live" society. They had a king, but his power was kept in check, and he could be deposed. Obviously, this Parthian Empire was nothing like the Roman Empire.

Let me ask you: Which of these empires acted with more civility to their fellowmen? Which of these empires would crucify somebody at the drop of a hat, or feed people to lions for sport? Which empire would decide someone's fate by the flick of a wrist–thumbs up or thumbs down? If you had had a choice of where to live in the second century, no doubt your choice would have been Parthia. I know mine would have been... and obviously of quite a large number of Jews!

But the Parthians were eventually conquered by the Persians. In the seventh century, the Arabs conquered that region, about forty years after Muhammad saw his first visions. And in the next one hundred years, another Arab group–the Abbasid Caliphate–set up their worldwide capital in Baghdad.

The Abbasid Caliphate

Jews were respected by the Abbasid Caliphate, but other Arabs were jealous. When the Abbasids lost power in the Muslim infighting, they started compromising. They invented yellow badges for Jews in 807 AD, as well as blue badges for Christians.

Jews could see that they were in trouble, that rival Arab Muslims would not be as kind to them as the Abbasids. What solution would

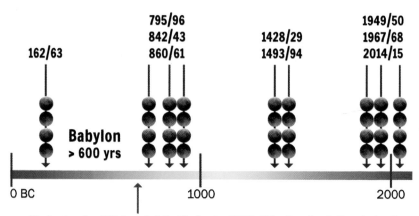

Babylonia (Abbasid Caliphate 750 AD: Capital Baghdad)

God provide? Starting in the early 800s, Abbasids started to move their seat of power–first to Syria, then to Egypt, and then on to North Africa. By 850 AD, the Abbasids had united with the Berbers, the Moors, and the Arabs of North Africa, and settled all along the North African coast. Many Jews came along for the ride. The Abbasids treated the Jews very well, and Jews could finally relax, knowing that they were safe again.

In one hundred years, these very same Abbasids would expand their borders to include Spain. The Jews followed them into the Iberian Peninsula in large numbers, initiating the 500-year-long

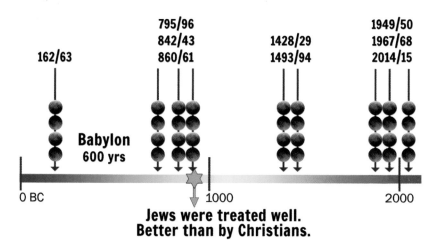

**Jews were treated well.
Better than by Christians.**

Golden Age of Spain. It was here, during this period of history, that Sephardic Judaism was born. But what about the Jews who were still left in the Roman Empire, where things were getting steadily worse? What happened with all the Jews in Greece, Macedonia, and Italy? Let's go back to 795 AD, the beginning of the first of the three Blood Moon tetrads in this period.

Charlemagne's Empire

Charlemagne, around that very same date, 795 AD, invited Jews from Italy to come and join him in the Frank kingdom, the forerunner of France.

When they accepted, Charlemagne installed some of them as his personal advisors, and out of that tiny migration of Jews from Italy to France came the very seedling from which Ashkenazi Judaism was born!

Charlemagne

• Invited Jews from Italy in mid 790s
• Jewish Advisors
• Thus begins Ashkenazi Judaism!

Unfortunately, the golden age of Jewry in France lasted only one hundred years. The treasure that came out of this period of the three tetrads of the 800s was the first Jewish prayer book, referred to today as the *Siddur*. This book, which would prove to be a unifying work, would keep Judaism much more cohesive in the years that followed.

More Trouble: The Spanish Inquisition

As we turn our story back to Spain, trouble comes for the Jews from Christians. Fast forward 500 years from the last Blood Moons Tetrad to 1391 AD, we find the turning point of the story of Spanish Jews, when the Jewish massacre occurred in Seville. As things progressed, the church began a season of forced conversions in 1411-1415 AD. You can see this precedes the first Blood Moon tetrad of this period.

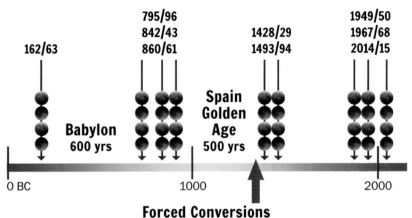

Forced Conversions

It seems that 1428 AD was a period of less intensity. There is no record of especially good things happening to the Jews in 1428 or 1429, so this exposes a crack in the theory. On the other hand, there was a great treasure that came out of the mid-1400s: Johannes Gutenberg invented the printing press. Many books, foremost among them the Bible, were distributed around the world.

A "silver lining" of the forced conversions was that opportunities opened for many Jews to move up into influential offices in government, the church, and the royal palace. But as those positions began to be filled by Jews, suddenly many Christians became "dissatisfied" with the sincerity of the conversions. In 1478, the Spanish Inquisition tribunals were created to test whether these conversions were genuine. Many Jews were considered guilty until proven innocent.

True to our theory that trouble precedes a Blood Moon Tetrad, the Jews experienced forced conversions before the 1428 Tetrad, followed by the Spanish Inquisition beginning before the second Tetrad. As we know, many Jews eventually migrated safely to South and North America; however, it would take one hundred years for the New World to be ready to receive them in any kind of large numbers.

How, then, would God provide for the Jews in the meantime? The answer is surprising: the Ottoman Empire! Sultan Bayezid II invited the Jews immediately when he heard that Spain wanted to give them up. Once again, God had prepared an immediate solution even as He simultaneously seeded the long-term solution.

First, Bayezid II dispatched his navy to evacuate Jews from Spain to Ottoman lands all over the Mediterranean, even allowing a few to move to the Holy Land. He demanded that his people treat the Jews well. He offered them citizenship. And he ridiculed King Ferdinand and Queen Isabella: "Why is Ferdinand considered a wise ruler when he impoverishes his own country and enriches mine?" The Ottoman Empire would retain peak power for another sixty-five years, while Spain began its long, slow decline.

Highlights in the Heavens

Moving to the 20th century, we don't need to remind you that WWII and the Holocaust preceded the establishment of the State of Israel. Another great treasure coming out of that first Blood Moons Tetrad were some of the most important documents found in thousands of years—the Dead Sea Scrolls.

So let's review:

1. The attacks of Rome... leading Jews to Babylon

2. The oppression of Islam... leading Jews to Spain

3. Roman persecution in the same timeframe... leading Jews to France, from which Ashkenazi Judaism spread all over Northern Europe

4. Forced conversions by Christians... leading Jews, first to the Ottoman Empire, later to South and North America, which was a way of escape for many Ashkenazis as well

5. WWII and the Holocaust... opening up the Land of Israel

This is my evidence that Blood Moons signal extra-special feast days, highlighting in the heavens that Jews are remembered. With each of those waves of Tetrads, signaling a "mini-exodus," the Jews were taking the next step in the journey toward their eventual homeland. **The times of the Blood Moons were not times of distress and panic for Jews, but times of relief and celebration.**

The Penumbral Eclipse

"I am with you."

A smart skeptic would ask me the following question: If the Blood Moon lunar eclipses were good for the Jews, what was going on with the moon during the worst years of Jewish history? That is a great question, and the answer is compelling.

In the terrible years of Jewish history, there were no tetrads and no lunar eclipses—*not even one*.

In fact, amazingly, there was a kind of eclipse called a *penumbral eclipse* that is usually invisible. That's the very least amount of lunar activity possible in a year. And that is what happened in the tragic years (for the Jews) of 70 AD, 135 AD, and 1492 AD. It happened again in 1933—the year the Nazis came to power.

It is notable that, in those periods, there were still eclipses, although they were invisible. This reminds me of God and what we often say about Him as we look back to our tough times: "I could not see Him or feel Him. It was only by faith that I knew He was still with us and for us." Indeed, the message of the invisible eclipses is that even when it seems God is invisible, He is still there, still faithful.

How clearly we can see that with the history of the Jewish people in the last 2000 years! **If He is faithful to the Jews, then He is faithful to us all.**

In summary, we have had nine Blood Moon Tetrads since the birth of Christ. These Blood Moon Tetrads each signaled a mini-exodus. But we needed to look at them as if they were waves of history that came in sets. And once we did that, the theory fit quite well, demonstrating how the Blood Moons are a sign of God's faithfulness to His ultimate plan for Israel.

We have looked back in time and established key patterns in history. In the next chapter, we will look forward and try to guess what may happen next! ✡

CHAPTER 7

A New Story Begins

My wife and I own an antique scale that sits inconspicuously in our living room in Austin. That scale speaks to a very old freedom which all humans should enjoy: the freedom to decide. Tellingly, the Hebrew words for "weigh" and "decide" are identical—*lishkol.*

You have just read our theory about the Blood Moons in the last chapter, but Gidon and I want to encourage you to make up your own mind. We report the facts. You decide.

But whatever your take on the Blood Moons, there is an important "takeaway" we hope you glean from this book. We have a question for you, and that question is much more important than our opinion—or yours—on this fascinating topic.

The question is this: Will you be content with your "findings" from the past regarding any particular issue—including the Blood Moons—or will you be willing to search for answers you don't yet have?

Jesus also used this technique when challenging His disciples. His first words in the Gospel of John pose a question. The answer? Another question. And do you remember how Jesus answered that question? By suggesting they take action to seek out the answer with Him! This is much like the approach that Gidon and I take with the sticky subject of the Blood Moons. Will you be satisfied with your present understanding? Or will you venture out with us into the unknown to uncover as much truth as possible? It's your decision.

One of my favorite places in West Texas is a mountain in Big Bend National Park named Casa Grande. As you gaze upon that mountain from the National Park headquarters, you have a choice of two different paths to take. The path to the left is beautiful and easy to walk on, but what you find at the end of that path is typical desert scenery. The path on the right is much more difficult; it is a steep climb thousands of feet into a high mountain forest. But when you make the climb and break through the dense forest, you're rewarded with a spectacular view! Both paths are available, but the decision is yours.

If you're still with us on the "high road," let's review our thoughts about the Blood Moons:

- We have said that Psalm 19 can be fulfilled specifically, but God's purpose is not to serve our interests, but His glory.

- We asked and proposed answers for three foundational questions, about science, history, and the Bible.

- We have stated our belief that the Blood Moons are a gift to reveal God's covenantal love for the people of Israel. God gives only good gifts to His children.

- We recognized that tetrads come in waves, because God also moves in waves. We saw that when trouble came for God's people in exile, He always provided an escape, culminating in the rebirth of a final homeland for the Jews.

In this chapter, we will focus on the most recent tetrads. After a period of 500 years of quiet, we are now in the middle of our third tetrad in sixty-five years: a series of three tetrads that began in 1949 and concluded in 2015.

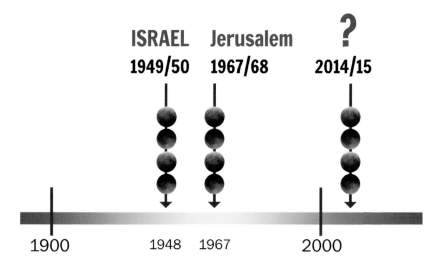

The Final of Three Tetrads

When I considered the model of "waves of history," I wondered if these three most recent tetrads of 1949, 1967 and 2014 might represent three phases of one big move of God.

The tetrad in 1949 was clearly related to the re-founding of the nation of Israel, and fittingly, all four of those Blood Moons were visible in Israel in 1949 and 1950. The tetrad in 1967 was clearly about the reunification of Jerusalem. What might the 2014 tetrad, the third tetrad in the cluster, signify?

I began to think of it as if we were looking down on earth with a zoom lens. Imagine traveling to Earth from space and first spotting the entire State of Israel. As we zoom in closer, Jerusalem comes into view. Once we narrow our focus, what else can we see?

The Temple Mount! We have no inside knowledge from God about His plans for the Temple Mount. This area is so sacred and so precious to God that the safest thing we Christians can ever do when discussing the Temple Mount is to simply proclaim: God will do what He wills to do!

However, an interesting tie-in from the solar eclipse of March 20, 2015 (that fell on Nissan 1 on the biblical calendar) is the Tabernacle, which was the forerunner of the Temple. The dedication of the Tabernacle is recorded in Exodus 40:

> 17 *And it came to pass in the* **first month** *in the* **second year,** *on the* **first day of the month,** *that the tabernacle was reared up* (*The first day of the first biblical month is Nissan 1*).

> 21 *And he brought the* **ark into the tabernacle,** *and set up the veil of the screen, and screened the ark of the testimony; as the LORD commanded Moses.*

> 34 *Then the cloud covered the tent of meeting, and the* **glory of the LORD filled the tabernacle.**

> 38 *For the cloud of the LORD was upon the tabernacle by day, and there was fire therein by night,* **in the sight of all the house of Israel,** *throughout all their journeys.*

If the glory cloud came down upon the Tabernacle on Nissan 1, and this amazingly rare solar eclipse was also scheduled to occur on that day, then why not observe the Temple Mount and see what might happen at sundown, the moment when the biblical day would officially begin. I rented a video camera online and controlled it remotely, using an online service provided by Aish HaTorah, an educational institution located directly across from the Western Wall that has a perfect view of the Temple Mount.

And the result? Nothing special.

It seems, however, that one place on the earth did have some interesting activity that day. Something happened a few hours before the beginning of Nissan 1, during the exact two minutes the shadow of the sun was passing over the North Pole.

Tom and Patricia Moore live in Northern Ireland, not far from the path of the eclipse. They had heard about our call to pray Isaiah 11:9 for those two critical minutes. From their home, they would have been able to see the moon cover about 90 percent of the sun, except they were so socked in with clouds that day, as was most of the United Kingdom, that they saw nothing at all. There was no reason for them to keep standing outside, so they went back into the room in which they often pray. While they were praying—during the precise two minutes of the eclipse over the North Pole—their prayer room was bathed in light, and they felt the strong presence of the Lord. Patricia said that the room was "filled full of angels."

Tom and Patricia Moore's House During the Total Solar Eclipse at the North Pole

They rushed outside to see the source of the light. A hole had opened up in the clouds just enough for the sun to shine directly down on their house. At that moment in time, the sun was eclipsed at the North Pole, but for the Moores in Northern Ireland, the sun was only partially eclipsed; there was plenty of sunlight shining on them. They snapped this photo soon afterward.

I couldn't help thinking of Isaiah 60:1-3:

Arise, shine; for your light has come, and Yahweh's glory has risen on you. For, behold, darkness will cover the earth, and thick darkness the peoples; but Yahweh will arise on you, and his glory shall be seen on you. Nations will come to your light, and kings to the brightness of your rising.

What does this photo mean? We don't know. We may know eventually, after the complete Blood Moons story unfolds.

With all these "indications" of God's move in history, and now a photo, it reminds me of a question that we have so far overlooked...

Where Are Tetrads in Scripture?

Many critics of the Blood Moons ask: Where are tetrads mentioned in Scripture? The answer is: *Nowhere.* You will not find four moons cited anywhere in the Bible, much less four lunar eclipses.

But we might ask another question: Is there anything in Scripture about Passover and Sukkot in one year being treated as a pair of events, followed by a reference to Passover and Sukkot in a second year also treated as a pair of events? No, not overtly, but what about a more general reference to some days in one year being connected to those same days in the following year?

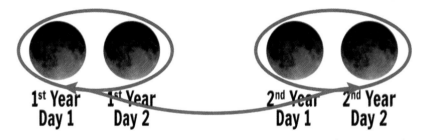

1ˢᵗ Year **1ˢᵗ Year** **2ⁿᵈ Year** **2ⁿᵈ Year**
Day 1 **Day 2** **Day 1** **Day 2**

From "Days" in Year 1 corresponding to "Days" in Year 2

Gidon and I believe there is such a reference. While we do not claim that our discovery is conclusive, it gives Christians an appreciation for the richness of the Hebrew language and how deeply Jews can probe into the Hebrew texts.

In Exodus 12:2, God designated Nissan 1 as the first day of the year. Then we read this in Exodus 13:

> 6 *Seven days you shall eat unleavened bread, and in the seventh day shall be a feast to Yahweh...*

> 8 *You shall tell your son in that day, saying, 'It is because of that which Yahweh did for me when I came out of Egypt...'*

9 *And it shall serve as a sign to you on your hand, and as a reminder on your forehead, that the law of the LORD may be in your mouth; for with a powerful hand the LORD brought you out of Egypt.*

10 *You shall therefore keep this ordinance in its season from* **year to year.**

Well, that's a start. At least, that passage includes the phrase "year to year." But this is where an understanding of the Hebrew language becomes incredibly important.

In Hebrew, the word for year is *shanah*, yet that is not the word used here. Take a look at the highlighted words in verse 10 above. In the original Hebrew, that phrase is written as below, from right to left:

Again, reading from right to left (letters 1 through 10), the expression is pronounced *Mi-Yamim Yamimah*, translated: "The Feast of Unleavened Bread (a holiday that consists of multiple days at Passover) is celebrated from year to year." Literally, those last three words are "from days to days."

This expression appears only five times in the Bible, yet within this brief expression is encoded Passover, *Sukkot*, Covenant, Shavuot, as well as four moons and a lunar eclipse!

- **Passover.** The tiny *Yod* (letters 2, 4, 6 and 8) in its name and pictograph form means hand, which hints at the hand of the

Lord (verse 9) that lifted them out of Egypt.

- **Sukkot.** The *Mem* (letters, 1, 3, 5, 7 and 9) in its name and pictograph form means water (*mayim* in Hebrew) for Jews. Water is associated with the Sukkot holiday. In addition, the Hebrew character Mem looks like the walls of a Sukkah when viewed from above. Just like the two forms of the Mem, the sukkah can have four complete walls (letter 5) or an opening (letters 1, 3, 7, and 9).

- **Covenant.** This expression Mi-Yamim Yamimah has ten Hebrew characters, one for each of the Ten Commandments, split into two words (two tablets) of five Hebrew characters each.

- **Shavuot,** the day the Ten Commandments were given. This is encoded in the fact that the expression Mi-Yamim Yamimah appears five times in the Bible, with ten letters each for a total of fifty characters, for the fifty days between Passover and Shavuot.

- **Four Moons.** The Four Yods in the expression could indicate four moons. One of the Hebrew words for moon is *yareach*, which begins with a Yod. Yareach is used in Psalm 89:37, where the moon serves as a witness to God's covenant with the House of David.

- **Lunar Eclipse.** This is the most amazing of all. Total lunar eclipses have five phases: (1) Penumbral, (2) Partial, (3) Total, (4) Partial and (5) Penumbral. These are represented by the five Mems, where the Total Eclipse is represented by the fifth letter, the "final Mem," perfectly whole and in the middle of the sequence!

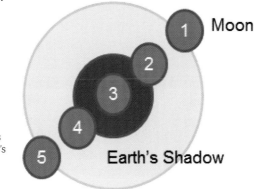

Moon Passes Through Earth's Shadow in 5 Phases

While the Blood Moons do not appear in Scripture *per se*, they may be encoded. Why would God go to all the trouble to encode four moons into the feasts? In the next chapter, we will share something about the original Exodus that, if correct, could explain everything!

Meaning of the Blood Moons, 2014-2015

Now for the most interesting question so far: What might the Blood Moons of 2014 and 2015 mean?

Do you remember how I found out about the Blood Moons? It started with Mark Biltz, then John Hagee, then my sister Laurie, and finally the message reached—me! When I was talking to my sister about the meaning of the Blood Moons, she texted me her thoughts and gave me permission to share them with you:

> The thing I love about this whole hoopla about the sun and moon eclipses is how God gives us something in a mystery. God loves a mystery. Marriage is a mystery. Christ and the Church, a mystery. Really, the very nature of God and His relationship with His creations is a mystery! It isn't critical to understand everything about the mystery intellectually. What's important is to lean in, to inquire of the Lord, to have fellowship with Him, and to ponder these things in our hearts, as Mary did. It's the secret of why Jesus spoke in parables. I just love that about our God!

Laurie's right! God doesn't expect us to figure everything out right away. I believe that God is pleased when we work on unraveling a mystery together. From the outset, we have emphasized: Nobody has a full picture of the Blood Moons yet!

I must also tell you how important that text message was to the entire North Pole Solar Eclipse Prayer project. It was Laurie's sentence:

I just love that about our God.

If she had not written those words, then in my development of the very first Root Source lesson on the Blood Moons, I would have not turned my face beyond the solar eclipses... to God. Without her text message, Gidon and I would have never discussed the possibility of praying during the eclipse. Without the prayer initiative, Tom and Patricia would have never sent us that picture. With the initiative, without Isaiah 11:9 on the mind of Rabbi Tuly Weisz, he would have not connected Bezalel to the shadow of God. It was after making that connection that Rabbi Tuly called Gidon and me and said, "*We are dealing with something here that is bigger than all of us!*"

Message from Gidon

Gidon, my co-author, offers his perspective on the meaning of the 2014-2015 tetrads:

In Jewish tradition, the Jewish people are likened in many traditional parables to the **moon**, and the nations of the world are likened to the **sun**. There are many ideas that branch out from this, but I think the tremendous interest in the current eclipses and Blood Moons emphasizes the **relationship** between these two celestial bodies and, in turn, the **relationship** between the Jewish people and the nations of the world. Throughout Jewish history, there is an almost uninterrupted tradition of fear and suspicion by Jews for the rest of the nations, with—I might add—good reason.

But in our generation, we are noticing **a tremendous outpouring of *teshuva* (repentance)** on the part of many righteous Christians: recognition of the historical wrongs perpetrated by Christians against Jews, remorse, and attempt to right these wrongs. This year's Blood Moon phenomenon is perhaps actually a **message from God to the Jewish people,** to recognize that this outreaching in friendship by Christians is a sign for us to recognize the sincerity of that overture and to **work together** to bring about the expansion of the knowledge of God amongst Jews, Christians, and all people worldwide.

I think Gidon is right. One of the things that may happen in the days ahead is that Christians and Jews will work together in ways we could have only dreamed of a hundred years ago.

It's already happening! Take Gidon and me, for example, an Orthodox Jew and a Christian writing a book together. And then there's Mark Biltz, who is a Gentile with Jewish blood. Mark's Jewish heritage is on his father's side of the family. His mother's side is Christian, through and through. So, in his *own family—actually, in his own body—*Mark represents the coming together of Jews and

Christians, a picture of a work God wants to take to a whole new level. And that, in my opinion, may be one of the reasons God chose him.

All of this point to the fact that only God could orchestrate such unusual connections. And He receives all the glory!

Civilizations on the Decline

In the preceding chapter, we mentioned that some empires were peaking in power about the time of the Blood Moons. The Roman Empire peaked around the early tetrad of 162-163; the Spanish Empire, around 1492, along with the Ottoman Empire, which remained strong for another sixty-five years. The Frank kingdom also peaked during the sixty-five years of the tetrads that started in 795 AD.

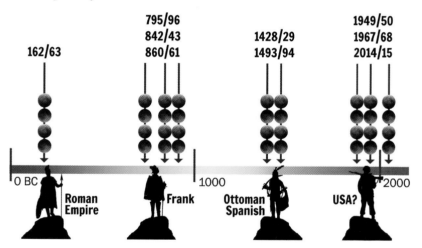

Where does the USA stand? I think we are also peaking. For now, let me encourage you: (1) do not fear, and (2) difficult times also bring opportunity. This book is an attempt to reframe a view of the future that puts you in a position to impact the future. But what about the present?

The End of the Beginning

Let's return to that center line of the United States. The states shown in the diagram below, indicated by green squares, are the states where people could view all four of the Blood Moons of 2014/15. I believe this line, clearly through the heart of the country, represents the entire country. In contrast, South America could not see all four. More significant, I believe, is the fact that the USA could view the last eight Blood Moons—the four in 1967 and 1968, as well as the most recent four! What does it mean?

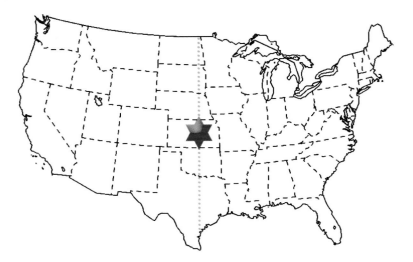

Who could see all eight Blood Moons in 1967/68 and 2014/15?

Since the Blood Moons are linked with Israel in indisputable ways—a gift from God to the Jews—we need to pay attention. Is He only speaking to the Jews in America? Our Root Source teacher, Rabbi Ken Spiro, says that both Scripture and history indicate American Jews will move back to Israel in much greater numbers than ever before.

Or is He warning Americans? God sends a warning before He sends judgment. And His Word clearly states that any nation that turns its back on Israel is in danger of His judgment. See Genesis 12:3.

We went to history and looked for patterns. Do you remember our discussion in chapter 4 about 1492, that the seeds of the USA were found in the voyage of Christopher Columbus? The great empire of USA was seeded by God in the solar and lunar eclipses of 1492. That pattern happens over and over in these waves of history. If the USA was seeded in the tetrads of the 1400s, what nation is being seeded now? What could the tetrads of 2014/15 mean? I was struck very strongly by something Benjamin Netanyahu said to the

U.S. Congress on March 3, 2015. He said that even if Israel has to stand alone, **Israel will stand.**

That speech was given to both houses of Congress, before the eclipse, before Nissan 1. As you remember, Nissan 1 was when the glory of the Lord came down upon the Tabernacle. What did that mean? What message did that glory send to the other nations of the world? I would say that from that moment on, any nation listening knew that **THE LORD IS WITH ISRAEL.**

Yes, tetrads come in waves. The last three tetrads clearly mark the planting of "the seed of Israel." And if you ask me what I think the final tetrad means, I will say that it is not the beginning of the end for Israel; rather, it's the end of the beginning. This is a story that was launched in the last sixty-five years. What we see today is not the closing act, but the opening one. Some may have thought this might be a short story, but it is becoming a novel of epic proportions. The story of Israel being back in the Land is not even close to ending. For those of us who love the God of Abraham, Isaac and Jacob, the wonder, the mystery, and–yes, even the fun–are just getting started. ✡

CHAPTER 8

The Importance of Being Wrong

In 1895, a play called *The Importance of Being Earnest* was performed at the St. James Theatre in London. Oscar Wilde called it "a trivial comedy for serious people." It stood out from the plays of that day because it did not take itself nearly so seriously, and it was often criticized for that. Surprisingly though, it is this play which has outlasted most of its contemporaries!

So with this theme in mind, we need to explore a principle that is even more important than being earnest: the importance of being wrong! The purpose of this chapter is to present a case that God's plan for you, together with His established principles, is that you and I have to acknowledge that we are wrong in order to ever hope to be right. While this sounds counterintuitive, hear me out.

Let us begin with a simple example: the scriptural concept of repentance leading to salvation.

As a boy of ten, I told my parents that I was ready to "become a Christian." My father called the assistant pastor of the Baptist church we attended, and the pastor agreed to come to our home. I still remember this dear, old man explaining the concept of repentance to me. He walked in one direction in our living room, and then turned and walked in the opposite direction. "Repentance," he began, "means to turn around and go in a different direction."

More recently, from my association with Israeli Jews in the past year, I have learned that they have almost the same view, but they add a twist to it: "Repentance means to return home," they say. Their view is embodied in the New Testament story of the prodigal son, isn't it? For some, repentance is coming home to what you left, even if you never knew you left it.

If you are a Christian, no doubt you know the three steps in repentance that lead to salvation:

1. Confessing that you have missed the mark.
2. Acknowledging that your current direction is wrong and renouncing it.
3. Turning and heading in the opposite direction.

We have to recognize—embrace!—the fact that we were wrong in order to repent. In fact, we cannot repent unless we do.

A preacher once gave this example:

Let's say you are driving down the road and you realize that you should have taken an exit many miles back. Confession is saying "I've missed my exit." Renouncing is saying, "I must stop going in this direction; it's the wrong direction. I need and want to turn around." But neither of these is repentance. Repentance doesn't happen until you actually turn around. Full repentance does not occur until you are going in the opposite direction.

And, we might add, restoration is when you can say, "I'm now back to the place where I should have been all along."

Being wrong—and acknowledging and acting upon it—is very important. Of course, there are a few beliefs I have no intention of ever renouncing: That God exists, that the Messiah is Jesus Christ, that the Spirit bears witness to my spirit that I am a child of God. But I may be wrong about many other things, including the truth about the Blood Moons.

Course Correction

What does repentance and being wrong have to do with the Blood Moons, the Shemitah, the Promises to Israel, and the Jubilee?

If I reveal to you more behind-the-scenes glimpses of the process God used in my life—how I made multiple course corrections before this material was ever published—then you will understand why I am so insistent about the importance of being wrong. I am not the only one who has to walk through this principle. You must, also!

Let's begin back on January 21, 2013, when I watched those Blood Moons DVDs by John Hagee and excitement welled up in me. That was the day I realized that the March 20 total solar eclipse was much rarer than the Blood Moons, probably on the order of happening only once every several thousand years. (It turned out to be once every 100,000 years!) This excitement motivated me to do some voracious research during the months of February through May of that year.

But there is something I haven't mentioned. When I saw that solar eclipse, I began to think about writing a book. My idea was to tie together all kinds of natural phenomena—eclipses, comets, earthquakes, meteors, volcanic explosions, and more. But at the time, the concept never got out of the starting gate. Why? Because the key verse I was using to confirm the Blood Moons, (Joel 2:31 and Acts 2:20) contradicted the theory.

What did I do? I prayed, then did more research, trying to find a way to make my theory work. When I had no positive results, I prayed some more, but God simply would not give me light on the topic, no matter what I did.

You see, He was trying to tell me something. He was trying to teach me the importance of being wrong—and admitting it. Looking back, I can see why God withheld His light from me. It was as if He were saying, "Hey, Bob, you need to reframe this. You need to see the bigger picture. You need a different orientation!"

What was I missing? It didn't seem to be anything in the data. Was it something else? Something in the heart? At first, I couldn't believe that there was anything wrong with my heart. I was a Christian, wasn't I? Loved God. Loved my fellowman...

The more I probed, the more uneasy I felt. Suddenly a new thought occurred to me: God was showing me that it was a matter of my attitude toward certain people. I needed to be willing to confess that I was wrong about my attitude...toward the Jews! What attitude toward the Jews? I found the answer in Romans 11:20: "Do not be conceited, but fear; for if God did not spare the natural branches, He will not spare you either." Paul warned Christians not to feel superior to the branches we Gentiles are grafted into—the Jews. Yet I suppose I did feel superior—because I had Jesus the Messiah in my heart.

God needed to break me of this mindset because He had a bigger plan for me than writing a book on the End Times. He was saying to me, although I could not hear at first: *Bob, I need to prepare you to help Gidon start Root Source.* That was a very difficult spring and summer—wondering, wandering, praying—not understanding why I couldn't go forward. But God was saying that I needed to go in a different direction. All this took place until October 2013, about six months before the first Blood Moon in 2014.

As God would have it, once I was willing to get on the same page with Him about the thing He cared about, then He would give me light about the thing I had once cared so much about—and that I had to release...

An Idea Reborn

That insight boiled down to this: a change of perspective. Rather than looking up at the eclipses of the moon and feeling that they were prophetic tools of the End Times because they occurred on biblical Jewish feast days, I looked down from the moon to Earth and began to realize that these objects in the sky bear witness to God's covenant of love for His Chosen People. Thus, the Blood Moons idea was reborn—as a witness to the Jews.

Exclamation Points in the Sky

One of our Root Source students, Linda Merchant, expressed this thought beautifully when she said, "The Blood Moons are like exclamation points in the sky over the earth!"

Another student, Daniel Camick, offered this Scripture:

But I will not break off My lovingkindness from him, nor deal falsely in My faithfulness. My covenant I will not violate, nor will I alter the utterance of My lips. Once I have sworn by My holiness; I will not lie to David. His descendants shall endure forever and his throne as the sun before Me. It shall be established forever like the moon, and the witness in the sky is faithful. Selah.

Psalm 89:34-38

Notice that these verses not only call out the sun and moon, but they call out the house of David. David was from the tribe of Judah and was therefore Jewish.

Right on the heels of that revelation about the Blood Moons came a test from God: *Now that you see this, I need you to let it go again. I have shown you some things, but I have not given you permission to write about them! I am going to test your priorities now. Are you willing to not share what I give you?*

Have you ever had the frustrating experience of God telling you something profoundly interesting and then asking you not to share it? Or you may be one who prefers to keep things to yourself. In either case, God sometimes calls us out of our comfort zone to undertake something that runs counter to our personality or even our desire!

The First Blood Moon

Beginning in October 2013, six months before the first Blood Moon, I had to go into silent mode. When I did try to share a couple times, the doors were all closed. It was becoming quite clear that the idea of writing a book was wrong—at least, at that time.

On the night of April 14, 2014, the first Blood Moon was visible over the entire continental United States. That lunar eclipse was a very red one—one of the reddest in a long time. Did you ever consider that if God wanted to discredit the Blood Moons theories, one of the easiest ways was for Him to have made sure that particular moon was NOT very red? But it was, or so I was told, as I was not in a position to see it.

On that night, I was in Jerusalem, at Christine Darg's *Exploits Ministries Passover Conference*. I was prepared to speak about the theory that tetrads come in waves, and that each wave is like a mini-Exodus – which brings me once again to the importance of being WRONG. *Bob, you need a reframe... a bigger picture... a different orientation.*

Only the day before, I had begun to sense that God was saying that somehow we as Christians needed to realize the importance of acknowledging that we were wrong in our approach to the Blood Moons—that the Blood Moons belonged to the Jews. Now I felt that God was asking me, *Will you be willing to repent publicly? And give others a chance to join you?*

I was stunned. What would that repentance even look like? After prayer and consultation with my wife, I asked Christine for permission to add a repentance prayer opportunity after my talk. She agreed! I learned later that an Orthodox Jew had recently confronted her with a complaint: "Why are you Christians taking our Blood Moons?"

That Passover night, after explaining the new theory of the Blood Moons—as a gift to the Jews and a confirmation of God's covenant with them—we spent some time repenting for the ways Christians have treated Israel in regard to End-Times prophecy. As for myself, I had a personal decision to make. What change would I be willing to make in view of my participation as a Christian? I decided to let go of publishing any material on the Blood Moons—*unless it was in partnership with a Jew.* You know the end of this story because you are reading this book; however, that would only happen much later.

I had met Gidon three months earlier in January 2014, and by February, we had agreed to collaborate on trying to bring his vision to life. In March, we began planning and organizing, and by April, we had officially registered Root Source with the Israeli government as a new company. But Gidon had no interest in the Blood Moons at that time. Yet, to be of help to me, he did suggest some names and made some introductions to other Jewish people who might be interested in co-writing a book. None of those were a good fit.

The Second Blood Moon

With the second Blood Moon upon us—October 8, 2014--we were running out of time. This year, I would be in the USA so I would be able to view it. There was only one problem—with my focus on October 8, I forgot that the eclipse would occur on the night of the 7th and very early morning of the 8th, and I slept right through the event! My only consolation was learning from a friend that it was cloudy that morning.

But something happened during that October. I had a new idea. I had been thinking that we had had 2000 years of tetrads. But what about the years prior to 0 AD? Now to be fair, I'd given this some thought many times, but without a reliable Jewish calendar for that time period, there was no accurate way to determine the exact dates of the Passovers. Much to my relief, I realized that there was a way to determine which of the many tetrads in that era were clearly Blood Moons Tetrads. I found several, including one in particular that seemed to stand out—the only one of its kind in a 500-year period of

Israelite history.

Referring to the biblical chronology table that I had been developing over the previous eighteen months, I checked the date and got the biggest surprise of my entire experience–even bigger than the solar eclipse at the North Pole:

There was a Blood Moons Tetrad the year of the original Exodus out of Egypt!

This could not be random. The chance that my Exodus date and the Blood Moon Tetrad dates being exactly the same was about one in 500! If all this was correct, the implications were absolutely staggering. It would forever seal the deal that the Blood Moons were a witness to God's eternal covenant to give the Israelites a homeland. It would also forever confirm that the Blood Moons were not a Christian "idea"–except in that we were grafted into Israel. It would have profound implications about how God interacts with us today. It would give us proof that he had left cosmic "breadcrumbs" so that those of us in the modern era might have a hope of coming to a consensus on certain key dates in history that otherwise would be the source of endless speculation.

You would think this would thrill me, but it was even more frustrating than before. God had given me another insight for which there was no open door. Now I had to keep both the solar eclipse at the North Pole and the possible connection of the Blood Moons to the original Exodus a secret.

The Third Blood Moon

Near the end of February 2015, three weeks before the total solar eclipse of March 20, I was forced to follow the example of many of my biblical forebears who also had to wait for the fulfillment of a dream – Abraham . . . Moses . . . Jacob . . . Joseph . . . Mary, the mother of Jesus. The words *"in the fullness of time"* took on new meaning.

And then, in a marketing meeting, Gidon suggested that I start teaching a class on the Blood Moons. He didn't know the secrets I had been keeping about the solar eclipse at the North Pole or the Exodus date!

As previously mentioned, God did steer our focus toward prayer, and we ended up praying Gidon's selected verse, Isaiah 11:9, for the two minutes during the solar eclipse on March 20. Then two weeks later, at the time of the third Blood Moon, we are pleased to say, we issued a call to prayer jointly with Blood Moons discoverer Mark Biltz. This time in Austin, I had the right date, but stormy weather prevented my seeing the eclipse. Finally on April 20, at the Root Source launch event in Jerusalem, held just prior to Israel's 67th birthday, we "gave the Blood Moons to the Jews" and publicly announced the *possibility* that a Blood Moons Tetrad accompanied the original Exodus out of Egypt.

In that presentation, my favorite slide was a table showing how God had released an incredible spiritual treasure to the world during each of the waves of Blood Moons Tetrads. The Torah was at the top of the list!

Spiritual Treasures Released to the World during Blood Moons

Blood Moon Tetrad Wave	Spiritual Treasure Revealed
1579/78 BCE	Exodus/Giving of Torah
1058/57 BCE	King David/Psalms
162/63 AD	Mishnah/Talmud
860/61 AD	Siddur Prayer Book
1428/29 AD	Guttenberg Printing Press
1949/50 AD	Dead Sea Scrolls & Israel Declared

Our website contains a fully referenced paper **www.root-source. com/blog/blood-moons-gift-to-the-jews/** that explains the Exodus and Tetrad calculations and assumptions. Those who have studied the Exodus date know that it is fraught with controversy, so we in no way expect this work to settle the matter. No other prediction in this book requires the Exodus date to be correct. That possibility stands on its own, and as the subject of this chapter states, that date may be proven wrong someday. What is very reliable and historical, though, is that on April 20, 2015, Root Source symbolically gave the Blood Moons to Israel as a gift to the Jews, and we revealed their possible connection to the Exodus.

I have gone into detail about my journey to show how God worked through the steps of my being willing to have my perspective changed and enlarged.

But there is one more bizarre piece to the story.

In preparing for the Root Source launch event on April 20, 2015, I was rechecking my work on the Blood Moon Tetrads in the years before the common era (BCE), and I realized that what I thought was a Blood Moons Tetrad was not one at all, because I had a mistake in the conversion between the Julian and Gregorian calendar dates. This meant that the entire connection to the Exodus had just fallen apart! This was a severe disappointment, news especially difficult to break to Gidon. But by then I was used to this whole journey having twists and turns. I assumed the Exodus thing was just a red herring.

But as I was doing a recheck of the chronology dates, I realized that one of the sources I was using had an error in it also! One of the books I was referencing had incorrectly summarized a conclusion by E.W. Bullinger in his landmark book, *Number in Scripture*, originally published over 100 years ago. When I went to the original E.W. Bullinger source, his conclusion was different from mine by 18 years. Since much of my chronology was based on his, this changed the chronology of my Exodus date by 18 years.

This was even more embarrassing—my Blood Moons calculations were off and my chronology was off! Why had I even bothered with this exercise in the first place? It was with great fear and trembling that I went back to the scientific calculations of tetrads to see what would have happened 18 years later. To my shock, not only was there another tetrad at that time, but it was a Blood Moons Tetrad—the only Blood Moons Tetrad for the next 500 years. And the icing on the cake was that with this new date, there was even another tetrad (not a Blood Moons Tetrad) exactly 40 years later, the year that the Jewish people would have entered the Promised Land. The Exodus idea was saved! When I told Gidon about the two-year errors cancelling themselves out perfectly, he said "Somebody (God) seems to be looking out for you!"

Indeed!

Who Can You Trust?

As we have demonstrated, God often corrects our course, so you have no way of knowing if the predictions we make in this book will be completely accurate or not. Our advice: Do not put your *full trust* in anything we might say—but neither should you discount it. In fact, I think I would say it like this: if you are the kind of person who trusts easily, then be very careful with our predictions. And if you are the kind of person who naturally distrusts what others have to say, then realize that perhaps God might be pleased to give you an absolutely key insight from this book.

I cannot guarantee that God won't correct my course again at some time in the future, but by His grace, I'm willing to be wrong and then be corrected. *"Hey, Bob, you need a reframe. You need a bigger picture, a different orientation."* With that in mind, I promise to tell you what I think may happen to whatever level of insight I believe God may have given. That kind of openness is how friends interact with each other.

So let me summarize once more: I understand that I may be wrong. I might need to be reframed by God, and He may choose this very public forum to do it. If I am corrected or reframed, I'll be sure to tell you about it on our website at **www.root-source.com** in our blog. You can put yourself on our mailing list by signing up for the free videos and newsletter. **www.root-source.com/free-newsletter**

What about you? Are you willing to be wrong? Are you willing to reframe? When was the last time you had a course correction? How recently? And what did you do about it?

Being wrong is not shameful; it's actually a place of honor—as long as you do something about it. Because as Psalm 25:3 tells us, God does not put to shame those that wait upon the Lord. Being wrong can be like pure gold. Pure gold comes from pressure. So here is a piece of pure gold that I offer you in this book: Being wrong is anything but wrong. It is the way up in this upside-down world, where the first are last and the last are first. The wrong can be right, and the right can be wrong. If you try to save your life, you lose it, but if you lose your life for His sake, you will find it. ✿

CHAPTER 9

The Peaking United States

We have shown that whenever a wave of tetrads moves through history, one empire is peaking. We suggested that the United States might be an example of an empire that is currently peaking.

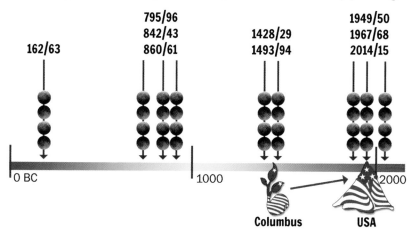

Whenever one empire peaks, however, another is *seeded*. For instance, as Spain was reaching its peak in 1492, the United States was in the process of being seeded, as America was discovered by Columbus. We then suggested that the current wave of tetrads–1949, 1967, and 2014–seemed to indicate clearly the seeding of the brand-new, yet ancient Israel.

Something in our hearts calls out for such a pattern. When one story comes to a climax, there is a desire in us to find the new story that is beginning. This pattern is often seen in Scripture:

> Then I saw a new heaven and a new earth; for the first heaven and the first earth passed away, and there is no longer any sea.
> And I saw the holy city, New Jerusalem coming down out of heaven from God, made ready as a bride adorned for her husband.

> *Revelation 21:1-2*

Even in the greatest story ever told, the ending heralds a new beginning. Conversely, a new beginning requires an ending. That is why this chapter takes a deeper look at the United States and its trend toward decline.

Is the United States on its Way Out?

When I say "the United States," I want to add that I also think this story applies—at the very least—to the British Empire as well. The British Empire and the United States have been closely connected for a long time, but I am not as familiar with this Empire as I am with the U.S. For those of you who live in the United Kingdom, Canada, Australia, South Africa or New Zealand, please consider this finding from your standpoint, too.

If you do not live in the British Empire or the United States, but are a part of Western Civilization, may I propose this theory: That we could possibly be looking at the peak of all of Western Civilization as we know it. I will not go so far as to say that this includes China and the Far East, but in terms of Western Civilization, I believe it is possible.

Let's look at the history of empires. How long do they take to rise? How long do they take to fall? In most cases, we are talking about at least a couple of hundred years on either side.

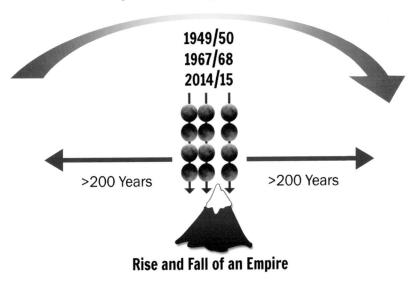

Rise and Fall of an Empire

When Blood Moons identify the peak of a civilization, it does not necessarily mean they are identifying the *end*. We are seeing some very long cycles with Blood Moons. Take the United States, for example. It has taken about 400 years for the United States to achieve the powerful standing we enjoy in the world today. And if the United States is peaking, it does not *automatically* mean that its decline will be coming very shortly. (Note: We will consider the case for a much faster decline later in this book, based on Shemitah cycles.)

Founded in 1607, Jamestown was the first colony. Most people think the first was the Plymouth colony in 1620, when the Pilgrims arrived on the Mayflower. Much credit is given to Plymouth because of the religious component, which is absolutely true, but there was also a religious component in Jamestown. If you do an Internet search on "Robert Hunt, Cape Henry, Virginia," you will find an interesting story about America being dedicated to the purposes of Jesus Christ in 1607–at the founding of that colony. The following diagram is based on the year 2015.

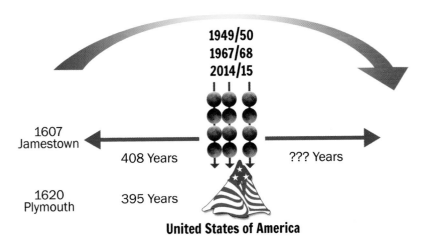

United States of America

We have repeated throughout this book that tetrads come in waves. For the three most recent tetrads, we asked, "Could these three sets of tetrads be identifying phases of the life of Israel?" We saw that the first tetrad in 1949 was connected with the founding of the State of Israel. The second tetrad in 1967 was connected with the reunification of Jerusalem as a result of the Six-Day War, which was a major event. While we were not yet sure of the meaning of the tetrads of 2014/2015, we speculated on several possibilities, including the groundbreaking idea that Jews and Christians might be coming together more closely than ever before.

But all that talk was about Israel. What might this "three phases" idea imply for the United States, the United Kingdom, and the West? Could the three tetrads in the last seventy years indicate three phases of the peaking of the United States? This chapter puts forward a case that these three tetrads in 1949, 1967 and 2014 indicate:

1949/50 The Moral Peak

1967/68 The Political Peak

2014/15 The Economic Peak

Let me explain how I came to this idea: it came first because of Israel. A few years ago, the pastor of our church, Geno Hildebrandt, began preaching a series on 2 Kings. Not too many pastors are bold enough to dive into the middle of all those kings and fit all those stories together. I remember his comment that the Northern Kingdom in the period just after Ahab and Jezebel, was, according to the historical commentaries, a period of strong economic activity.

In addition, in his book *The Harbinger*, Jonathan Cahn identified Isaiah 9:10-11 in connection with the United States. In other words, the Northern Kingdom, led by the tribe of Ephraim and in the region of Samaria, parallels the United States in some ways.

If the economic peak of the Northern Kingdom came later, when might its political and moral peak have occurred?

MORAL PEAK	POLITICAL PEAK	ECONOMIC PEAK
Period of David	Period of Solomon	Period of 2nd Kings
2 Sam 7:1-28	1 Kings 4:21, 4:34 10:21-24, 11:9-14	Isaiah 9:10-11
Desire to Build A House for the Lord	World-wide Respect	Ephraim & Samaria

The Three Phases of the Peaking of Israel

Moral Peak: David's reign. There is no question that the moral peak of the Kingdom of Israel came during David's reign. Read 2 Samuel 7:1-28 and you'll see David's true heart. Although he was a man of war, his heart's desire was to build the house of the Lord. What an amazing moment! See how the Lord responds to him. God also calls David a man after His own heart. Yet there was hidden sexual sin in David's life, as we know. He tried to hide his sins with Bathsheba, but God said that future sexual sin would be known to all Israel. Nor was David permitted to build the Temple.

Political Peak: Solomon's reign. There are a number of references in the narratives of Solomon that speak of how Israel is perceived from the outside—its wealth, Solomon's wisdom, etc. But the thing that creates a political peak is respect—respect from peers. This was the period in Israel's history when it was strongest politically and engaged in the fewest wars. It was an era of peace. The nation had much influence, but there were problems, too. For example, open sexual sin—King Solomon set a poor example with his wives and their practices. Toward the end of Solomon's life, Israel was no longer invincible, and God raised up Hadad, the Edomite, to harass Israel in some of its territories.

With Israel as a model, how might the phases illustrated here correlate to the phases of the United States?

MORAL PEAK	POLITICAL PEAK	ECONOMIC PEAK
1949/50	1967/68	2014/15
Winning WWII	WW Freedom	Militant Islam
Building a Home for the Jews: Israel	Putting a Man on the Moon July 20, 1969	Markets Reach All-time Highs

The Three Phases of the Peaking of the United States

Three Peaks of the United States

Moral Peak: 1949/50: The United States played a key role in winning World War II, a war that was not waged on its own soil until a surprise attack by Japan at the naval base at Pearl Harbor, in the U.S. territory of Hawaii. The European War was fought for the sake of other nations. Yes, it took us awhile to get involved prior to December 7, 1941, but when we did, our whole country rallied and sacrificed to help win the war by 1945. In 1947 the United States led efforts in the UN to pass a vote in the General Assembly to establish a

Jewish homeland. But that vote to legalize a State would not actually create it upon the expiration of the British Mandate one half year later. The new birth would still require the full backing of the United States again in 1948.

Against the desires of most of the world, Harry S Truman, convinced by his best friend, Eddie Jacobson, met with Chaim Weizmann. Dr. Weizmann was turned down several times before. Even though powerful forces did not want the United States to support Israel, Harry kept his promise to Eddie. Dr. Weizmann met secretly with President Truman. Dr. Weizmann became the first president of Israel.

Dr. Weizmann had to enter through the East Gate of the White House so he would not be noticed by the press. During their meeting, President Truman gave Dr. Weizmann his word that he would support Israel's statehood. (Used with permission from the book *Harry and Eddie: The Friendship that Changed the World*).

Along with the enthusiastic support of the American people following the Holocaust, Truman's efforts to ensure that the Jewish people would have a homeland of their own was *the most righteous act ever instituted on American soil in the sight of God*. I think these years in our history stand out as the moral peak. Like David in the days of Israel, we did have our sexual sin. In the countries where the Yanks fought or visited, they were well known for their sexual appetites. In the United States, though, this aspect of the war was concealed, kept out of popular media and literature, but common knowledge among the ranks.

Political Peak: 1967/68: During those years, the United States was a bastion of freedom; no country messed around with us. We were known for standing for freedom worldwide. Even with the Soviet Union as a major foe of the United States, there was really no aggression toward us after the early 1960s. It was well understood that the United States was the most powerful nation on the face of the earth.

The "marker" of this strength was putting the first man on the moon—planting an American flag there—on July 20, 1969. This placed the United States on the map, not just within its own era, but in achieving a first in the history of the world! This monumental achievement might actually have been a reward for the righteous acts that occurred in the 1940s.

When I look at dates, I often calculate the Hebrew calendar date, and I noticed something interesting about our "man on the moon." That mission lifted off on the 1st of Av. We landed on the moon on the 5th of Av. We touched back down into the Pacific Ocean safely on the 9th of Av. I find it interesting that this mission ended on the 9th of Av, which, on the Jewish calendar, is a day of great sorrow for the nation of Israel. I do not know what this means except for a biblical prophecy that the days of mourning will turn into days of joy for the Jews. This was certainly a day of joy for the United States, possibly a positive harbinger of the future.

While we peaked politically, we also sowed a seed of destruction that would be reaped like the whirlwind many years later. Like Solomon in the days of his reign in Israel, we had our sexual excesses in the 1960s, the Free Love Movement brought about by the release of "the pill" in the early 1960s. We followed that with the decision to legalize the killing of our children through abortion on demand in 1973.

Interestingly, during that same time period, we began to lose the lives of our young people in Vietnam. Up until that time there was a saying in our country: "The United States has never lost a war." This was no longer heard after Vietnam, when we got kicked out. Once again, this fits the pattern of the political peak of Israel, where they began to be frustrated by their enemies toward the end of Solomon's life, also coming after his decision to dive headlong into sexual sin.

Economic Peak: 2014/15: During these two years, we saw many all-time highs set in the financial markets. The stock market reached several all-time highs in the Dow, NASDAQ, S&P 500, and the dollar was among the strongest currencies in the world. However, there was a general sense that those peaks were not created on as solid a foundation as in past years. It reminds me a bit of the way it might have felt in Israel when the Northern Kingdom was doing well economically, while trouble was brewing.

Now, what many feared has come upon us: the Supreme Court decision to force gay marriage to be recognized in all fifty states. (Chapter 15 is devoted entirely to this subject.)

In addition, militant Islam is an enemy that is real and fierce and will not back down, gaining territory almost daily despite the efforts of its coalition enemies. Interestingly, the enemy we face in ISIS is from the exact same region of Syria/Iraq that the Northern Kingdom of Israel faced in its day, the Assyrians. Jonathan Cahn wrote *The Harbinger* well before that threat, but the connection he proposed between the Northern Kingdom and the pattern of the United States is now even more appropriate!

"For the Sake of the Father!"

Another pattern that was instituted by God during Israel's peak period was this: "For the sake of the father." In other words, God delayed certain unpleasant consequences of the sin of the people until other key people had lived and died.

> So the Lord became angry with Solomon, because his heart had turned from the Lord God of Israel...
> ...I will surely tear the kingdom away from you and give it to your servant.
> Nevertheless I will not do it in your days, for the sake of your father David; I will tear it out of the hand of your son.

1 Kings 11:9-12

Hence, because of the righteousness of past fathers of the faith, God may delay certain difficulties coming upon a nation. How might this apply to the United States?

The presidents that were alive during World War II are gone. The presidents who were alive in the 1960s are gone. From that standpoint, judgment could come upon us at any time, but there is one other factor, a perspective that I often ponder on: The generation that fought World War II was called "The Greatest Generation" in our country. In that generation, 16 million Americans served their country. The number of living veterans is obviously decreasing every year, as we see in this chart:

Notice that 2015 was the year that number decreased to below one million veterans. Interesting! Does God keep a calculator ready and say, "I am going to delay judgment until there are less than a million veterans left?" Or 50,000? Or 50? I doubt it. Another interesting question is: When will the last WW II veteran die? Based on actuarial tables, that death is expected to take place in the year 2036.

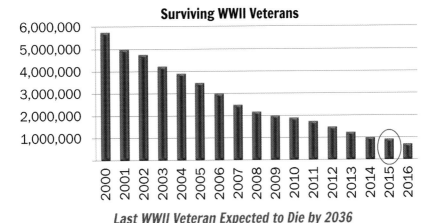

Surviving WWII Veterans

Last WWII Veteran Expected to Die by 2036

The general principle is this: God considers the lives of some of His saints very precious and preserves their lives in trying times, ending their lives before trouble comes. Isaiah 57:1-2 says:

"The righteous man perishes and no man takes it to heart; And devout men are taken away, while no one understands. For the righteous man is taken away from evil, He enters into peace; They rest in their beds, each one who walked in his upright way."

That may have well been the case in the passing of Lance Lambert, who died on Sunday, May 10, 2015, at the age of 84.

Lance was a friend of Israel. He was a Jewish Christian who had made aliyah (immigrated to Israel) and was working in his own ministry, along with the highly respected Jerusalem organization, Christian Friends of Israel, founded by Ray and Sharon Sanders.

I, Bob, was introduced to Israel by Lance Lambert when I heard him speak in the early 1970s at a Christian conference in Virginia. I have always held him in the highest esteem.

Here is what Gidon wrote to Christine Darg, who had hosted Lance's last public appearance at her April 2015 Passover Convocation:

I am humbled to have spoken to your group, Christine, just following Lance's last public appearance. His were shoes too large to fill. I am sure that his teaching and impact will continue in this world, way beyond their influence while he walked among us.

Our Tribute to
A True Spiritual Father
Lance Lambert
1931 - 2015

We are grateful for the blessed memory of Lance Lambert, and we close this chapter with his last formal prophetic word on March 15, 2015:

> *Everything in Israel will change, upside down and inside out. Nothing will be where it used to be. They will seek to destroy Israel, but they will see that they are destroying themselves. Bibi Netanyahu has been faithful. Everything will change, and the only certainty is this: "I am The Lord. Do not fear, I will defend Israel and I will save her. You will suffer, and suffer greatly, because I will turn everything upside down and inside out. I will not fail you and I will not fail Israel. Take note when you see these things. I am in the battle and I have won. Keep your eyes on My power and you will be safe."*
>
> *We have to know the Lord and the power of His resurrection. It's not enough to be a dead Christian. If The Lord says it's going to be unparalleled, then it is going to be unparalleled. It's worth it all—knowing Him and trusting in Him.*
>
> *"Watch Russia, for she is up to no good. Watch her carefully,"* *says the Lord. "With your own eyes, you shall see My triumph over darkness and evil. Trust Me,"* *says the Lord.* ✿

CHAPTER 10

The New Ancient Israel

Before we conclude our section on the Blood Moons and move on to the Shemitah, we will attempt to connect them to a subject of interest to many people: their own wallet.

The United States is a nation that is peaking, and has reached its economic climax. The message we presented in the previous chapter was bleak, to say the least. It is news that investors do not want to hear. As an investor myself, there was no joy in writing that chapter.

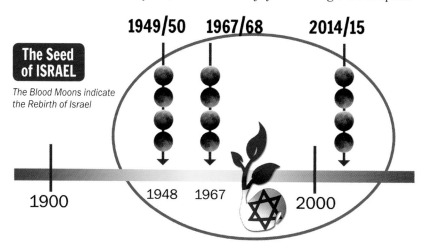

The Seed of ISRAEL

The Blood Moons indicate the Rebirth of Israel

1949/50 1967/68 2014/15

1900 1948 1967 2000

When one empire is peaking, however, another begins its rise. Israel is a nation that is presently being seeded. Both new and old at the same time, Israel's story is unlike anything we have ever seen in the history of the world. Since the year 2000, people refer to Israel not just as a survival miracle, but as an economic miracle.

The Rebirth of Israel

According to the pattern of the Blood Moons, the seeding and sprouting of Israel has happened much faster than in the case of the United States. Seeded by the voyage of Christopher Columbus in 1492, the United States was founded 115 years later in 1607 at

Jamestown, then declared its independence 169 years later in 1776.

The founding of Modern day Israel was at Petah Tikvah (literally the Door of Hope) in 1878, followed in 1882 by three more settlements. Baron Edmond de Rothschild was a main financial backer. The declaration of independence came 70 years later in 1948. Now in 2015, a mere sixty-seven years later, few would argue Israel's position as a world leader in many respects.

Consider that all of this has happened to Israel in its "seedtime." Could it be that what we are seeing is nothing compared to the sprouting we might see in the next few years? Even as other parts of the world deteriorate, would it not be just like God to advance Israel at an accelerated rate in these momentous times?

We see hope in the nation of Israel. There are many opportunities, especially financial opportunities. And that is the subject of this good news chapter! Jews have won a total of 41% of all the Nobel Prizes in economics. Not bad for a population that represents about 0.2% of the world's population. Over 20% of all Nobel prizes awarded were awarded to Jews.

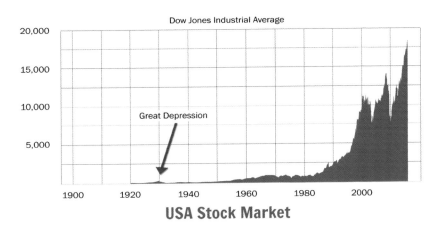

USA Stock Market

Back to the USA

Let's look at a snapshot of America's financial history to see where Israel may be headed. This graph tracks the rise of the U.S. stock market since its inception in 1885. Notice the general trend!

The little bump on this graph with the red arrow is the Great Depression, when the stock market crashed. That little bump does not look like much of a crash on this graph, but that's because the scale on the left compresses everything that happened in the early years. Now look at the exact same data, with a logarithmic scale, and you will see much more easily "how it felt" to live in those earlier years of the stock market.

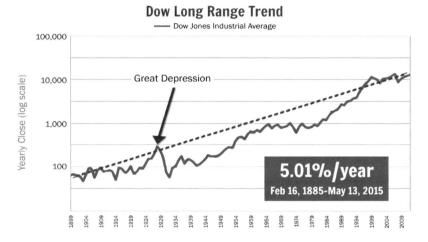

USA Stock Market
U.S. Stock Market Averaged 5% Growth for 130 Years

The dip below the red arrow shows the Great Depression—by far, the largest and most difficult problem in the history of the stock market.

Next, notice the dotted red line. The general slope of this curve shows growth of the value of the thirty most important companies in the U.S. market (the Dow); as such, it is a partial measure of the overall financial health of the United States along with NASDAQ and the S&P 500. We start from 1885, when the Dow Jones Industrial Average was first instituted, to May 13, 2015, the date of the end point of this diagram. You can see that this growth averages 5 percent per year. Some years less, some years more, but you make an average of 5 percent over the long haul. This is since inception. From the end of the Great Depression through 2015, the total return is much higher. A 5 percent growth rate year after year for 130 years is outstanding – abnormally high in the history of the world! Americans have been lulled into taking this growth for granted. Other economies in other times have not thrived nearly as well.

For Those Who Bless Israel?

But there is something even more astounding. Look what happens if you divide this chart into before and after Israel was founded.

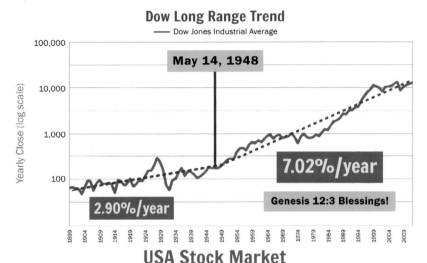

Dow Long Range Trend
—— Dow Jones Industrial Average

USA Stock Market
U.S. Stock Market Before and After Israel

Before Israel was established as a state in 1948, market growth in the U.S. averaged about 3 percent a year. After that, our economic growth averaged over 7 percent per year. That is an outstanding return over a more than fifty-year period.

Could it be that the United States' participation in the establishment of Israel as a state has brought economic blessing? You don't have to convince me! I believe this fact even outweighs our assisting the Allies in World War II, although I believe they are related, since the end of the War brought an end to the Holocaust. (Even while we helped, we were not blameless in that horrendous episode, as will be covered in much more depth in Chapter 17.)

While it is a useful tool, the stock market doesn't speak to overall growth of a nation. There is a better measure of the health of an economy: the gross domestic product (GDP) and its growth rate.

In this graph, we see that from 1948, when the stock market was growing at 7 percent per year, the growth of the overall economy was fluctuating, averaging 4 percent. Note that the highest growth rate of the U.S. economy was in the period immediately following the establishment of Israel.

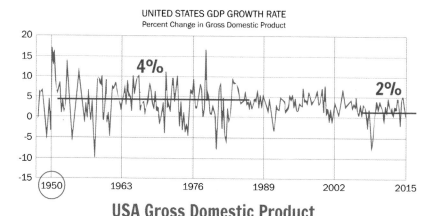

USA Gross Domestic Product

When we examine more recent periods, the past decade or so, we can see that the GDP is only growing at an average of about 2 percent per year. This is one reason why people do not feel so comfortable about the all-time market highs reached in 2015. This 2 percent growth is not just true of the United States; indeed, all Western nations were growing at a similar, reduced rate.

Israel is an exception to that rule. During the same period of time, Israel is averaging about 4 percent per year GDP growth. This brings to mind the heyday of the United States!

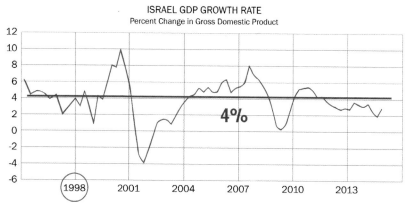

Israel Gross Domestic Product

There are some GDP drops associated with the declines that we had in America—the drop-off in 2001 and 2008—but even with those drops, Israel is still averaging 4 percent a year.

Strong Families = Strong Economy

One of the fundamental reasons for the stellar performance of Israel's economy is their birth rate. Every couple has, on average, 3.5 children; this is a strong influence, and will continue to drive future growth. Even more impressive is the fact that for religious couples, that rate increases to an average of 4.5 births.

On a visit to Israel a few years ago, an Israeli friend said to me, "Half of all first-graders now come from religious families." This means that not only is there growth in the population of Israel, but the biggest percentage of growth is coming from religious, morally principled families. Bringing up morally principled people helps any economy!

I heard an anecdote recently about two Israeli politicians who were debating one another. As this story goes, one was from a party representing religious Jews, while the other candidate represented secular Jews. Each was trying to make the case for which position would be better for the future of Israel.

At one point in the conversation, the religious politician turned to the secular one and said, "I have a question for you. Do you have any grandchildren?"

"Yes" was the reply.

"How many?"

"Well, I'm pleased to state that I have two beautiful children. One of them is married and now has two children, so I am privileged to be the grandfather of two."

The religious candidate then said, "I'm sorry, but I win. I have *one hundred children and grandchildren*, so it really doesn't matter about your opinions or policies. My grandchildren will be voting in another twenty years. When they can vote, it's 'game over.'"

Grow Israel Grow!

I am not credentialed in any way to recommend investments to other people. But I promised I would be open about myself and any decisions I might make. You already know that I can be wrong, and with that reminder, I *will* tell you that I am impressed by the GDP of Israel, their overall growth rate, their birth rate—not to mention the religious nature of that birth rate—and other impressive indicators. (For further information, read the best-selling book, *Start-up*

Nation.) Therefore, I have some of my stock holdings in Israel. I own some shares in an Israeli stock index fund called EIS, an Israeli stock mutual fund called ISL, as well as some individual Israeli stocks listed on U.S. stock exchanges.

I will caution you: Israel is an emerging economy, considered to be quite small overall, and easily influenced by world events. For example, they were hit pretty hard by past United States declines. Israel had negative growth for a few quarters after 2001, and its growth stalled in 2009, yet never went negative.

I consider Israel as a personal long-term investment only! I do not monitor those stocks carefully, nor do I attempt to buy or sell frequently. I probably won't even sell those shares if the overall market declines. Why? Because selling a company's stock brings down the value of that stock, and I enjoy the idea of financially supporting Israeli companies.

When considering investing in Israel, there is another top concern—the ever-present possibility of war. In Chapter 6 we showed that the pattern of the Blood Moons does not indicate major wars immediately after the Blood Moons are completed. Be aware that this observation contradicts what some others are predicting about the meaning of the Blood Moons! I may be wrong of course, but based on the historical pattern I am not expecting a war against Israel in the near future. The even larger point is that I am not letting the fear of war affect my Israeli investment decisions.

In summary, the question I am asking myself is: Where in this world could I invest some money today and expect 7 percent return on average for the next sixty years? That is an incredible investment return! But where? The United States? Western Europe? Communist China? Hindu India?

To me, investing in Israel now seems like investing in the United States in 1948, with the strong probability of increasing your investment 183 times over 67 years – an excellent long-term investment.

Of course, we do not know the date of the Messiah's return, nor the end of the age. But should He tarry, and should we desire to leave something to the next generation, I personally believe **there is no better long-term investment than the country of Israel.** ✡

Section TWO:

SHEMITAH

CHAPTER 11

The Jewish Background of the Shemitah Year

This chapter is written by Gidon Ariel, an Orthodox Jew, from a fully Jewish perspective.

As we explore the global and eschatological implications (some would even say apocalyptic) of the Shemitah and Jubilee years, it behooves us to understand the Jewish background of these two important cyclical events in the biblical calendar.

Outside of Jewish circles, remarkably little is known about these two years. Even within Jewish circles, broad familiarity is found only among the Orthodox. And even there, actual observance is limited to those who live in Israel. Beyond Israel's borders, observant Jews generally know the basic laws, but rarely to a depth that does justice to the importance of both Shemitah and Jubilee.

To partially remedy this dearth of knowledge, we include this chapter and chapter 19 as a means of familiarizing readers with the core biblical verses and rabbinic teachings. Our goal is to present this material in as clear and concise a manner as possible, employing the "who, what, where, when, why, and how" questions. (This chapter will cover the Shemitah year, and chapter 19 will cover the Jubilee year.)

What is Shemitah?

What is Shemitah? First of all, *Shemitah* is a Hebrew word, found only in the book of Deuteronomy, with a variation in Exodus. An expansion of the Exodus law is found in Leviticus.

Here are the relevant verses (original translation throughout this chapter from the biblical Hebrew by the author):

> *"You shall plant your land for six years and gather its produce. On the seventh year you shall let it rest [Hebrew: tishmitenah. This is a variation of the word Shemitah] and withdraw from it, so that the poor of your people will eat and*

the remainder shall be eaten by animals of the field; and you shall do the same with your vineyard and olive grove." (Exod. 23: 10, 11)

"Speak to the Israelites and say to them: When you come into the land that I give to you, the land shall have a rest period—a Sabbath for Hashem. For six years you shall plant your field and prune your vineyard and gather your produce. The seventh year will be a Sabbath of Sabbaths for the land, a Sabbath for Hashem—you shall not plant your field nor prune your vineyard. You shall not harvest the crops that grew on their own or the grapes of the unpruned vines—it will be a year of rest for the land. And the Sabbath of the land will be food for you and your male and female servants, your hired hands, and residents who live with you. All of the produce shall be food for the domestic and wild animals of your land." (Lev. 25: 2-7)

"And when you ask: 'What shall we eat in the seventh year for we didn't plant or gather our produce?' I shall direct my blessing to you in the sixth year and it will provide enough produce for three years. You will plant in the eighth year and eat from the old produce until the ninth year, until the new produce comes you shall eat from the old." (Lev. 25: 20-22)

"At the end of seven years you shall do Shemitah (the remission of debts). This is the matter of Shemitah: every creditor shall remit any debt owed by his neighbor and shall not demand it of his neighbor or his brother, for the Shemitah of Hashem was proclaimed... Take care that you do convince yourself of the selfish idea that the seventh year, the year of Shemitah, is coming, and you look unkindly upon your poor neighbor and refuse to give him anything, for he will call out to Hashem and you will be guilty of sinning. Definitely give to him and don't look suspiciously about giving to him, for because of this thing Hashem your God will bless you in all of your efforts and in all that you attempt." (Deut. 15: 1-3, 9-10)

So, after all that, what exactly is Shemitah? In the strictest sense, it refers to the mandatory remission of debts that comes at the end of the seventh year of a seven-year cycle. In this context, the word means "remit," as in "letting go of," forgiving a debt. This is an explicit commandment in the Torah that comes with warnings and blessings. Debts must be cancelled and claims must not be pursued. Furthermore, one must not succumb to the temptation of refraining from lending money with the approach of the seventh year–despite the impending requirement to forgive the debt within a short period of time. How one is supposed to avoid this temptation is not clear, as it seems there will be greater risk of the debt never being repaid. But corresponding to this risk is the promise of blessing if these laws are observed. It's a trade-off: be generous with your money, and Hashem (God) will bless you and your nation economically.

The second contextual use of Shemitah is in the resting of the land, as stated in the verses of Exodus and Leviticus. This, perhaps, is the more familiar use of the term, though the actual term Shemitah is only used peripherally in these passages. In this case, the term refers to the commandment to refrain from planting or harvesting produce or pruning vineyards during the seventh year of the seven-year cycle. The rabbinic elaborations of this commandment are quite extensive, but for our purposes, suffice it to say that virtually all manner of agricultural work that involves food-producing plants or trees is prohibited. Any way you look at it, this is a difficult commandment to keep. Not to plant, prune, or harvest crops would be virtual suicide in an agriculturally-dependent society like the Israel of biblical times. How were they supposed to eat? The Torah actually poses this very question on behalf of the Israelites. The answer, of course, is that promise of a bountiful sixth year.

However, one detail must be added to this difficult scenario. The Torah specifically states that the resting of the land will be "food for you"–for the landowners, for the poor, and for animals. How could the resting of the land result in food? Again, the obvious answer to this question is, in fact, the answer Torah provided–that it will come from that bountiful sixth year. But there is a second answer that reveals a crucial detail of the seventh year. This is the rabbinic explanation that harvesting of crops is only prohibited when done in a purely private and selfish manner–meaning keeping it all for oneself. Crops can be harvested if they are treated as common property, allowing anyone–whether landowner or not–to come and harvest what is needed for their family. The prohibition on harvesting really involves selling the produce for economic gain but does not prohibit its use for personal consumption.

We can now understand that the agricultural commandment has two aspects, both of which have something to do with the word Shemitah. First, there is the aspect of letting the land rest, which the Torah refers to as a "Sabbath of the Land for Hashem." Shemitah fits into this definition in the sense of "letting go" of your control of the land and allowing it to lie fallow. The second aspect is "letting go" of private ownership of the land so that it becomes common property and allowing the harvest to be shared by all. This is also a Shemitah, in the sense that one temporarily relinquishes private ownership over the most valuable item in an agricultural society—his land.

We would be remiss if we did not emphasize in this section that the commandment of Shemitah as commanded in the Torah, like almost all agricultural commandments and many others, only applies in the Land of Israel, and is only incumbent upon the People of Israel there. Like many commandments of the Torah, the concept and spirit is universal, eternal and infinite—but the application is limited to a defined time, place, and/or person(s).

How to Observe Shemitah

How does one observe this commandment? The two aspects listed in the previous paragraph tell the whole story. The first aspect is not to work the land—no planting, transplanting, pruning, or any other activities that stimulate growth of produce. This applies only to things growing directly in the ground that produce edible food.

The second aspect concerns the harvest. Gathering food for personal use is permitted, but a large harvest for commercial purposes is not, unless that harvest will be shared with the community. Produce that is harvested according to the law is considered to have a certain unique quality, commonly called *Kedushat Shevi'it*, or "holiness of seventh-year produce." This uniqueness results in several restrictions on how the produce must be consumed, the details of which are beyond the scope of this book. Suffice it to say that it must be consumed in a respectful manner and treated as products of the Holy Land, grown during God's Sabbath year according to the laws of the Torah.

Who Observes Shemitah?

Who must observe this commandment? In general, the Torah's commandments are directed to the Israelites and their descendants, the Jews. In the case of agricultural commandments, another limitation kicks in—they only apply to Jews in the Land of Israel. While there are exceptions to this in certain agricultural laws, Shemitah is not one of them. Thus, non-Jews may farm in Israel during the Shemitah year.

Whether the laws of Shemitah apply to the produce grown on Land in Israel owned by non-Jews is an open issue. The common consensus today is that they do not, and consequently Jews who observe Shemitah do not have to consider such produce to have "seventh-year holiness." This is the basis for two well-known leniencies in contemporary observance of Shemitah. The first is being able to eat produce grown by Arabs or other non-Jews living in Israel without any concern for Shemitah issues. The second, which is better known and much more widespread, is selling the upper topsoil of the entire Land to a non-Jew, thus making it permissible for Jewish farmers to work the land. This leniency of Jews working non-Jewish-owned land is highly controversial today. The practice of selling the land before the Shemitah year is standard in modern Israel and is authorized by the Israeli rabbinate. Needless to say, as with most and perhaps even all leniencies, there are plenty of observant Jews in Israel who do not accept this view.

Where Does Shemitah Apply?

Where does the commandment apply? Only in the Land of Israel. Whether Jews (or non-Jews) ever attempted to observe this commandment outside of Israel is unknown and highly unlikely. Of course, crop rotation and letting fields lie fallow was practiced widely in ancient times and even today, but none of them really match the laws of Shemitah. In particular, the concept of declaring all the land to be common property may be unique to the Bible.

With regard to the biblical boundaries of the Land of Israel for the purposes of the geographic map of Shemitah observance, these are subject to a certain amount of dispute within Judaism. In general, they consist of modern Israel, including the so-called "West Bank" (Judea and Samaria) areas, minus approximately the southern half of the Negev area, which itself is the southern half of Israel. They likely do not include the Golan Heights on the northeastern border or certain coastal strips like Gaza and the area north of the city of Acco (Acre). They may extend into modern Lebanon, though how far is unclear.

(If you are in one of the questionable locations, consult your rabbi.)

When Is Shemitah Observed?

When is this commandment to be observed and when has it been observed? This is probably the most debatable of these questions and the one most relevant to this book. From the Torah, it is clear that it occurs once every seven years. Jewish tradition has it that the count (year 1 of the first cycle) started in the year that began after the Israelites conquered the land of Canaan and divided it up among the tribes.

The biblical Jewish calendar started traditionally one year after creation. We entered year 5776 this Rosh Hashanah (September 14, 2015). The Exodus took place in year 2448 (1456 BC). There were forty years of travel in the wilderness and fourteen years of conquering and dividing the Land, so that puts us at year 2502. Thus, year 1 of the first Shemitah cycle was in 2503 (there are slight disagreements on this year and other subsequent dates in this chapter, but the minority opinions do not concern us, so we will ignore them).

Jewish tradition generally agrees that the count stopped with the first (Babylonian) exile and the destruction of the First Temple. It began again in 3416 (according to most opinions) when Ezra the Scribe returned with a large group of exiled Jews to set the newly built community in Israel on firm footing. The count continued even after the destruction of the Second Temple, but with a possible change in the method of counting the cycles. This has to do with the Jubilee year, the subject of Chapter 19. In that chapter we shall cover the details of how the Jubilee year fits into the Shemitah cycle. For now, we will state that since the destruction of the Second Temple, Jews have traditionally counted the Shemitah years in a simple seven-year cycle, seemingly ignoring the Jubilee year. Current Jewish tradition has it that the Second Temple was destroyed in a Shemitah year, which would put it in the Jewish year 3829 (69 AD), though this is debated by some. A destruction date of 70 AD would be the first year of the subsequent Shemitah cycle, or 3830. The past year, 5775, is 1946 years after the Shemitah year 3829. This number is evenly divisible by 7 so it is also a Shemitah year. (For a detailed discussion of the Jewish opinions of the date of the destruction of the Second Temple, see www.bit.ly/temple-destruction-date.) The rule of thumb for deciding if a given Jewish year is a Shemitah year (according to standard Jewish tradition) is that if the year is evenly divisible by 7, it is a Shemitah year. There is nothing mystical about this. It is simply an arithmetic outcome of the way Shemitah is counted and the way the Jewish year is counted.

As to when Shemitah has been observed in Jewish history, we have surprisingly little to go on. The Bible has nothing to say about the actual observance of Shemitah. There is a verse at the end of 2nd Chronicles (36:21), which interprets the purpose of the destruction of the First Temple and the exile of the Judeans: "to fulfill the word of Hashem through the mouth of Jeremiah: Until it (the Land) is satisfied with its rest, it shall rest all the years of desolation–70 years." This is traditionally interpreted as a forced desolation of 70 years to make up for 70 Shemitah years that were missed. This means that there was a period of 490 years in which the Israelites were not observing Shemitah. Since Jewish tradition maintains that the entire period from entering Israel until the first exile was 850 years, there must have been 360 years in which they were observing Shemitah. Classically, this is believed to have been the first 360 years of Israelite settlement in the Land.

We also have evidence from the Apocryphal book of Maccabees I, which describes the Jewish revolt against Greek rule that began around the year 165 BC: "But there were no provisions in the storeroom, because it was a sabbatical year" (6:53). Exactly what year this was is difficult to know, so it does not help us in determining the Shemitah calendar. But it is clear that Jews were observing the Shemitah year during this time. Jewish tradition has it that Shemitah was observed during the entire period of the Second Temple, and possibly for decades beyond its destruction.

Shemitah observance restarted with the return of large numbers of Jews to Israel. During the sixteenth century, there were sizable Jewish communities in both Jerusalem and Tzfat (Safed) in the Galilee area. There is much rabbinic correspondence concerning how to observe Shemitah, especially the question of whether produce from non-Jewish-owned land was subject to the laws of Shemitah. Unfortunately, we have no hard evidence that Jewish farmers were actually observing the laws, as we have no records of Jewish farmers existing during this period at all.

It was only with the beginnings of the Zionist movement in the 1880s and the slow but steady immigration of Jews to Israel that serious consideration of Shemitah began. Almost from the beginning of the new settlement, the question of Shemitah was posed. The rabbinic approval of selling land to non-Jews dates from the Shemitah year of 1888-1889. Since then, it has been renewed every Shemitah year, and currently is a virtually automatic process, though subject to considerable disagreement and controversy. Notably, there are a small number of farms that actually let their land lie fallow during the Shemitah year. Driving along certain roads in Israel one can see signs proclaiming that a roadside field, which obviously has not been farmed, is in fact resting, observing its Sabbatical year. There is little firm evidence that farmers who observed Shemitah experienced a bumper crop during the sixth year, but stories to this effect abound.

How much faithful observance of Shemitah year will increase in the future is unknown. It depends on many factors, including Jewish observance in general, outside economic support for farmers, alternate sources of produce, alternate methods of agriculture that does not violate the prohibitions of Shemitah, and, perhaps most importantly, faith in God. It is this last factor that leads us into our final topic to examine—the "why" of Shemitah.

A Sabbath for Hashem

Why should Shemitah be observed? From the Torah itself, the answer is obvious. The verses from Exodus state that it enables the poor to have food to eat. Presumably, this is because the land is ownerless and anyone can eat the produce of the fields. A second reason comes from the verse in 2 Chronicles, which stresses the need for the land to rest. This seems to stem from very practical considerations—the land needs a break every once in a while, and Shemitah fulfills that need. But there is a third reason that is easily missed in the technicalities and the laws. This is the subtle reminder that, ultimately, Shemitah is "a Sabbath for Hashem."

What does this mean? Does Hashem need to rest? Does letting the land lie fallow allow God to relax and take the year off? From a simple reading of the verses, it may appear that such is the case. However, Jewish tradition interprets this phrase differently.

The ancient rabbinic teachings on individual verses of the Torah go by the collective name *Midrashim* (singular: *Midrash*). This word essentially means "teachings," but more precisely, it means "a deeper interpretation." Regarding the phrase, "a Sabbath for Hashem," the Midrash makes what appears to be a very simple statement: Just as the Torah points out "a Sabbath for Hashem" when referring to the Sabbath of creation (the sixth day), in the Ten Commandments, Leviticus 25:2 also declares "a Sabbath for Hashem" for the seventh year.

In both of these commandments, the identical phrase is used, stating that the resting that is commanded is not simply a day off from work or a year off from farming. It is a rest that is not really for us or for the land—but for Hashem. How is this to be understood? Perhaps the meaning of this is that when we rest or when we allow the land to rest, Hashem is able to rest from something. From what labor does Hashem need rest? From the labor of creation—the very tiresome and demanding task of having to deal with the needs and problems of creation.

We are not referring to the problems of nature and the physical world. Those problems were solved when nature was set in perpetual motion eons ago. Nature is God's constant. It works according to schedule and follows set rules. It's a walk in the park compared to the whims and fickleness of those creations that have a will and an agenda and an ego of their own. That's us. We cross lines and make demands that stress, in a sense, even God. Maybe God needs an occasional break from all this stress.

We work all week and insist that we be compensated adequately for our efforts. We want more for less and are never really satisfied with what we have. We work the land, expecting it to keep coming through for us. We rarely appreciate the great blessing that comes from the miracle of the earth. We just consume what it produces. Perhaps we need to take some time off to gain a deeper perspective on our lives, on our time, on our earth, on our land—and understand that these are all precious gifts from God. Resting on the Sabbath and allowing the land to rest during the seventh year give God a little break from all our bellyaching and our self-oriented personalities. We rest and the land rests, and so does God.

This, more than anything else, is the real message of Shemitah. It is a time to reflect on the blessing of the earth, the land, our food, our money, and to regain the awareness that it all comes from God.

Shemitah may be difficult. To give up on debts that are owed to us, or to refrain from working the land when we need the food or need the extra cash that it can bring in, is not easy. But if we gain from it a new perspective on life and a new appreciation for all that we have, who can deny that the gains outweigh the losses? That is the true beauty of Shemitah. It's a way of giving back to God, who has given it all to us in the first place. ✡

CHAPTER 12

How Powerful is the Shemitah?

In the 1600s, a cosmic question was being debated in Europe—the power of the sun. Copernicus had introduced a new theory that he claimed fit the observational data better: that the earth was not, in fact, the center of the universe; rather, the sun.

When we look at the sun today, it's hard to imagine anything other than the understanding that this object is massive, by far the largest object in our solar system! But in Copernicus' day, this idea wasn't so clear. You could look down and see a very large earth beneath your feet, and certainly you could look up and see a very bright and hot object in the sky, but its size was not fully appreciated at the time.

The question was: How powerful is the sun?

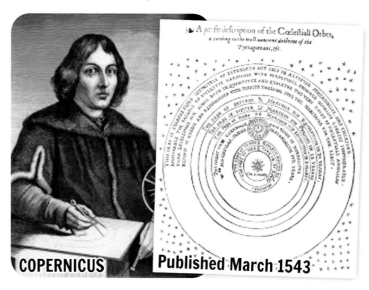

COPERNICUS   Published March 1543

Copernicus published his manuscript in March of 1543. He had delayed publishing it, editing and re-editing it for a period of ten years, sensing perhaps that a debate might follow. When he finally did publish it, he died two months later. The debate that did follow was actually made possible by the printing press that was invented 100 years earlier.

Copernicus offered us a new way to view the universe. It's not that the universe changed because of Copernicus; it's just that our perception of the universe changed. It would have been quite disruptive to be alive during the time that this debate was ongoing, as it is unsettling to think about a structure that is different from what you expected, different from what you may have even believed on religious grounds. And with that introduction, I present to you...

The Power of the Shemitah

Today we live in the Internet age, which means that not only can books be published, but information can be shared and new ideas introduced so fast it is almost impossible to censor them, as the church attempted to do in the case of Copernicus.

A significant matter that is being debated today–thanks to Jonathan Cahn's groundbreaking books, *The Harbinger* and *The Mystery of the Shemitah*–is the power of the Shemitah.

To orient ourselves, we need to be clear about the beginning and ending of the Shemitah year. We begin with a traditional Gregorian calendar. We have placed the months here on a circle in black, with January being where 1 would be on a clock and the twelve months of the year appearing on the chart in a clockwise position. The seasons–winter, spring, summer and fall–are noted in the same way. The Hebrew Calendar months are added in purple.

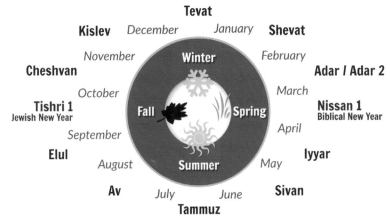

The Hebrew Calendar

The Hebrew Calendar is a hybrid of solar and lunar, and its months do not align exactly with the 12 Gregorian months in our traditional calendar. While normally comprising 12 months per year, the Hebrew calendar months are only 29 or 30 days, depending on the moon's cycle; therefore, an additional thirteenth month (Adar 2) must be added every so often, about 7 out of every 19 years.

In what Hebrew calendar month does the year begin? There are actually two beginnings. The first is Nissan 1, as has been discussed with the Blood Moons, referred to as the Biblical New Year. Nissan is the first month of the biblical year, established by Moses, when God commanded him: "This shall be the first month of the year for you" (Exodus 12:2). The biblical calendar follows this particular New Year.

On the other side of the diagram, marked in red, is another new year—Tishri 1. This is the observed Jewish New Year. Both of these New Years are associated with some major holidays. Let's run through them very quickly.

Beginning with Nissan, the first major holiday is **Passover**, followed immediately by the seven-day-long **Feast of Unleavened Bread,** and then by the counting of 50 days to **Shavuot** (referred to by Christians as Pentecost).

On the Tishri side of the calendar, Tishri 1 is the **Feast of Trumpets** when the shofar is blown. Ten days later is **Yom Kippur** (the Day of Atonement); 5 days later, another week-long feast, the **Feast of Sukkot,** that begins on Tishri 15 and lasts for 7 days. The biblical feasts calendar is concluded with **Shemini Atzeret**, the eighth, additional day of Sukkot.

When does the **Shemitah** year begin and end? The Shemitah year is aligned with the observed Jewish New Year, so it begins on Tishri 1.

This diagram below lays out a 7-year period; the Shemitah year is the 7th year or Sabbath Rest Year after 6 Work Years. Every year in the Jewish Calendar begins with Tishri 1, the 1st day of the month of Tishri, and accordingly so does the Sabbath Rest Year. The last day of the year is Elul 29, the last day of the month preceding Tishri.

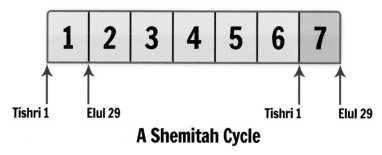

A Shemitah Cycle

To demonstrate better, let's add some real years into the mix. The first year of the current Shemitah cycle began on Tishri 1 of the Jewish year 5769, which fell in the fall of 2008, and lasted until Elul 29, 5769, the fall of 2009. The last, seventh, year of the cycle, called the Shemitah Year, was the Jewish Year 5775 (fall, 2014 through fall, 2015), which ended on Elul 29–September 13, 2015.

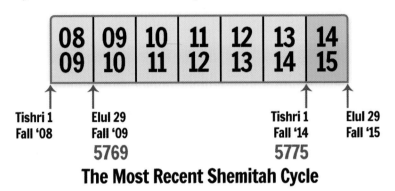

The Most Recent Shemitah Cycle

As mentioned in the last chapter, the current seven-year count was set up by Jews and has been running since before the fall of the Second Temple in 70 AD. Since Jews have been keeping track of the yearly cycle for thousands of years, they tell us when the Sabbath Year starts and ends, and the rest of us mark it down on our calendars.

The following chart shows the Shemitah cycles over the past 100 years:

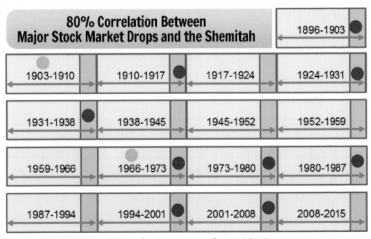

Shemitah cycles since 1896

Looking at all of these cycles together, we can now see why the Shemitah is considered to be a very powerful indicator. The dots indicate the eleven major stock market drops since 1900, including nine in a Shemitah year. In total, 9 of 11 major corrections in the stock market since 1900, over 80 percent of them, are correlated to a Shemitah year, or the first month following that year. If stock market drops were random, we would expect to see a Shemitah year involved in one-seventh of the corrections, less than 20 percent of them. What are the two exceptions? From the standpoint of a major stock market correction, the two big corrections not involving a Shemitah year since 1900 were in 1907-1908 and 1968-1970.

Furthermore, many of the single-day drops have also occurred in a Shemitah year or the month that follows it, including the large single-day drops in 2001 and 2008. The two biggest single-day drops from a percentage standpoint that did NOT fall within a Shemitah year were Black Monday and Black Tuesday in 1929. We will suggest an explanation for these drops in Chapter 17, as we believe they are unrelated to the Shemitah.

In short, the Shemitah does not connect to every correction, but it is occurring at times closely related to most stock market corrections. All this seems beyond coincidence! The Shemitah year is a powerful year, but how powerful is it? How pervasive? How much should it change the fundamental view we have of the workings of the economic cycles on the earth? *This is what is at stake.*

In order to answer this, we should examine the data further. First, it is interesting that this cycle of correlation with the Shemitah year started happening to the United States even before Israel became a nation. So, clearly we are dealing with something even bigger than just Israel coming back into their Land. Look at the original verses in Leviticus 25:1-2:

The Lord spoke to Moses at Mount Sinai, saying:

"Speak to the children of Israel and say to them, When you come into the land which I shall give you, then the land shall have a sabbath to the Lord."

As explained in the previous chapter, rabbis have associated this verse with the Land of Israel. The verse says, "When you come into the land which I shall give you, then the land shall have a sabbath to the Lord." And yet, there seems to be something going on with this Shemitah effect that transcends the presence or absence of the Jewish people in their own Land.

So, let's see if we can solve the riddle. Leviticus says, "When you come into the land which I shall give you..." Might the meaning of this clause be general enough for that verse to apply to the United States? Since America was founded by Christians and based on Biblical principles, could the beginning of the United States have coincided with a Shemitah year?

In other words, was July 1776 the beginning of a Shemitah cycle? The answer is no. July 1776 fell in the sixth year of a Shemitah cycle, not the first year of a new cycle. What about the Peace Treaty after the Revolutionary War? That was signed in 1783–also the sixth year of a Shemitah cycle.

Let's go back further still: Did the 1620 founding of the Massachusetts Bay Colony begin in a new Shemitah cycle? The answer is no. The nearest Shemitah cycle began in 1623. What about the earliest founding of all, the Jamestown Colony in 1607? No, it did not begin or end a Shemitah cycle, either.

The U.S. is the largest nation to be founded according to God's principles. Many of the early founders considered themselves to be carrying out a divine mission, the work of God, in bringing forth this new nation. Given that the cycle does not fit the founding of America, a reasonable question would be: Are the Shemitah cycle and the stock market drops even a U.S. phenomenon?

Below is a graph showing the stock market indexes of some of the major stock markets around the world. This chart covers the largest world indexes in Asia, America and Europe.

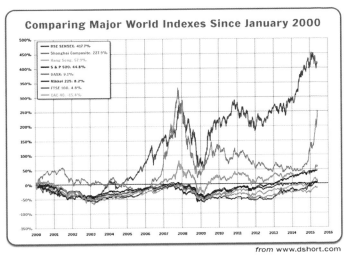

from www.dshort.com

Do you see the general correlation? Do you see that in 2008, when we had a very deep drop in the U.S., the entire world was affected as well? Such correlations are not surprising or new. Major world stock markets have affected each other for over a hundred years.

Much about the Shemitah understanding is new. Yet many Christians view the Shemitah as only affecting the United States, because the United States was uniquely founded upon God's principles. They see the United States, being one of the most important nations in the world—the largest nation economically—as causing the other nations to be affected as well. I *completely disagree*.

I believe we're talking about a fundamental shift in the understanding of what is the center of gravity of economic activity around the world. And I think it looks like this.

The Hebrew Calendar is at the center of all nations, including the United States. Why would I say that?

First and foremost, if the United States was the center, then the Shemitah cycle should have begun at its beginning, in 1607, or 1620, or 1776.

Secondly, I believe that a careful economic study would indicate that the nations of the world are affected by the Shemitah cycle in their own right, not simply because of their relation to the United States. This was more easily seen one hundred years ago when the United States was not so dominant an economy. But, even this year, the China market began to drop in early June 2015, leading the decline around the world and pulling down other markets with it. China's

...ν was 20%-30% while the U.S. was about 2%. China's drop was the worst of the major indexes. Greece also had a lot to do with the market losses.

Nobody expected this idea even 10 years ago! Nobody expected a fundamental shift in the way that we view worldwide economic cycles. The Jewish rabbis who have studied the Shemitah for years don't seem to have predicted this either.

What are the implications of all this? The thing that we thought was a minor issue in Israel—a Sabbath rest for some farm land in a single country—reveals a principle that is now central to the world economy. This is going to take some time to adjust to! This feels like the sun has now moved to the center of the solar system instead of Earth!

Shemitah—a Seismic Shift

How could such a huge shift in understanding ever be justified from Scripture? The following ideas are my own. I cannot cite any support from Jewish rabbis. As I said before, this whole topic is so new that it is catching everyone by surprise. Leviticus 25:1-2 states:

The Lord spoke to Moses at Mount Sinai saying: "Speak to the Children of Israel and say to them, when you come into the land which I shall give you, then the land shall have a sabbath to the Lord."

The first explanation I will propose actually came to me as a result of a discussion I had with a Jewish rabbi, who told me that the reason God gave the Torah to Israel in the desert and not in the actual Land of Israel was because God desired that His principles would apply to the whole world. That is an earth-shattering comment! Now let us take that comment and apply it here. This verse specifically calls out the fact that the Lord spoke to Moses "at Mount Sinai," which can be seen as an indicator of something more general in impact.

The second possible explanation comes from the second verse: "*Speak to the Children of Israel and say to them, When you come into the land...*" The Hebrew word for *land* is actually *eretz*, which also means earth.

So, reading it with the Hebrew, we have:

"*Speak to the Children of Israel and say to them: When you come into the eretz which I shall give you, then the eretz shall have a sabbath to the Lord.*"

Now the word *eretz* is used in Genesis 1:1 when God created the "heavens and the *eretz*," so the word can certainly apply to the entire earth. Is there any justification for why we might translate *eretz* in Leviticus as "the whole earth"? This idea is verified by a verse from the New Testament. *And He made from one man every nation of mankind to live on all the face of the earth, having determined their appointed times and the boundaries of their habitation."* (Acts 17:26)

We see from this verse that Paul is explaining that it is not possible for man to move to a new location on earth (some even suggest even a new house or apartment) without God's approval and appointment.

Take this principle and apply it backwards, into Leviticus 25:1-2:

The Lord then spoke to Moses at Mount Sinai saying, "Speak to the Children of Israel and say to them, When you come into the land which I shall give you, then the land shall have a sabbath to the Lord."

I think we could possibly interpret this as follows:

"Speak to the Children of Israel and say to them, When you come into the eretz (land) which I shall give you, then the eretz (earth) shall have a sabbath to the Lord."

Of course we can and should still read this Scripture as applying to Israel: When the people of Israel move into their Land—that Land given by the Lord—then that Land shall have a sabbath to the Lord. I'm just proposing that it has a double meaning. Perhaps it can also be read that the movement of the Children of Israel into their own Land triggers a principle that applies to the entire Earth.

At this point, you may ask a valid question: "Isn't this whole set of principles about the Jews?" Let us examine the Scripture again.

The Lord then spoke to Moses at Mount Sinai saying, "Speak to the Children of Israel and say to them, When you come into the (land) which I shall give you, then the (earth) shall have a sabbath to the Lord."

We can translate the "Children of Israel" as applying to Jews, and that is certainly valid, but I think it is worth asking: Where are the Children of Israel today? The answer may be found in both Scripture and in history—the Children of Israel have been scattered all over the earth. The tribe of Judah, identified with the Jewish people today, is, for the most part, back in the Land. We know that the tribe of Benjamin has been closely associated with Judah. We also know that some Levites are back in the Land. But the location of most of the other tribes remains unknown. Scripture indicates that they're scattered and dispersed widely. So even if you take this Scripture as applying only to those to whom it was spoken and their descendants, we could make a case that the descendants of those people are in many different countries, and so the words that were spoken to their forefathers still apply to them.

Furthermore, from a Christian perspective, we as Christians see ourselves as being spiritually grafted into the Seed of Abraham. Therefore, those nations which were founded on Christian principles could claim the promise of that Scripture on the basis of being grafted in, even if their descendants had no connection with the Ten Tribes. Don't we, as Christians, take Scripture from the Old Testament and find ways to apply it, personally, in our lives and our churches? So, there's really nothing new here; all we are suggesting is that there is yet one more Scripture which has never been applied to Christians, and which is also applicable.

What is God doing in all this? What's He after? What's His purpose in this shift of understanding?

God's Omnipresence

I believe that God wants His Light to shine before the whole world in every area. Today in the area of science, God's principles can be seen in the countless indications of an intelligently designed universe, to the frustration of godless scientists. In the area of the arts, godless artists find that, once again, God is frustratingly present. For instance, the attempt to express and explore meaning and beauty in art becomes shallow and hollow unless the art acknowledges that man is part of a redemption story greater than himself.

Now we have a whole new area—finance, business, and economics—where God will become more and more perceptibly present. Perhaps wise business people will make key business and investing decisions using the seven-year cycle, aligned with the Hebrew calendar. God is making Himself known.

Ultimately, I do not believe we will ever find a field of endeavor where God is not present or does not want to be present. He wants a witness of Himself made known to everyone. Man may choose to ignore it or may deny it, but every person will be without excuse.

I also believe that the Shemitah will be an increasing source of frustration for nations that do not acknowledge God. Politics and elections tend to be fueled by good business environments, so there's nothing like an economic cycle to affect and steer what will happen politically.

The Shemitah will also give Israel a new opportunity to be used by God. God is showcasing His principles in the Nation of Israel to the whole world. This is very good news! God is on the move. God is taking action. God is doing the work of reframing our view of economics to coax people to acknowledge that He exists and that nothing happens without His permission.

So, how powerful is the Shemitah? Powerful enough to move nations to acknowledge God's existence and to pay Him the honor and tribute He deserves. A fundamental shift is underway. A new way of looking at business, finance, and economic cycles that is forcing us to put God at the center of things again.

It is our generation that is privileged to see this shift, a shift so important, so powerful in scope and implication; it is as if we were living five hundred years ago and had just been told that the sun is now the center of the solar system. ✡

CHAPTER 13

Always Pray, But Sell in May?

While those who have no interest in finances and investments can just skip ahead to the next chapter, the practical financial observations we present in this chapter will set up a fascinating *spiritual* question: To what extent and in what way—if any—should Christians observe Shemitah?

For those of you who do not have a background in the stock market, this chapter will not race past you. We will explain everything step by step, and those who are well-versed in this area will get a quick refresher.

What do people mean when they say, the *stock market*? Most will lump several categories together:

- Stocks: shares in a company
- Bonds: lending money to others and getting interest back on the loan
- Commodities: like oil and gas, gold, and real estate
- Money: certificates of deposit, money market accounts, foreign currencies

Strictly speaking, a company's stock is a way to invest in that company since the stock is a measure of its value. For instance, if a company has issued one million shares and those shares are worth $20 each on the market, their company is worth $20 million dollars (market capitalization). You often hear about the stock price of a company, and that price is a number. That number can be either a big number or a small one, and it moves up and down. What does it mean when a stock price moves up and down?

Market Merry-Go-Round

In the example of a company that has one million shares outstanding, this would mean that that company's overall value is moving up and down as the stock price fluctuates. So, when a stock price goes up or down by $2, the value of this company is going up and down by $2 million dollars.

$20M   **$20M**

$18M   **$18M**

A Company's Valuation Changes When Its Stock Price Changes

Stated another way, depicted in this graph, this company's value in the market went up by 10 percent, then down by 10 percent, then back up by 10 percent (numbers rounded for simplicity). Clear so far? Now let us look at the stock market in a couple of different ways. What makes a stock price move up and down, anyway? One way to think about it is as "Buy Demand" versus "Sell Demand." If a stock price is stable, then it means that the average person thinks the price is fairly representative of the company's value. If the demand to buy the stock increases, then the price will begin to rise until it reaches equilibrium again.

In reality, because people are involved, something else happens. When demand increases for a stock, that demand does not stop when it reaches that equilibrium. The demand actually often creates further demand until the stock price ends up overshooting the real value. After it overshoots, there will

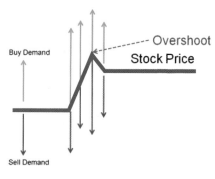

be a decline until it regains its equilibrium.

This overshoot is human nature. The momentum of something causes you to expect that its momentum will continue longer than it may actually deserve to continue. This is sometimes referred to as a "bubble." These bubbles are a lot harder to predict than you might think.

The Dow Jones and the S&P 500

In the U.S., there is a measure called the Dow Jones Industrial Average, and this average goes up and down, too. The Dow is the most quoted and publicized market index in the world.

Dow Jones Industrial Average

18000   18000

16000   16000

Sum of Stock Prices of 30 Top Companies

This big number is tl the stock prices of the 30 largest companies in our economy. They are not all industrial companies. Financial service firms represent about 25% of the index while Industrials comprise 19%. Other sectors represented are consumer services, technology, health care, and oil and gas companies. They add up the stock prices and adjust for splits (getting a higher number of shares for a single share). Those numbers are then multiplied by a scaled average to get to the end number. Those 30 large companies are mainly stocks that trade on the New York Stock Exchange. The stocks, often referred to as blue-chip stocks, are picked to reflect the overall economy but, of course, that reflection is not perfect. Even so, the Dow Jones is one of the most common measures of how the U.S. stock market is doing.

Another important index in the United States is the Standard & Poors 500, referred to as the S&P 500. This is a broader index of large cap U.S. equities. This index was invented by a company called Standard & Poors in 1957.

This index moves up and down as well, but unlike the Dow Jones, it is not simply the sum of selected stock prices. The way you can think about it is as the weighted average of the valuations of the Top 500 U.S. companies. This is a much better indicator of the stock market (the overall market) because it will not be swayed too much by any one company. For instance, the Dow Jones includes Apple, and Apple's performance as a company can affect the Dow Jones much more than it would be able to affect the overall S&P 500.

If you could only pick one measure of the world's stock market, the S&P 500 would probably be the best single graph to show. Here is a chart for the S&P 500 over the last 20 years along with some key points of interest.

This chart also has a graph for volatility at the bottom. Volatility is the measure of the instability of the market. You can see that in times of trouble, the volatility goes up, as would be expected. You will also notice that since about the middle of 2012, the volatility has been very, very low—uncharacteristically low for the market.

What should we notice on this chart? The first thing you can see is that the drop in 2008 was the most severe drop on the chart.

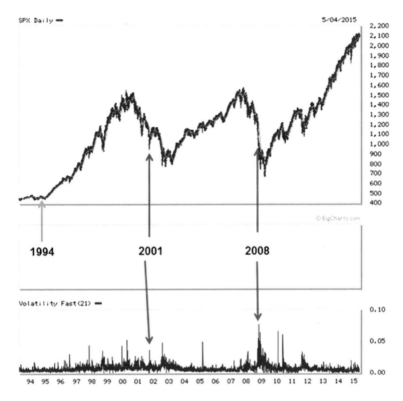

SPX Daily —   5/04/2015

1994   2001   2008

Volatility Fast (21) —

94 95 96 97 98 99 00 01 02 03 04 05 06 07 08 09 10 11 12 13 14 15

Second, the drops tend to happen faster than the rises. (We will return to this chart later on in this chapter.)

What Happens when the Stock Market Drops?

Many people are surprised at how fast the market can drop when the news is bad. How can people lose much of their life savings in the stock market in a matter of days or weeks? Why don't they have time to "get out"? This is called a stock market crash.

To understand why stock markets crash, we first need to ask: What is being measured here if the value of a company, based on its stock price, is said to be $20 million dollars?

When a company is said to be worth $20 million dollars at a certain point in time, this simply means that

What is Being Measured Here?

$20M

$18M

Future Value

Stock Markets Measure
Future Value, Not Current Value

this is the value you should be able to get if you sold the company. Indeed, when companies on the stock market are sold, they tend to fetch at least their stock price. However, that is not the key answer.

The key point is that a company is being measured *now* as a prediction of what it is expected to earn over a period of time. *The value of a company is a prediction of its future value*, its ability to make profits going forward. When you invest in something, you want a return over time, right? You want to get your money back and then some. The profits are that return. Profits come later, not right away. That is why the measure of a company's worth is always a look into the future.

Furthermore, the measure of a company, its value, is not just about how much profit it is expected to earn in the next year. It is also a measure of whether those profits might be increasing or not, even later on in time. That is why a company in a hot, new growth segment of the market may be considered to be worth a lot more than a stable company, because people expect that it will be making more a year from now than it is right now, and even more later.

How a Stock Can Crash in a Single Day

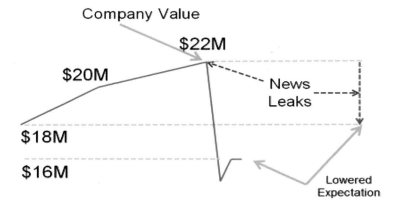

To understand how a stock can crash, first notice the darker blue line indicating increasing company value. The value increases from $18 million, to $20 million, then up to $22 million. Remember: the value of $22 million is based on the expectation that profits in the future will justify that price. Then, let us suppose that when the price reaches $22 million, news leaks that the future profits of the company will not justify a value of $22 million, but only $18 million.

Because of this news, the value of the company would reduce to $18 million. The company is *still going to make money*, but it is just not going to be making money at the rate that was expected. When news gets out, the stock drops fast. And according to human nature, it undershoots the real value. Notice how even after it settles out and reaches its equilibrium at $16 million, its equilibrium is lower than what is being reported as reality. Strange, but true! Companies are punished for bad news even to a greater degree than they might deserve. This is caused by a lack of trust and an impression that *more bad news* will probably follow the initial bad news.

Have you ever been in an airport, waiting for your flight, when a delay of 20 minutes is announced? What are you thinking? *Oh, right. They're going to come back and announce another delay soon, because they don't want to give us the bad news all at once.* It's the same thing with performance in the stock market. There is a belief by investors that perhaps not all the bad news is being reported at once. It's just human nature to think that more bad news will follow. Now we will apply this idea to the overall market.

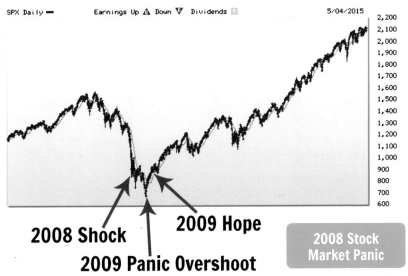

We see here that in 2008 there was an initial shock of the drop. This drop was unlike 2001, because there was no bounce back. Then some months later, valuations reached the low point, essentially an undershoot of the real value of the market. This is when a second wave of panic set in for many people. I know people who sold most of their holdings at this very lowest point, thinking, *We just don't know how far this is going to drop, and we must save whatever we can.* After that, a period of hope was reinstated in the market, opportunists began buying, and the market began to rise.

The Shemitah Year Connection

How do these stock market drops relate to Shemitah years?

The initial stock market drop in 2008, the one-day drop on Elul 29 that we labelled "2008 shock" and was associated with the Shemitah, did not end up defining the lowest point of the market. The lowest came only in March 2009.

Was there a drop corresponding to the end of the Shemitah cycle in 2001? Yes! This drop—that occurred on the first day of trading after the notorious 9/11—was a very steep decline, for sure, but the market bounced back very quickly after that drop.

Was there a drop in the market seven years earlier, in the Shemitah year of 1994? There was no drop that year, although there was a strong increase following the conclusion of that Shemitah year that continued through the rest of the 1990s. We could say that 1994 was an example of a normal Shemitah. **The design of the Shemitah is not to punish a nation,** but to simply give it a chance to rest before it continues to forge ahead economically. In that sense, 1994 was almost a perfect Shemitah year.

I love it when new theories can offer explanations to long-standing mysteries. The theory Jonathan Cahn introduced in his book, *The Harbinger*, about the Shemitah offers a great example.

An investment practice that some have used has been tossed around as a slogan within the financial community for many years. That slogan is: "Sell in May and Go Away."

Recently Bespoke Investment Group published a report testing that slogan with the following scenarios:

- From 1945 to 2012, if you were to invest $100 in the S&P 500 in October, investing *only* for the seven-month period until the end of April and then selling, and then repeat that behavior of buying for seven months in October, then you would find that the $100 you started with would have yielded $9,329.

- If, however, in the same time period, you invested your $100 in the beginning of every May and sold at the end of every September, the same $100 would be worth $99, a little more than *just one percent* of their value if the "Sell in May" slogan were followed.

So, there is a *huge* difference in the market when upturns happen. This is pretty amazing when you think about it: The market delivers such a big difference in return over a certain seven-month period versus a five-month period.

Why don't people ever take advantage of this, and only invest during those seven months? A few reasons:

- Effort. It is not easy to sell your entire portfolio and re-buy it every year.

- Taxes. You would pay the highest possible taxes if you did this because you are buying and selling every six months. In most countries, you get a tax benefit for maintaining a longer investment, such as a year or more in the United States.

- Dividends. A number of stocks give dividends, and if you hold on to those stocks, you can earn from 2 to 7 percent a year. That is like earning a percentage on your money which if reinvested, buys more shares. You can invest in more shares or cash a check sent to you for the dividend value.

There is another big reason not to "sell in May and buy on Columbus Day" (October): If you were to leave your money in there continuously from 1945 to 2012, you would have earned the same amount as if you tried to "sell in May and buy on Columbus Day." In other words: **Don't buy in May and sell at the end of September!** Rather, buy and hold.

The Greater Investment

I believe there is a greater principle in play. Something *spiritual* is going on here.

Should we as Christians not attempt to view our material possessions and holdings from a spiritual perspective, and appreciate that God might be at work? So let me make a proposal that I think carries profound implications:

What if a person sold in May every Shemitah year, and repurchased in October, five months later?

The following chart shows what would happen.

Oct 1 1945 to Selected Dates		
	$ 100.00	$ 100.00
	Sabbath	Continuous
1-May-52 $	139.80	$ 139.80
1-May-59 $	323.44	$ 340.87
1-May-66 $	475.74	$ 508.23
1-May-73 $	578.20	$ 502.38
1-May-80 $	492.86	$ 441.07
1-May-87 $	1,196.40	$1,243.61
1-May-94 $	1,677.75	$2,018.33
1-May-01 $	4,753.12	$5,943.36
1-May-08 $	6,997.77	$7,094.94
1-May-12 $	8,579.54	$7,241.82
1-May-15	$ 11,645.00	$9,829.31

In the table above, two people invested $100 on October 1, 1945. The first person sells on April 30 of every Sabbath year, and reinvests the following October 1. The second person leaves their investment in the market continually. You can see that the selling every 7th year actually turns out a bit better on some of the earlier years (1973, 1980). Then, in 1994 and 2001 (before 9/11), the continuous investment actually was more profitable. More recently, since the drops of 2001 and 2008, we find the Sabbath year method is ahead once again—by about 20 percent in 2012 and by 15 percent in 2015. (The date of May 2012 in the table was included to allow comparisons with the Bespoke Investments article previously cited.)

This method does not only produce better results, but it also avoids the disadvantages mentioned previously.

- Selling every seventh year requires less effort.

- A seven-year investment would qualify for the lowest possible tax rates. (Some might say it is better to delay paying taxes as long as possible, but I would point out that there is nothing wrong with supporting your government and paying taxes on your investments from time to time.)

It is true that during the five "off" months of this experiment, you would not be receiving any dividends. But is that really so bad? What about faithful, observant Israeli farmers? They let their land rest for an entire year every seventh year; in this experiment, we are only letting our investments rest for five months.

Why did we choose a five-month off period? No special reason, other than we were just trying to compare to the alternative of "Sell in May then Go Away." To do this every seventh year for fifty years would not cost us much, and for some of the years, it would have significantly benefited us.

Now for a spiritual question: Is letting our investments rest in a Sabbath year a spiritual decision? Could it honor God if we were to do it as an act of worship or an act of faith? I do not have a solid answer. I have never been asked this question by anyone before, nor had I considered it myself until recently.

While I do not have a firm answer for you, I will tell you what I did for the first time ever this year. I moved my biggest retirement account from stocks into cash on May 6, 2015, immediately after preparing this material for a video lesson on our site Root Source. It only took one phone call. If you call in to make this change, the person on the phone will probably ask, "Why are you doing this?" My answer to that question was the truth, that upon consulting with my financial advisers, we decided to increase our cash positions.

I understand that the personal story I just told you may frustrate many people who are reading this chapter after the Shemitah year has ended on September 13, 2015. Most people may rightly ask: "Why did you publish a book just when my opportunity to "sell in May" has passed?" But hold on! A later chapter concerning the Jubilee will make the case that September 14, 2015 begins a Jubilee year that *was also commanded to be treated as a Shemitah year from the standpoint of letting the land rest!* So, as you will read later, if you agree with our Jubilee calculations, you may still have time to participate in this exercise.

The investment we can all make, regardless of our financial situation, is the investment of prayer. Prayer is an investment that need not ever lie fallow! How does one invest in prayer for one's economy and government?

My guiding answer is found in 1 Timothy 2:1-2:

First of all, then, I urge that entreaties and prayers, petitions and thanksgiving, be made on behalf of all men, for kings, and all who are in authority, so that we may lead a tranquil and quiet life in all godliness and dignity.

I have taken this particular Scripture and implemented it in a very specific way. I have decided that in my prayer list—when I come to the place of praying for others—I will apply this Scripture very literally and place kings and those in authority at the top of my list. My very first prayer for any specific persons is for the President of the United States, and my second prayer is for the Prime Minister of

Israel. Praying for these leaders causes me to focus outside of myself and my family. It forces me to focus on an important matter: that if the LORD will bless them and they do well, then many other things—including the economy—will do well.

After I pray those prayers, then I move on to my wife and family, and many other individuals and locations, including specific places like Jerusalem. My primary prayer for my own country is for repentance and spiritual renewal.

So when I consider the phrase "Sell in May and Go Away"—I do not want to go away at all! I want to be fully engaged in asking that the LORD would bring good things for us and for our country. I hope you are doing the same.

"I Will Always Pray, but I Sold in May!"

And if/when I buy again, I will be happy to let readers of this book know. Once again, you can get current updates about what we are thinking, and any corrections that we post at **www.root-source.com.** If you sign up for our free videos and newsletter with your name and email address, we will notify you about changes without your having to monitor that web page regularly.

Regarding this selling and praying, I wonder if taken together they will be seen by God as an act of worship, of honoring God? Is it an act of worship if I am willing to say before God: "I am not addicted to earning the maximum amount I can possibly earn, and I am willing to let some of my investments rest as an act of honor to the King of the Universe"?

Yes, I think a careful approach makes sense because of the coming judgment. And truthfully, for me, this whole idea started out as a defensive measure to protect myself from God's judgment. But even more, it makes sense as an act of standing against the pressure of always trying to make more money, to accumulate more possessions or a healthier portfolio, to work the land continuously. But maybe this is really a course correction from God, a point where He was showing me the importance of being wrong, because my initial motive was not right. Could the simple act of letting investments rest—for me, not a Jew, nor an Israeli, nor a farmer—be viewed in heaven as an overt, tangible way of honoring God's Sabbath year on this earth?

I'm still pondering on this one. What do you think? ✿

CHAPTER 14

Joseph: Feast and Famine

The Shemitah examination we have presented thus far has just been that—an examination. We have learned its Jewish history. We have projected the big picture of how God might leverage the Shemitah as a facet of His witness to a fallen world. We have looked behind the stock market numbers to see if living by Shemitah principles is economically and spiritually advantageous.

But this chapter is different—it is a biblical story. In this chapter, we will experience two seven-year economic cycles through the eyes of Joseph, the son of Jacob. Yes, his life predates God's revelation of the Shemitah. But without knowing it, he was being given a view of the distant future in cycles of seven years. From this, we hope to gain insights about how to live our lives at the onset of a new seven-year cycle, which begins in the fall of 2015.

In 1889, Oscar Wilde wrote: "Life imitates Art far more than Art imitates Life." The life of Joseph also imitates a symmetry, an artistic symmetry which shaped his calling.

For instance, in Genesis 37:2, we read:

These are the records of the generation of Jacob. Joseph, when **seventeen** *years of age, was pasturing the flock with his brothers while he was still a youth...and Joseph brought back a bad report about them to their father.*

Our story begins with Joseph at the age of seventeen. We also see that after Jacob moved with his family to the land of Egypt, he lived there for seventeen years.

Jacob lived in the land of Egypt seventeen years; so the length of Jacob's life was one hundred and forty-seven years.

Genesis 42:8

Symmetry in the Shared Life of Jacob and Joseph

The life that Jacob and his son, Joseph, shared on this earth was first seventeen years together, then about twenty-two years apart, and finally seventeen years spent together—symmetry!

There are other examples of symmetry in the life of Joseph. When he was a boy, he had *two* dreams that brought his relationship with his brothers to a critical turning point. In Egypt, he interpreted *two* dreams, of the cupbearer and of the baker. And then later, he interpreted *two* dreams of Pharaoh.

Joseph's tunic was taken from him *twice*: the first time, his coat of many colors was ripped off him by his brothers; later, Potiphar's wife stole his robe and used it against him. In both cases—the coat and the robe—these garments were used as evidence of betrayal. Indeed, Joseph was betrayed twice!

He was cast into prison after his master's wife falsely accused him of violating her. There he excelled, interpreted his fellow prisoners' two dreams, asking one of them, the cupbearer, to remember him when he was released back into the service of Pharaoh. When the cupbearer forgot his promise, Joseph remained in prison for *two* more years. After that period, in the fullness of time, Pharaoh also had two dreams—the seven fat cows coming out of the marsh, and the seven gaunt cows rising to eat the fat ones. In the second dream, he saw seven fruitful ears of grain, followed by seven thin and scorched grains that devoured the seven fruitful ones.

So much symmetry! Joseph's life imitates God's art. Yet the most important symmetry of all would be two seven-year periods during his lifetime that would change history.

Joseph, by God's grace, was given the gift of interpreting dreams and was specifically placed in a position where he was available to do so for Pharaoh. Not even the Ruler's wisest men were able to do that. Having interpreted the dreams for Pharaoh, Joseph was able to see fourteen years into the future. Imagine being able to foresee that far ahead! Imagine God telling you or me what your life would be like for the next fourteen years. That would be amazing!

Joseph's fourteen-year period was divided into two segments: seven years of abundance and seven years of famine. God's mercy was so bountiful to him! He gave Joseph an opportunity, a time of preparation before a time of trouble.

On Mount Sinai, God instituted for all generations that which was a one-time event in the life of Joseph. God instituted the seven-year Shemitah cycles into Israel's cycle of life after they entered the Promised Land. It was to become part of their world view.

You who have read up to this point have enough background on the Shemitah for your world view to change as well. You and I are like Joseph, in that we are looking ahead in cycles of seven years.

What principles can we take for ourselves from Joseph's life? We will cover this in stages:

- The seven good years.
- The transition from abundance to famine.
- The seven years of famine.
- Concluding principles.

Seven Good Years

How was Joseph treated during the seven years of abundance? Three ideas come to mind: he was tolerated, he was separated, and he was targeted to fail.

Joseph was tolerated. Pharaoh was very pleased with Joseph. He had a strong, vested interest in Joseph doing well because he had granted him that job. But how did other Egyptians feel? The priests? The servants in Pharaoh's court, who were jockeying for a better position? Here is this new ruler, who had come out of nowhere, and now they had to bow down to him whenever his chariot appeared!

Joseph hadn't been in his position as second only to the Pharaoh long before he instituted a tax: 20 percent of each landowner's grain to be collected and put in a storehouse. For this alone, I imagine that Joseph was, at the very least, tolerated, disliked, unappreciated. The word on the street must have been: "Pharaoh has another pet project underway. We're just going to have to put up with it. Smile and nod, because at least for now, this young man is Pharaoh's new favorite."

Joseph was separated. He identified himself from the very beginning as a Hebrew. Therefore, he was subject to all the "stigmas" of that despised race. He could not even eat with the Egyptians. (See Genesis 43:32.)

In the last seven years, in general, Christians have been tolerated—at least, in the free world—not particularly liked, but tolerated and allowed to live in our separateness. Others may not have wanted to associate with us, but they did not intrude on our lives.

On June 26, 2015, that changed when the Supreme Court of the

United States handed down the Gay Marriage decision, *which came at the end of the last seven years.* Overall, I would say that the last seven years have been marked by tolerance and separation.

Joseph was targeted to fail. Behind the scenes, when Joseph was the topic of conversation, don't you imagine they were waiting for him to fail? With the seven years of abundance, they must have been saying: "Man, this guy lucked out! Egyptian experts are telling us that we're undergoing 'climate change' right now, and this Joseph character managed to time it perfectly! When the eighth year comes around, and we're still seeing abundant harvests and we are still producing wonderfully in the ninth year, he's going to change his tune and say: 'You know, because we have prepared so well, this Elohim has spoken to me again and has changed His mind!' Yeah, just you watch...the economy will continue to roar forward and this little upstart is going to fall flat on his face, right in front of Pharaoh!"

When we Christians speak about judgment and consequences just around the corner, aren't people just waiting for us to fail? Aren't they thinking, *we will get through the Blood Moons and this Shemitah stuff they're talking about...yeah, yeah...and we'll all see that there's really nothing to it.* They can't wait for us to fail!

The seven years of abundance were also a time for physical preparation, given that the land was taxed at the level of 20 percent. This was probably a shock for the Egyptians. Although we aren't sure of their taxation policies prior to Joseph's reign, the Bible tells us that he was the one who instituted the 20 percent rate, a law that was still in force at the time the book of Genesis was written by Moses, hundreds of years later. Joseph filled the storehouses to the point that there was so much abundance they eventually stopped counting it all. Wow, what an economy! By that point, most of the taxation complaints would have stopped because of the continual bumper crops.

(Note: Mirroring the physical preparation Joseph embraced, I hope that we Christians—we who have been wondering about the judgment of God—have been saving up during the past seven years of abundant times.)

Besides the physical preparations that Joseph initiated, I see those years as a time of spiritual healing for him. You see it in the names of his children: He named his firstborn son Manasseh, meaning "God has caused me to forget (Hebrew: *Nashani*) my trouble and all my father's household." He named his second son Ephraim, meaning

"God has made me fruitful (Hebrew: *Hiphrani*) in the land of my affliction." Do you notice that Joseph's focus and interest were very personal in nature? "God has caused **me** to forget. God has made **me** fruitful."

In good times, doesn't our focus as Christians tend to become very self-centered? We are thinking about our walk with God. We are thinking about His plans for us in our own, personal journey. While that is not wrong, God had a much larger plan in store for Joseph. And like for Joseph, in God's grace, He has much more for us.

From Abundance to Famine

Unlike Joseph, we do not know what is ahead of us. We don't know if we are looking at a year or a few years of hard times. Could we be entering a period of seven years of difficult times? Yet, the principles we can take from this lesson should apply to us, no matter how long the season might be (the seven-year cycle that began in the fall of 2015).

In Joseph's story, we see that God has a surprise in store! Pharaoh's dream was for Egypt. At least, that's how Joseph interpreted it. Yet God had something bigger in store: His plans for economic trouble were bigger than Joseph's interpretation.

> All the land of Egypt was famished, and the people cried out to Pharaoh for bread; and Pharaoh said to all the Egyptians, "Go to Joseph; whatever he says to you, you shall do." When the famine was spread over **all the face of the earth**, then Joseph opened all the storehouses, and sold to the Egyptians; and the famine was severe in the land of Egypt. All the earth came to Egypt to buy grain from Joseph, **because the famine was severe in all the earth**.
>
> Genesis 41:55-57 (author's emphasis)

While the dream *was* about Egypt specifically, that same dream was applicable on a far larger scale. This, I believe, is another principle we can take from Joseph's story. When we enter a transition, we must get ready for a surprise. In this case, the surprise was that God's plan for judgment was more complex, more extensive, and more pervasive than imagined by either Joseph or Pharaoh.

The good news is that God's plans for redemption are also greater. Whatever comes, His plans for good are beyond anything we can imagine! We must remember, we must have faith that God has a plan for good—a plan to give us a future and a hope. (See Jer. 29:11.)

The Seven Years of Famine

What happened in Egypt during the seven years of famine? What was Joseph learning? And what lessons can we take from his experience?

First, Joseph thought that redemption meant personally *forgetting* the past, and moving on from the pain of the past. But God had other plans. God wanted Joseph to *remember* his past because He wanted to redeem it. We see this in the occasion when Joseph saw his brothers for the first time after so many years:

> And Joseph's brothers came and **bowed down to him** with their faces to the ground... Joseph recognized his brothers, although they did not recognize him... Joseph **remembered** the dreams which he had about them, and said to them, "You are spies..."
>
> Genesis 42:6, 8-9

It all came back to him. Joseph had wanted to forget, but God used the famine to bring to remembrance the things He wanted Joseph to deal with again.

We are often tempted, as Christians, to think that judgment is about somebody *else*, that punishment comes as a result of someone else's sin. We must learn that trouble is not only *about us*, it is *for us*. That is how good God is! To bring up things in our past that we have not yet had the inclination or courage to face—things that can only rise to the surface in times of serious trouble—is a sign of God's grace.

Joseph gained something else in his life through the famine. Joseph thought that redemption was all about success, freedom, personal wealth. But God's plan was not just for Joseph's benefit; it was for the entire family of Jacob, all of the Children of Israel! He had placed Joseph in that privileged position to bring about fruitfulness, not just for himself, but for all of God's people.

> Now Israel lived in the land of Egypt, in Goshen, and they acquired property in it and were **fruitful** and became very **numerous**.
>
> Genesis 47:27

Joseph knew this and shared it with his brothers:

> "You intended to harm me, but God intended it all for good. He brought me to this position so I could save the lives of

many people."

Genesis 50:20

Once again, God's plan for fruitfulness was larger than any individual plan.

We need to look for this pattern in our lives as well. God wants a level of fruitfulness that extends not just to ourselves but to many, many others. Would God use us to bring about a new level of fruitfulness to others in His kingdom?

Thirdly, in the seven years of famine, Joseph's plan was to save Egypt. God's plan was to feed the whole world, and to save His chosen people, Israel—once again, a much grander scheme of things. Joseph must have realized this when people began to come from all over the earth to buy grain.

All these wonderful benefits in Joseph's life—the great good that God intended—came through the famine. Yet God did not wait until the end of the seven-year famine to reveal all this. It only took about two years, so he told his brothers:

*Now do not be grieved or angry with yourselves, because you sold me here, for God sent me before you to preserve life. For the famine has been in the land these **two years**, and there are still **five years** in which there will be neither plowing nor harvesting.*

Genesis 45:5

He got it! By the end of two years, Joseph understood God's purposes.

My belief is that we are in the same situation. We do not fully understand God's purposes for the next seven years. We do not understand what He is fully trying to accomplish. But if we press into Him, we will know. It should not be too long. Give us a year or two, into 2016 or 2017 at most, and we should be able to see God's larger plan. We will understand where our view is too small, and we will behold God's "bigger picture." We will see God's heart and embrace His greater purposes as we begin to understand.

The other amazing thing is that the next big story near and dear to the heart of God *begins during* the famine! The famine is the time in which Jacob (Israel) brought his family down into Egypt where they would stay for hundreds of years. The next God story begins during times of difficulty.

This is another reorientation for us. We must begin looking for

God to do a new thing soon, to launch something important within a two-year span.

Are you beginning to get excited to look ahead and say, "I would love to know what God is up to"? What sort of redemption will He bring out of this trouble? Will there be a worldwide revival? Will there be a new aspect of God that is revealed on a large scale? Will there be a physical movement of His people in a more profound way than we have seen; perhaps large numbers of American Jews making Aliyah to the Land of Israel? What is in God's heart? What's going to happen next?

Concluding Principles

We have looked at the seven years of abundance, the transition to the famine, and the seven years of famine. Let us look at the entire fourteen years and see what general insights we might glean from them:

1. **Famines always bring collateral damage.** Imagine the children who were harmed during this period of worldwide famine. Imagine the difficulty in traveling to Egypt to buy food and provisions. The lame, the aged, the infirm—all of whom also had to make the long journey on the back of a camel or donkey. No SUVs. No Delta jets. Not even a Greyhound bus. Heartbreaking, but it happens. While our hearts go out to those who suffer during these times, we have to be willing to try to help where we can.

2. **How quickly the haughty are humbled!** For seven years, the Egyptians had enjoyed a robust economy. But after only a year of famine, they were running to Pharaoh and Joseph, crying, "We're hungry! Give us bread!" Their attitude did a 180. No longer did they barely tolerate Joseph. Now they were completely dependent upon him. One great benefit of a famine—or any disaster—is that many people will awaken out of their stupor, humble themselves, and admit they need help.

3. **The Egyptians refused to prepare.** Scripture does not tell us that Joseph went around broadcasting the news that there would be seven years of good crops and seven years of famine. Yet, what would Joseph have answered to those who asked "Why are you taxing us?" He probably answered honestly. And even if he was quiet, the reasons for the taxation were certainly known to all the priesthood, because they had tried to interpret the dream; no doubt, they had also heard Joseph's interpretation. And even in a day when there was no instant

communication, news surely got around. At some level, everyone would have heard about the plan. So why didn't the Egyptians prepare? They could have stored up their own grain too. They could have saved it for a day when it could be sold for much more; instead, they lost everything.

4. **Famine brings opportunities for the godly.** When the family of Israel moved in to Goshen, they ended up acquiring property. They were able to use the money they had saved in the good times to purchase assets and to make the land a better place than it was before. That is our job too–*tikkun olam*–to help repair the world and provide in times of trouble. Famines do bring opportunities for those who love God.

5. **For those who do not love God and are living a life apart from Him, a famine brings slavery.** Within the first year, all the money the Egyptians had saved up had to be spent on food. By the following year, they had to give up their livestock and trade it for food. The year after that, they had to sell their property. That was Joseph's last demand until the famine was over, and then he provided seed for them so they could plant crops.

The people promised to pay their taxes again once they could get re-established. Yet, stunningly, at the end of that whole process, the Egyptians were slaves. They were no longer landowners, but tenant farmers.

In times of difficulty, people move toward drugs, alcohol, and other forms of addiction. Some will move even further down that path to escape the difficulties surrounding them. In future days, there will be a segment of our society that will go into slavery. Maybe they are slaves to sin now, but it will get even worse. They will be in more debt. They will endure even worse forms of addiction that will take hold of them. Let us pray that many will be saved out of that deep abyss through God's mercy.

6. **With regard to those who are enslaved, we Christians need to hear the word: *Beware.*** I personally struggle with the way Joseph enslaved an entire people. I do not see in Scripture that Pharaoh required Joseph to deliver all the money from the sale of land to him, or transfer every piece of property, except for that which was controlled by the priesthood and by Joseph's own family members, to him.

Think how Joseph must have been viewed by those who had to pay high taxes on their crops, and then had to buy back that same wheat at much higher prices later. Eventually, even their land was taken from them. Joseph's wife was from a family of the priesthood, and the priesthood was fully exempt from the tax law. Joseph's family was now living in Goshen, and they were doing well, able to purchase property of their own. A privileged class now emerged for both the Hebrews and the priesthood.

Do you think the Egyptians remembered that? Do you think that, hundreds of years later, when the Egyptians had the upper hand, their great grandchildren would not relish the chance to turn the tables and put the Hebrews into slavery?

When people are in trouble, and we have the means to help them, we need to remember the freedom which God wants all to enjoy. God does not want us to be slaves, nor to enslave others. It is for freedom that Christ has set us free. (Galatians 5:1)

7. **Seventy persons were saved.** That is how many people came down to Egypt with Jacob. Seventy is also the number of the nations. What this says to me is that God's purposes are global. Yes, He has great purposes for Israel and the Jews, His people, but He has a global plan and global purposes as well. That gives me great comfort.

8. **The situation turned around all because of one brother–Judah.** It was Judah who pleaded with Joseph to allow their youngest brother, Benjamin, to return to his father. Jacob would be heartbroken without him. Judah had promised the old man that he would look out for the boy, and offered to take his place as a slave to Joseph and Pharaoh. This was the point at which Joseph lost his composure, broke down, and revealed himself to his brothers.

How beautiful to see the selfless actions of Judah, the forefather of the Jewish people. In this pivotal story in world history, he made the first move. We should remember this and honor the Jews today.

The venture Gidon and I call Root Source was Gidon's vision, not mine. He made the first move. Thank you, Gidon, for keeping Judah's tradition alive and well. ✿

CHAPTER 15

Shemitah and Society

All sin has a common denominator in that it separates us from God. In that sense, all sins are equally damaging. But the Bible says that the outworking of sin, the impact of sin, can vary. Take sexual sin, for example:

> *Flee immorality. Every other sin that a man commits is outside the body, but the immoral man sins against his own body.*
>
> 1 Corinthians 6:18

In that case, the results—physically, emotionally, mentally, and spiritually—can be damaging, even disastrous.

Three Categories of Sin

If we consult the writings in what Christians call the Old Testament and Jews refer to as the *Tanach*, or the Hebrew Bible, we see three categories of sin:

- Sin—*chattah* or *cheth*
- Rebellion—*pesha*
- Iniquity—*avon*

A verse that is often quoted to define and contrast these three different kinds of sin is found in Exodus.

> *Then the Lord passed by in front of him and proclaimed, "The Lord, the Lord God, compassionate and gracious, slow to anger, and abounding in lovingkindness and truth; who keeps lovingkindness for thousands, who forgives iniquity (avon), transgression (pesha) and sin (chattah), yet He will by no means leave the guilty unpunished, visiting the iniquity (avon) of the fathers on the children and on the grandchildren to the third and fourth generations.*
>
> Exodus 34:6–7

These three Hebrew words, describing three different kinds of sin, are used in the same verse, with the word *avon* (iniquity) being used in a special sense, with some additional consequences.

1. **SIN** means to "miss the mark." While this word can apply to all sin, this particular form of missing the mark is one that is not willful.

It is not a blatant desire to dishonor or to anger God, but it is simply a mistake. The cause can be ignorance, or it might be forgetting to do what was promised. For instance, David tried to move the Ark of the Lord without first researching the precise method God had commanded. Out of David's ignorance, a man died, which had a very serious consequence for the man and his family.

2. **REBELLION** implies knowing that something is wrong, but crossing the line and doing it anyway. There can be hundreds of reasons for this kind of sin, including thinking we are not going to get caught, or that the action is worth the consequences. Human nature affirms that there is a certain pleasure derived from sinning. If we decide that we will receive more pleasure from the sin than pain from its punishment, then we may make a fateful decision to do it anyway. We can be afraid, like Saul was (1 Samuel 15:24) and cross the line—doing something we are told not to do. Or it can be a decision to do it now and fix it later. "I will ask for forgiveness later, I will make reparations later, I will do whatever I need later, but I've got to get this done now."

3. **INIQUITY** means "to exchange the truth of God for a lie." This third category of sin is really quite different from the other two. In this form of sin, iniquity actually means to believe that what we are doing is right, to believe that it is not sin at all!

> Woe to those who call evil good and good evil, who substitute darkness for light and light for darkness, who substitute bitter for sweet and sweet for bitter. Woe to those who are wise in their own eyes and clever in their own sight.
>
> Isaiah 5:20

This is really the essential element of iniquity: to take something that is wrong and call it right, or something that is right and call it wrong. I would add that if we teach others to do that which is wrong, then, by definition, that too is a form of iniquity.

Of these three kinds of sin, it is iniquity that has the most serious consequences, according to Scripture. While much can be said about it, I would summarize it in this way: **The consequences of iniquity are both generational and "twisting".**

We know, from God's Word, that sins can be passed down through generational lines, including the tendency to sin sexually (Psalm 51:5). In addition, there is a self-deceptive element to the consequences of iniquity that we might call "twisting." It is not possible to twist the truth into a lie; any attempt to do so will only result in that person becoming "twisted" instead. This kind of distortion can result in a physical manifestation that can be observed outwardly—especially in the case of sexual sin. It can also change the way we think until our minds cannot even make a "reasonable argument toward the light." Cain complained to God (Genesis 4:10) that his punishment (Hebrew: *avon* for iniquity) was unfair treatment placed upon him by a God who did not care. But the good news for us all, even today, is that what is twisted by iniquity can be straightened out again by God's grace!

Shemitah: Release and Remission

The Shemitah cycle, as we have explained, is a seven-year cycle, with the Shemitah year being the seventh of those years. It is a time to reflect on the blessing of the earth, the resting of the land, the provision of our food and our money—and to regain the awareness that all of it comes from God. There is also a consideration of the poor, the necessity of community, and the relinquishment of ownership in submission to God's principles.

There is beauty here, a beauty of release and remission that we find in this seventh year:

> You shall sow your land for six years and gather in its yield; but on the seventh year you shall let it rest and lie fallow, so that the needy of your people may eat; and whatever they leave the beast of the field may eat. You are to do the same for your vineyard and your olive grove.
>
> Exodus 23:10–11

If we manage the earth according to God's design, even the animals benefit and the environment is enriched!

So, the seventh year can be said to be about restoration and wholeness. It gets even better: God says the sixth year will be a year of great blessing, so we are not to worry about what will happen if we let our fields lie fallow for a year. In His beautiful plan, the sixth year will be a year of abundance—enough to carry us through until we are ready to sow and reap in the next Shemitah cycle.

Shemitah and Society

The two biggest Supreme Court decisions in the United States in the past fifty years were the Abortion ruling and the Gay Marriage ruling. Both of these rulings occurred in a Shemitah year: the Abortion ruling in 1973 and the federal Gay Marriage ruling in 2015. Let us cover each in turn.

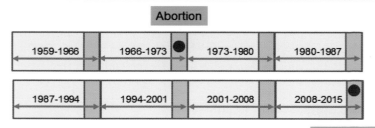

The Two Biggest Supreme Court Decisions of the Past 50 Years
As relating to Society

Abortion

| 1959-1966 | 1966-1973 ● | 1973-1980 | 1980-1987 |

| 1987-1994 | 1994-2001 | 2001-2008 | 2008-2015 ● |

Gay Marriage

Roe v. Wade, 1973

The abortion ruling of 1973 was essentially a license for a mother to choose whether the child growing inside her body would live or die. This court decision, which declared the mother's privacy and privilege to be of more value than the life of the child, had twisted the relative priority of personal choice and God-given life, and was therefore a ruling of iniquity. It was made on January 22, 1973, which was right in the middle of a Shemitah year.

Why would such a horrific societal decision occur during the Shemitah year? My opinion: The Shemitah is actually a spiritual opportunity for social change. God's desire and purpose for the Shemitah is for social restoration and reorientation; however, this can equally become an opportunity for man to defile God's ways. What a tragedy that we would take a time period designated for rest, restoration, holiness, and community, and use it to create new forms of iniquity against Almighty God.

Shemitah year social changes do not have to be negative. The 14th Amendment to the United States Constitution was signed on July 9, 1868–a Shemitah Year. This amendment required the states to ensure that former slaves receive all the benefits of other citizens, including life, liberty, due process, and equal protection. This amendment was just and honorable before God. Ironically, it was that very amendment's "due process" clause that, combined with the privacy right, was later twisted into the 1973 Roe v. Wade ruling to force all states to allow abortion.

What Happened after the Abortion Ruling

| 67 | 68 | 69 | 70 | 71 | 72 | 73 |

↑
January 22, 1973 Roe v Wade

Oil Crisis • Recession • Inflation • Post War Boom Ended • Affected Western Nations • Gold no longer backs the Dollar

What was God's response in 1973? The oil crisis began to hit in 1973. A recession set in. We had inflation, high unemployment, no growth, high gasoline prices with long lines to even get gas, etc. which is termed *stagflation*. In addition, the stock market, which had been rising steadily since the end of World War II, began to decline. The booming economy came to an end in 1973, a downturn that affected not only the United States, but also many other Western nations. The final straw came when the decision was made to no longer back our dollar with real gold, which shocked the markets at the time. The overall impact of the 1973 recession lasted for almost ten years, until the early 1980s.

NYSE DJIA 1970s

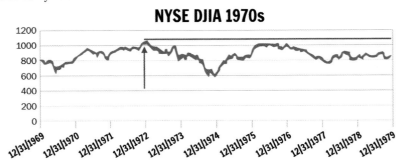

Same-Sex Marriage Ruling, 2015

Gay marriage was legalized in the United States by a 5-to-4 ruling on June 26, 2015. Once again, ironically, the 14th Amendment was used to effect this change. Its "equal protection" clause was interpreted so as to justify gay marriage, forcing all states to legalize it.

The nations that have legalized gay marriage are as follows:

1. The Netherlands (2001)
2. Belgium (2003)
3. Spain (2005)
4. Canada (2005)
5. South Africa (2006)
6. Norway (2009)
7. Sweden (2009)
8. Portugal (2010)
9. Iceland (2010)
10. Argentina (2010)
11. Denmark (2012)
12. Brazil (2013)

Recent Gay Marriage Laws Enacted

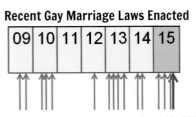

June 26, 2015
Gay Marriage in 50 States
US Supreme Court 5-4

13. France (2013)
14. Uruguay (2013)
15. England/Wales (2013)
16. New Zealand (2013)
17. Scotland (2014)
18. Luxembourg (2014)
19. Finland(2015)
20. Ireland (2015)
21. United States (2015)

Was the USA Event the Capstone of the Gay Marriage Arch?

The first law protecting civil partnerships was passed in Denmark on June 7, 1989, but the first gay marriage law came from the Netherlands on April 1, 2001. That was followed by the second gay marriage law on June 1, 2003, in Belgium. The third gay marriage law came on July 3, 2005, in Spain. Canada, that passed the fourth gay marriage law, was also the first country outside of Europe to bring in such a law on July 20, 2005. And since the 2008 recession, many more countries have followed suit. The United States was the 21st nation to make gay marriage legal.

Implications of the Gay Marriage Ruling

Is the United States event the capstone of the gay marriage arch? We are the largest country in the world to pass such a law to date, and it seems the structure of this new social paradigm has been solidified by our decision. The date this law was passed—June 26, 2015—is, on the Hebrew calendar, the 9th of Tammuz. The 9th of Tammuz, 586 BC, was the date that Nebuchadnezzar's army breached the walls of Jerusalem. If you do the math, you can see that from 586 BC to 2015 is about 2600 years. The 2015 Gay Marriage ruling is the 2600th anniversary of the breaching of the walls of Jerusalem.

The breaching of the walls was the point at which hope that the city could be saved was lost. Once the walls were breached, everybody knew that destruction and exile were imminent. It would take another whole month for the Temple to be destroyed, but the turning point of the battle was the breaching of the walls at Jerusalem.

I see this as a marker that our Christian nation could be on its way to "exile."

What might it mean for us to be in exile? To live in a land that is not your own, under rules you do not make, adhering to the will of a people who sneer at your former way of life. There have been many opinion pieces, tons of blog posts, and endless talk about how our country no longer feels like our own anymore. It isn't that we're being physically cast out of the country, but we are being asked—and even forced—to live under a kind of rule that's not ours.

An Unholy Separation... an Unholy Union

The 1973 ruling on abortion was not only a decision involving life and death, it was a decision of *separation—separating the life of a preborn baby from the safe sanctuary of its mother's womb!* And, indeed, this is iniquity. But the gay marriage situation is different. The 2015 Gay Marriage decision redefines the sacred covenant of marriage, which is a *joining, a union.* How appropriate that the founders of that movement would look to the rainbow as their symbol. What does a rainbow represent? The covenant between God and man (that He will never flood our earthly home again.) So not only do the founders of this movement redefine the marriage covenant, they use another symbol of covenant as their flag to celebrate their iniquity. And this, too, is iniquity. Finally, this sin is aimed directly at God. It is a direct affront to Him even more so, if that were possible, than it is a travesty against humanity.

After the decision was announced, I asked myself: *Why does this decision somehow feel even worse than the abortion decision?* My sense is that the ramifications of this *joining* are somehow going to bring even worse calamity than the ramifications of that *separation.* Perhaps an example in physics can express this idea: **It is the difference between the atomic bomb and the hydrogen bomb**. The atomic bomb separates atoms that normally belong together and, therefore, releases energy in the process. The hydrogen bomb, however, can destroy with one hundred times more intensity than the atomic bomb. The hydrogen bomb joins elements in a runaway reaction that releases much more energy. Gay Marriage is the hydrogen bomb.

Another analogy comes to mind after reading this sentence from Judge Alito's dissenting opinion in the Gay Marriage case:

> *Today's decision will also have a fundamental effect on this Court and its ability to uphold the rule of law. If a bare majority of Justices can invent a new right and impose that right on the rest of the country, the only real limit on what future majorities will be able to do is their own sense of what those with political power and cultural influence are willing to tolerate.*

While he doesn't use these words, what he seems to be describing could be referred to as **Constitutional Cancer**. Cancer, of course, is the uncontrolled growth of abnormal cells that the body is not able to fight because they cannot be distinguished from the real cells. Based on the precedent set by this case, this same means to an end will spread, and will sicken and ultimately kill the U.S. Constitution.

The final analogy of the Gay Marriage decision is a newly opened door to another room filled with many already-open doors.

What Is God Going to Do about It?

1. God may give us seven years to correct our course. Because He is slow to anger and abounding in lovingkindness, He may give us a few years to come to our collective senses and reverse this specific Gay Marriage decision. We will discuss a potential seven year delay in the next chapter.

2. God may judge our sexual sin harshly—with death and adversity. Because of the massive, dominant sexual sin culture that has taken hold in our Western nations, God has every right to judge us severely, and that response is ripe to begin immediately. This could include some measure of financial distress, since money always seem to get the attention of people, and it may also include large losses of life through war or natural disasters. But the main consequences before us are death and adversity. We will discuss this more specifically in the next chapter.

See, I have set before you today life and prosperity, and death and adversity.

Deuteronomy 30:15

3. God may create a response we have not seen before. Regarding gay marriage specifically, we should begin looking for what may be a "new" kind of response from God. My hope and prayer is that God will choose to unleash confusion on false marriage covenants, just as he did with the Tower of Babel. The world's first great dictator, Nimrod, organized a building committee to build a tower to heaven, with the goal of redefining how man would interact with God. God responded by confusing their languages, dispersing the nations, and preparing to choose a man from which to create a nation unto Himself.

Many centuries later, Nebuchadnezzar, who had previously sacked

Jerusalem, was walking on the roof of his palace. As he gazed at everything he had done and took all that glory unto himself, God brought confusion upon him and he went mad. He roamed like the beasts of the field for seven years until he came to his senses—and immediately praised God. The beauty of confusion is that it is not only God's weapon, but it propels God's overarching story forward as well.

We can look back to the 1970s and see several examples of things that were both confusing and new. One was the oil crisis, the first *oil war*; that was the first time those two words had ever been combined. Another new phrase at the onset of 1973 was *stagflation*, a stagnation (recession) occurring at the same time as inflation. Then came the monetary decisions to put the faith and credit of the United States ahead of God's gifts to the earth: gold, silver, etc. (Some decisions are not paid for immediately, but they set the stage for that which happens later.)

4. Christians may be "exiled." If the secularists have their way, we Christians could be placed in virtual cultural exile, attacking us with legal ramifications and challenges, if not outright imprisonment. But we must take heart that even exile is not the end. In fact, God performed more miracles for the Jewish people during their Babylonian exile than He had for many years before that. He is able to work in exile. We also believe that where sin abounds, grace abounds even more. I believe in the coming days, we will see greater miracles taking place to restore and heal battered individuals from sexual sin—yes, even homosexual sin.

5. We may no longer be a "Christian" nation. Yes, we Christians might lose the right to refer to our homeland as a Christian nation, but even if that happens, we will never lose our deeper identity in God. May we be prepared, in the days ahead, to be light and hope to the world around us. May we be loving and approachable. May we remember to offer mercy to others, even as it has been offered to us. May God complete His task of bringing forth redemption on the earth. ✿

CHAPTER 16

Shemitah: God's Seven-Year Forecast

Just as the Supreme Court ruling for Gay Marriage on June 26, 2015, fell on the 9th of Tammuz—the date that Nebuchadnezzar breached the walls of Jerusalem in 586 B.C.—Independence Day 2015 fell on the 17th of Tammuz, the date that the Roman army breached the walls of Jerusalem in 70 A.D.! Before we rush to conclude that this is a warning to our nation, we need to consider one more fact: The United States Declaration of Independence on July 4, 1776, also fell precisely on the 17th of Tammuz! Such coincidences will happen about every 30 years. The point is that facts, dates, meaning, theories, etc., are not always tied up in neat little packages, complete with bows.

One of the best pieces of advice I ever received was this: *When things don't line up perfectly with your theory, don't force it to fit.* Just continue to move forward, holding everything loosely until the pieces come together. The meaning of the 17th of Tammuz for the United States is a perfect example of something we will hold loosely for the time being.

What we can say with certainty, though, is that when proposing a theory, one cannot have too much Scripture. The more corroborative passages of Scripture there are, the better. This is why we considered the whole book of Exodus as the basis for our understanding of the Blood Moons. It is also why we looked at the life of Joseph over the seven years of plenty and the seven years of famine. This gave us scriptural context to explore how God might reveal Himself over seven-year time periods.

When, but not What

What we know about the Shemitah is that its impact is very precise in time. **We know *when* it will happen, but not *what* will happen**. And the main reason that we don't know what will happen is because we only have few verses that mention the Sabbath rest year or the word Shemitah in Hebrew—only a handful. My question: **What if there were a model in Scripture that explained what might happen in a particular Shemitah year?**

What you will read next is probably going to push the envelope more than any other chapter in this book. Once again, you will need to decide for yourself if this idea was given by God or whether it just came from man. If it came from God, we will know soon enough. If the "prediction" proves correct, then we must worship the Almighty God for His graciousness in giving us wisdom and understanding about His plans on the earth.

If it turns out to be incorrect, we will correct ourselves on our website, **www.root-source.com,** as we will be tracking the large number of predictions being made in this book, and will issue a report card on ourselves as we go along! From this point on, this chapter assumes that the theory is correct—but don't forget our disclaimer!

The 28-Year Shemitah Cycle

If you study patterns in history, in nature, and in life, you will find that they either reveal truth or cause you to dig for more. These "random" findings often lead me to search the Bible for insight. Nothing is recorded in the Bible by accident, and nothing is left out by accident.

I, Bob, was impressed with the research done by Jonathan Cahn in his book, *The Mystery of the Shemitah.* For example, he found that the concept for the Twin Towers in New York City was conceived in 1945, which was a Shemitah year, and that it was not completed and dedicated until 1973, also a Shemitah year. In his book, he also points out that this is a 28-year period, covering four Shemitah cycles. This was a brand new idea to me.

Cahn then goes on to show multiple 28-year cycles in the history of the United States. He points out that 1917 was the year the United States began its rise to world power, peaking in 1945. (We refer to the moral peak of the U.S. in Chapter 9 of this book. We date the moral peak just after the establishment of the State of Israel, in 1949 and 1950, so Cahn's theory and ours are very close.)

Another 28-year cycle began the year after the dedication of the Twin Towers and ended in 1973, marking the year in which the Supreme Court elected to make abortion legal in America, a pivotal decision in the life of this nation. The next 28-year cycle began in 1973 and ended in 2001 when those very same Twin Towers fell to a terrorist attack. Now, here we are at the end of the second of two seven-year cycles.

When I read those observations from Jonathan Cahn, I was stunned. A 28-year cycle was NOT what I was expecting. I had never even thought of the idea of a 28-year cycle. What cycle would I have thought of? Well, I would have thought of a seven-Shemitah cycle, in other words, a 49-year cycle. This 28-year cycle was unexpected. But if you lay out these Shemitah years in order, as Jonathan Cahn described, you'll see 1917 to 1945, then 1945 to 1973, then 1973 to 2001. And here we are, past 2001, and we're now at the end of the second seven-year cycle.

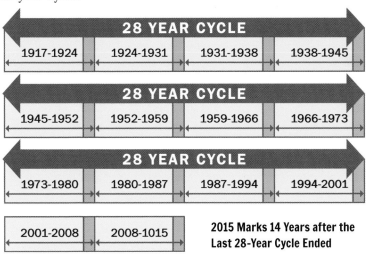

2015 Marks 14 Years after the Last 28-Year Cycle Ended

The last Shemitah year on our graph above, 2015, is the subject of a concluding chapter in Cahn's book, entitled "The Last Shemitah." He encourages readers that this Shemitah cycle is an excellent opportunity to get right with God. Amen! Clearly Cahn believes that something very serious, even dire, is underway.

But what if—and we want to be clear that we are no longer quoting from Jonathan's book, but putting forth our own question—**What if we are now reaching the halfway point of a new 28-year cycle—a 28-year cycle that is going to decide the outcome of our nation?**

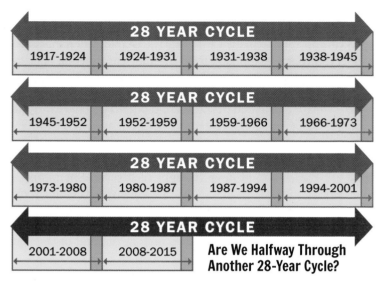

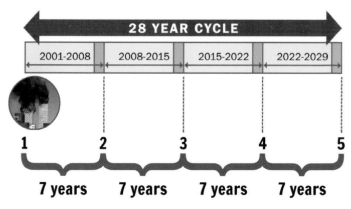

Noting this kind of pattern should cause us to search the Bible. So I began my investigation, looking for Scriptures that might point to a 28-year cycle. Cahn had found parallels in life and history, but he had not offered any scriptural backup. What we would need to find, I concluded, was essentially some kind of starting point associated with the 9/11 terrorist attack, followed by four seven-year cycles. To be clear, I needed to find five descriptions in Scripture and four seven-year periods between them. Would I be successful?

Once I got underway, it was really quite simple. I did a search on the word "seven" and looked for patterns where it appeared four times in the same chapter. Stop here and try it for yourself. Join in the discovery!

To search, start in Genesis with a concordance or Bible search program. Simply look for any chapters that have the word "seven" listed four times. When you find such a chapter, ask yourself if those four "sevens" could in any way be related to a 28-year pattern we are searching for above. You *will* find a couple of chapters that do not fit, before you find a chapter that does.

Have you finished searching for yourself? The answer is below.

They are found in Leviticus.

They are found in Leviticus 26, right after Leviticus 25 quoted earlier, explaining the Shemitah and the Jubilee in detail. Leviticus 26 cites the word "seven" four times, beginning with the blessings of obedience, followed by the penalties of disobedience.

The Blessings of Obedience

Walk with me through God's principles for living according to His Word. These principles of obedience from Leviticus 26 are paraphrased below:

- Don't make idols.
- Keep My Sabbaths (both the day of the week and the Sabbath Rest year).
- Revere My sanctuary.
- Walk in My statutes.
- Keep My commandments.

If we obey, these blessings will follow:

- You will have rains in season.
- Your lands will yield produce.
- Your trees will bear fruit.
- Things will happen for you at the right time.
- You will eat until you are full.
- You will live securely.
- God will grant peace in the land.
- He will eliminate harmful beasts.
- You will chase your enemies (and be successful).
- You will be fruitful and multiply.
- He will confirm His covenant with you.
- The new will come in so fast that it replaces the old (a good thing).
- He will make His dwelling with you.
- His soul will not reject you.

- He will walk among us.
- He will be your God.
- You will be His people.
- You will be free.
- You will walk tall.

That's some pretty good stuff. It seems that following His instructions—obeying His commandments—would be really, really rewarding.

The Penalties of Disobedience - The First List

On the other hand, if we disobey, we are in for some pretty stiff punishment. And we can't say we haven't been warned. Read this:

> "If you do not obey me and do not carry out all these commandments, if your soul abhors my ordinances so as not to carry out all my commandments and then so break my covenant..."
>
> Leviticus 26:14

With this heads-up, we should listen when God spells out the "reward" for our disobedience:

I will turn and do this to you:

1. I will appoint over you a sudden terror,
2. consumption and fever that will waste away the eyes and cause the soul to pine away;
3. also, you will sow your seed uselessly, for your enemies will eat it up.
4. I will set my face against you so that you will be struck down before your enemies;
5. and those who hate you will rule over you,
6. and you will flee when no one is pursuing you.
7. If also after these things you do not obey me...

As you examine the list, notice that there are seven items. (The numbers are not referencing verses; this is merely my organization of the ideas. A Jewish Rabbi, whom you will meet later in this chapter, remarks about the seven-fold nature of this passage.) This is the first of five lists, and the word *seven* occurs four times, in between the five lists. So, from our perspective in this timeframe, this pattern seems like it could be a list of things that kicked in after the 9/11 event.

Did these seven things happen, beginning with the 2001 event? Certainly the appointing of a sudden terror—the 9/11 attack itself. As for the rest, all I can say is that these comments are not final; we have had so little time to study them. But we will offer some of our thoughts as to how these Scriptures might apply in that seven-year timeframe. Perhaps you will have your own ideas, too!

1. *Sudden terror.* When I read those words, my first thought, of course, was of the 9/11 attack in New York City. No other event has so impacted the nation—indeed, the entire Western world—quite like that particular event.

2. *Consumption and fever that will waste away the eyes and cause the soul to pine away.* I see that as the fear of terror that has settled upon our country. We now have Amber Alerts, airport screening, and the Department of Homeland Security. The constant threats of radical Islam have entered our social consciousness and have begun to sap our strength.

3. *You will sow your seed uselessly.* We had the dot-com bubble burst in that time period. That whole seven-year period was not a period of growth; it was a period of stagnation. Large global corporations were afraid to invest in our economy. Others kept their cash safe and did not launch major innovations.

4. *I will set my face against you so that you will be struck down before your enemies.* I can see this in a couple of ways: One is Osama Bin Laden. We couldn't get him for many years, although we tried. He struck us, and we couldn't retaliate. Secondly, the fact that we moved into Afghanistan and then into Iraq and suffered casualties.

5. *And those who hate you will rule over you.* This was a period in which China began to rise in power and absorb the debt of the United States. I definitely do not think these Scriptures imply that the nation of Israel was going to be fully overtaken and captured by another country in this first list, but it implies that the nation will have to answer to leaders from other countries.

6. *You will flee when no one is pursuing you.* I think of the new air travel security measures that affect everyone. I also think about Iraq and the weapons of mass destruction. We were sure they had weapons of mass destruction and were coming after us, when in fact, they had none. It was a tremendous embarrassment.

7. As if this were not enough, God goes on: *And if also after these things you do not obey Me.* God is looking for our response, He is

looking for obedience. But if we respond with disobedience, let us now see what happens.

If we are to follow our pattern, we will need a "seven" here between lists.

*"Then I will punish (Hebrew 'yasar' also means "chasten") you **seven times** more for your sins.*

Leviticus 26:18

Second List

1. I will also break down your pride of power;
2. I will also make your sky like iron
3. and your earth like bronze.
4. Your strength will be spent uselessly,
5. for your land will not yield its produce and the trees of the land will not yield their fruit.
6. If then, you act with hostility against Me
7. and are unwilling to obey Me...

According to our interpretation, this series of seven refers to the years 2008-2015. Let's consider these, one by one.

1. *I will break down your pride of power.* Since the recession of 2008, there is hardly an American who would not agree that our standing in the eyes of the world has been greatly diminished; we are certainly not regarded with the same level of respect as before. In 2015 (at the end of a Shemitah cycle), after signing a nuclear arms deal with Iran on July 14, 2015, the only reason given by our Secretary of State for rushing forward with a limited agreement is that the coalition of nations willing to enforce an embargo on Iran was "falling apart." The coalition fell apart because the United States no longer has the power to hold it together. It is a startling admission of weakness, confirmed by this verse!

2. *I will make your sky like iron.* During this seven-year period, parts of the United States have suffered severe drought conditions. Texas experienced a three-year drought, but recovered significantly in the spring of 2015. In the summer of that year, the U.S. Drought Monitor declared 99 percent of California to be in a "severe," "extreme," or "exceptional" drought for the past three consecutive years. On the East Coast, unusual storms and blizzards pounded the land.

3. *And your earth like bronze.* Because of the prolonged drought, areas of California that were not pumping up groundwater for irrigation were parched and brown. Water-thirsty crops were plowed

under.

4. *Your strength will be spent uselessly.* This last seven-year period has seen some of the worst unemployment numbers in history. Formerly hard-working Americans were wasting away on the sidelines. And even at the end of that seven-year period, employed workers were not receiving pay raises. This lack of wage growth was a new thing for the nation.

5. *For the land will not yield its produce and the trees of the land will not yield their fruit.* Weather conditions, of course, adversely affected the agricultural segment during this seven-year period, but so did the second largest recession in the history of this nation, trailing only the Great Depression. The 2008 recession had the slowest economic recovery in over fifty years, according to many analysts.

6. *If you act with hostility against Me...* This is the first of a conditional two-part phrase, intended as a warning to God's people. When I read these words, I think immediately of the Gay Marriage ruling issued by many Western nations as an act of hostility directly against God. The Hebrew gives additional insight. The word 'hostility' (Hebrew: *Keri*) can be translated as 'frivolity' or 'contrariness,' but it also has another meaning: a seminal ejaculation that is unable to create a pregnancy! The word 'against' (Hebrew: *im*) is now used for the first of seven times in Leviticus 26.

7. *...and are unwilling to obey Me...* Here we are reminded of the foundational quality required to reap His blessings—obedience. The offer is repeated once again from the prior list.

Third, Fourth and Fifth Lists

This brings us to a third list of seven consequences that, according to our model, began in the fall of 2015. It begins in verse 21:

*Then I will increase the plague on you **seven times** according your sins:*

1. I will let loose among you the beasts of the field,
2. which will bereave you of your children
3. and destroy your cattle
4. and reduce your number
5. so that your roads lie deserted.
6. And if by these things you are not turned to Me,
7. but act with hostility against Me...

(We will comment in detail about this third list later in this chapter.)

Let us move on to the fourth list, which would be, according to this model, commencing in about 2022 (starting in verse 24).

Then I will act with **hostility** *against you and* **I, even I,** *will strike you* **seven times** *for your sins.*

1. I will also bring upon you a sword which will execute vengeance for the covenant;
2. and when you gather together into your cities, I will send pestilence among you,
3. so that you shall be delivered into enemy hands
4. When I break off your staff of bread, ten women will bake your bread in one oven and they will bring back your bread in rationed amounts,
5. so that you will eat and not be satisfied.
6. Yet if in spite of this you do not obey Me,
7. but act with hostility against Me...

Notice how God summarizes this list before it begins by saying, "I will act with hostility against you (this is the first time the word 'hostility' is used toward us) and I, even I, (so now 'I' is mentioned three times in one sentence) will strike you seven times for your sins."

We conclude with the fifth list, which begins in verse 28.

Then I will act with wrathful hostility against you and I, even I, will punish you **seven times** *for your sins.*

1. Further, you will eat the flesh of your sons and the flesh of your daughters you will eat.
2. I then will destroy your high places, and cut down your incense altars, and heap your remains on the remains of your idols,
3. for My soul shall abhor you.
4. I will lay waste your cities as well and will make your sanctuaries desolate,
5. and I will not smell your soothing aromas.
6. I will make the land desolate so that your enemies who settle in it will be appalled over it.
7. You, however, I will scatter among the nations and will draw out a sword after you, as your land becomes desolate and your cities become waste.

Preceding this fifth and final list, the word *seven* appears four times. According to the Leviticus model, these are things that could happen 14 years from now *after* the 28-year cycle is complete if we do not repent. God forbid that this passage would ever become relevant to our nations. But the result of all this, as it continues in verse 34, is that the land would enjoy its Sabbath rest years that it was not able to enjoy before—clearly a connection in scripture is now made between the Shemitah and the judgment of a nation!

The Leviticus 26 Model

Does this Leviticus 26 model work for American and Western nations? One reason I hesitated when I read these passages is because of the words *seven times*. God doesn't say that He will punish *for seven years* for the sins of the people or *in seven years*, which is needed to connect these passages to a 28-year Shemitah cycle. But could a deeper look at the passage bring understanding?

When the Bible talks about something happening *seven times*, as was translated in The New American Standard, this is usually written as *Sheva paamim*. Two words: *Sheva* is translated "seven," and *paamim* "times." Multiple examples exist in Scripture for this, including Genesis 33:3, when Jacob bowed down "seven times" to Esau and also in Leviticus 4:6, when the priest sprinkles the blood "seven times" before the Lord. But *paamim* is absent from the Leviticus 26 passage.

Each time that *seven* is written in Leviticus 26, the literal translation in Hebrew is: *Then I will increase the plague on you seven according your sins.*

What does the phrase "seven according to your sins" mean? This has been a matter of Jewish debate. The Jewish sage, Rashi, one of the most famous Jewish Bible commentators, suggested that this 'seven' means seven kinds of punishment for seven kinds of sins. This is the reason I organized the punishments into lists of seven.

I suggest that these sentences are written in the way they are written precisely because they are intended to have multiple meanings. So, the passage can mean *seven times harsher* or *seven kinds of additional punishments*, or even *over the next seven years* since the Bible is full of examples in which God works out his plans in seven-year cycles. In fact, I'll even suggest this possible idea that perhaps the passage has *seven different kinds of meanings*!

To summarize, when we combine the historical pattern noticed by Jonathan Cahn with a passage in Leviticus that fits a 28-year pattern we are seeing today, along with a series of verses that refer to "seven" in a generic way, we now suggest this as a possible biblical model.

God's Seven-Year Forecast: 2015-2022

In 2015, we entered another seven-year cycle. Let us look at the third list of seven to examine what might happen. We are attempting to interpret these Scriptures in a modern-day context, which means that you as the reader are perfectly free to interpret them for yourself as well.

Attempting to Interpret God's Forecast for the Next Seven Years

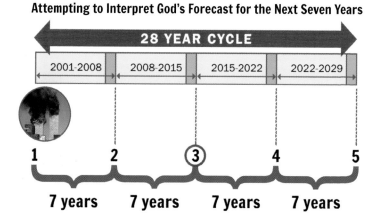

The third list, repeated, is:

Then I will increase the plague (Hebrew: makkah) on you seven according to your sins.

1. I will let loose among you the beasts of the field,
2. which will bereave you of your children
3. and destroy your cattle
4. and reduce your number
5. so that your roads lie deserted.
6. And if by these things you are not turned to Me,
7. but act with hostility against Me...

1. *I will let loose among you the beasts of the field.* We suspect that this has multiple meanings, multiple ways in which this statement may be fulfilled.

The first is literally that wolves, bears, animals may be more active against humans. We should monitor this going forward. The first forewarning was the increase in shark attacks on the East Coast of the

United States in the summer of 2015.

The second meaning for this may be embodied in the very term that is being used today: "Lone Wolf killings." These are deadly forms of Islamic terrorist attacks that are almost impossible to prevent. So what is meant by the use of the word *beast* in this Scripture? A beast may not necessarily be an animal; it may be something or someone you cannot reason with. There are people in this world who are so deranged and so demonized that they are beyond reason. On July 16, 2015, a lone wolf killing at a recruiting center in Tennessee was tweeted by ISIS fifteen minutes before it occurred, making it possibly the first ISIS-sponsored attack on American soil. There is a biblical basis for attaching ISIS terrorism to attacks by beasts. In the initial description of Ishmael, God speaks prophetically over Ishmael, in Genesis 16:12, and says that Ishmael will be a "wild donkey" of a man. That is very much a "beast."

The third interpretation of this passage could be microorganisms that may come upon animals or migrate from animals to humans, like a swine flu or a bird flu. Over 46 million chickens and turkeys have died or been killed as a result of bird flu. This has had a tremendous economic impact on the farmers that saw their flocks destroyed in a few short weeks, as well as on consumers that saw eggs double in price in the summer of 2015. Ebola is said to have come from bats, and the first person to contract Ebola in the United States was Thomas Eric Duncan on Tishri 1 of 2014 (September 25), the beginning of the Shemitah year. Is that meant as a prophetic indication? Could the fact that Legionnaire's disease has once again broken out, this time in New York City in July 2015, also be a sign of things to come?

For each of these meanings, we will be watching for a great acceleration in numbers or severity beginning Fall 2015 to be considered a sign of fulfillment.

2. *Which will bereave you of your children.* Whatever these "beasts" may be, they are going to harm our children. What a horrible thing for a nation to have to undergo. Financial distress is one thing, but losing our children is unimaginable! Diseases passing from animals to humans is one possibility, God forbid, for such things to happen.

3. *Destroy your cattle.* Again, this could be fulfilled literally. Some kind of "Mad Cow Disease" could enter the United States, like what the United Kingdom experienced. But more than the literal interpretation, what do cattle represent? In Scripture, cattle seem to be a symbol of strength, something that landowners point to with pride. What are we most proud of in our economy? Somehow it's "the beasts of the field" that destroy these "cattle." So, what might "lone wolf" terrorists do to

destroy our pride of ownership? What would they be attacking? Our savings accounts? Our homes? We don't have a solid answer.

4. *And reduce your number.* I can think of three possible ways for our number to be reduced. The first is emigration to other countries, due to concern about what is happening inside our country. The second is death through whatever might come upon us, God forbid. And the third idea is a reduced birth rate. After the 2008 recession set in, the birth rate in the United States dropped to an unsustainable 1.9 births per female, rising again in 2013 and 2014. (It takes 2.1 births to sustain a population without immigration). A significant drop in birth rate indicates that people are reluctant to bring children into the world in times of trouble, thus fulfilling this prophetic word.

5. *So that your roads lie deserted.* This, too, could be literal, in terms of people being afraid to travel, whether by land, sea, or air. But the Hebrew for *"roads lie deserted"* could be translated as *"so that your ways are desolate."* In that larger context, we could think about this as being related to trade.

Austin, Texas, was on the Chisolm Trail on which cattle were driven from South Texas to Fort Worth in North Texas. A depletion of cattle, whether literal or symbolic, could very well lead to a reduction in exports from the United States.

But one increasingly essential ingredient to trade and commerce today is the Internet. Imagine the impact of attacks that compromised the safety and security of information exchange. We have seen government-sponsored spying, attacks from one country upon another to unleash viruses, breaches of key servers, and the stealing of personal data of millions of people already. This passage might indicate that what we will see in the next seven years is much greater than we have seen so far.

6. *If by these things you are not turned to me.* Our job as Christians is clear. We are to call for our nation to turn back to the Lord in the next seven years.

7. *But if you act with hostility against Me.* Without repentance on our part, we can definitely see the open door of Gay Marriage leading to much more depravity in the next seven years. Those other doors would advance the hostility against God.

Let's step back and make a few big-picture comments about the three lists of seven we just covered.

The text is not clear as to whether each list of seven is an addition to what was already in place. In some cases, it seems so; for example, the fear of terrorism has escalated with the rise of ISIS. In other cases, relief was granted later. The climate for business investment has improved in the last few years compared to the stagnation of the early 2000s. If a drought begins in the second seven years, does it continue unabated forever? Even in biblical Israel, the longest total drought, called into effect by the Prophet Elijah, was three and a half years. God's mercy is still somehow present in the midst of these judgments, and so we need to hold our predictions loosely.

Looking at this third list of seven, though, we see a big difference emerge from this list, compared with the first and second lists. This third set of responses from God is not as economically focused as in the first two cycles. *Therefore, we may see that the financial correction this time around may not be as drastic as it was in 2008, but if that is the case, then response will be more deadly this time around, God forbid.* It will be felt much more personally. Please note that this comment is related to the impact of the Shemitah only. We have not yet discussed the impact of a curse upon America if we turn away from Israel. That is a different effect and will be discussed later.

The Big Picture, Gazing at 2022-2029

Before we close this chapter, we would like to take a long look down the path to 2022, the year the fourth list will begin to go into effect:

Then I will act with hostility against you and I, even I, will strike you seven for your sins.

1. I will also bring upon you a sword which will execute vengeance for the covenant;
2. and when you gather together into your cities, I will send pestilence among you,
3. so that you shall be delivered into enemy hands.
4. When I break off your staff of bread, ten women will bake your bread in one oven and they will bring back your bread in rationed amounts,
5. so that you will eat and not be satisfied.
6. Yet if in spite of this you do not obey Me,
7. but act with hostility against Me...

These are dreadful statements. We can only process them one at a time:

1. *I will also bring upon you a sword which will execute vengeance for the covenant.* This is the first specific use of the word covenant in any list. Here's my interpretation: God may give us seven years for the Gay Marriage court decision—the decision impacting the marriage covenant—to work its way into our system and examine the impact on our society. We will have seven years of data and experience to show how badly it is working, even for the people involved. But if we don't change, and if we add to those laws more laws still, then there will be a judgment in 2022 that will come specifically against the breaking of that covenant. It may affect all of us; it may affect only the people associated with that. We don't know, but it will come, and it will include death, God forbid.

2. *And when you gather together in your cities, I will send pestilence among you.* This sounds like a very specific reference to disease attacking many. It is larger in scope that disease spreading from the beasts of the field in 2015-2022, and is now spread solely from human to human contact. Widespread disease seems inevitable in this period of time. We can only pray for God's mercy.

3. *So that you shall be delivered into enemy hands.* One of our Root Source students, Tj, has pointed out that the European nations that have enacted gay marriage are the very nations in which Muslim troubles have been increasing. Could this sentence refer to the large-scale enactment of Sharia law in these lands? Root Source teacher Avi Lipkin has predicted that Islam is in the process of conquering Europe and America through future waves of immigration and a high in-country birthrate. (For existing birthrate details, see www.bit.ly/birthrate-data. As you look through the list, you will notice many enemies of Western nations having birth rates over 5.)

4. *When I break off your staff of bread, ten women will bake your bread in one oven and they will bring back your bread in rationed amounts.* This is a strange response from God. The statement involves a shortage of ovens (industrial resources), and a reduction in consumer products, returning to their owners in measured or weighted amounts, as part of a system that is not under full control of the owners. One way this might be fulfilled is through a devaluation of our monetary currency. We mention this also because the devaluation of the dollar has been the topic of much speculation among Christians for 2015-2016, yet this model suggests it might be delayed for another seven years. We could be wrong, of course.

5. *So that you will eat and not be satisfied.* This could refer to the amount and quality of the consumable items, as well as to other kinds of vile appetites and cravings.

6. *Yet if in spite of this you do not obey Me.* Even at the very end of the 28-year cycle, hope remains to halt the decline through obedience.

7. *But act with hostility against Me...* This is the third wave of hostility towards God and it is the last action taken in the 28-year cycle. To 'not obey' can be to ignore, but to act with hostility against God is to decide that God is the reason for our problems. And so, the cycle ends not with a judgment from God but a judgment from man, calling out the One who gives all life and all good things as the source of our problems. It is the ultimate iniquity, the ultimate twisting of the Truth into a lie.

In summary, and as we close out the Shemitah portion of this book, this chapter has presented a scriptural model that seems to describe a 28-year cycle. This book is being published at its very midpoint. We don't know if the model will ultimately be shown to be correct or not, but we will know a great deal more in two years. While the forecast in this chapter is grim, remember that we will also see great moves of God that will powerfully release many from bondage. God will also unleash surprises and opportunities for grace to abound even more than the sin that abounds around us. May we be, and may we become even more, God's servants who are ready to move with Him and bring help to those who need it. We can be certain that God is on the Throne. He is in control, He is our strong tower, and when we need it the very most, He is our hiding place. *Shalom.* ✡

Section THREE:

PROMISES TO ISRAEL

CHAPTER 17

When God Reluctantly Cursed America

When the stock market fell during the Great Depression, those losses were not fully recovered until 1954, more than twenty years later. During the Great Depression were two Shemitah years: 1930–1931 and 1937-1938. Neither of those years, however, matches the typical Shemitah pattern. That pattern shows a significant drop at the *end* of the Shemitah year.

The drop in 1929 was two years too early, and the drop in early 1937 was one year too early to fit the normal Shemitah pattern. It is precisely because so much of Jonathan Cahn's book explained so many things so well that this difference in such a major event in United States history stands out like a sore thumb.

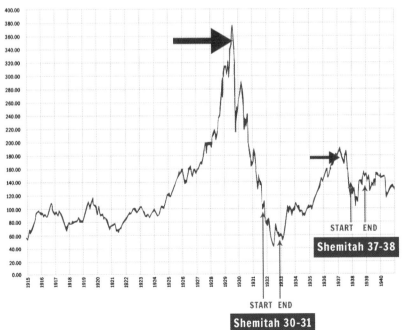

DJIA 1915 – 1940

When we consider the start date of the Great Depression, we do not think of 1931–a Shemitah year–but 1929. Why? Because the "three black days" occurred in 1929:

- Black Thursday (Down 11 percent at Opening Bell, but recovered)
- Black Monday (Down 13 percent)
- Black Tuesday (Down 12 percent)

On Black Thursday, October 24, 1929, the market opened at 11 percent below. That means that at the opening bell, the offers being made were 11 percent below the offers made the previous day. By the end of the day, trading had recovered. Then, on Friday and Saturday (the stock market used to be open on Saturdays), the trading was somewhat balanced. By Monday, stockholders began to sell. Monday saw the real drop–13 percent by the end of the day, and then another 12 percent drop on Tuesday. This was a 25 *percent drop* over a two-day period! This is what made the Great Depression "great" in the minds of the people who lived through it. Yes, 1929 was the beginning of a dark era in our history. Since this event did not exactly line up with the Shemitah cycle, should we simply consider it to be an aberration, or could we find an explanation that actually fits the data and unlocks yet another principle of how God moves on the earth?

Seeing History through the Lens of Israel

Where would we go to look for an explanation to 1929? How do we really see history through God's eyes? We see it through the lens of Israel.

Israel was not yet a nation-state in 1929, so what is the next closest thing? It is the Jewish people, overall. We have come to an opinion that an explanation for the Great Depression is found in Genesis 12:3: "*I will bless those that bless thee, and the one who curses you I will curse.*"

A Nation of Immigrants?

This chart clearly shows how immigration into the United States dropped significantly in the decade from 1931 to 1940. Why is that important? The answer, I believe, is that this drop reflects our sin against the Jews.

From the early 1800s to the early 1900s, immigration to the United States experienced a huge increase, upwards of a million people in some of the peak years of the early 1900s. How big an impact would a million people have on the United States? In 1900, our population

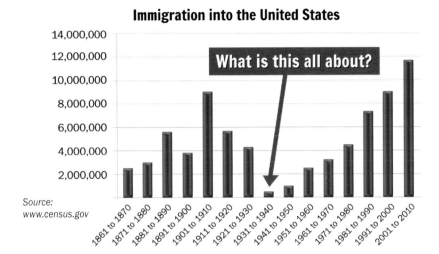

was about 100 million, so we are talking about adding approximately 1 percent population growth from immigration every year during those peak years, the last big year being 1913, the year before World War 1 erupted in Europe.

A huge percentage of immigrants were European Jews. During WWI, immigration was, of course, greatly reduced due to wartime conditions. Following the end of WWI, immigration numbers began to rise once again. At this point, the U.S. Congress began to take steps to limit immigration, and passed a law in 1921 to reduce the number of immigrants to around 350,000 people per year; in 1924, another law was passed, further reducing that number to around 165,000 people a year.

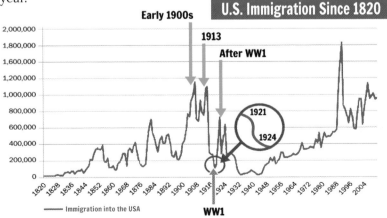

What might possibly be the reasons for the U.S. to take such action? After the war, speculations were circulating wildly as to what would happen because of the influx of immigrants. There were claims that 2 to 8 million people might be ready to immigrate immediately, that Europe was moving to the United States because everyone wanted out. These claims were never substantiated, but they got people's attention.

Three main reasons were given for the restrictive immigration laws that were about to be put in place. The first reason was *unemployment*. The U.S. was still struggling from post-war unemployment, although that would not have been an excuse for very long in the 1920s. The second reason was the claim that *the United States did not have enough space* to bring in so many new immigrants, that the United States could not possibly hold 200 million people. Today, we have a population of 320 million people. The biggest reason—and this was not concealed, but discussed openly—was the *type of immigrants* that were coming in and the fact that our racial mix was changing.

The Rise of Anti-Semitism in America

Let us particularly look at the Jewish issue and how that affected things.

Jewish Immigration, 1820 to 1930

YEAR	JEWS IN AMERICA	JEWS CAME MAINLY FROM	IMMIGRATION
1820	3000		250,000
1820-1880		Central Europe	
1880	300,000	Central Europe	
1881-1924		Eastern Europe	2,500,000
1930	4,500,000 (3.6%)		

In 1820, there were only 3,000 Jews in America. Between 1820 and 1880, about 250,000 Jews immigrated over that period, bringing the total to around 300,000, most of them from Central Europe. Beginning in the 1880s, huge numbers of Jews—2.5 million—emigrated from Eastern Europe, from Poland, and especially from Russia. By 1930, the total count of Jews had reached 4.5 million, or 3.6 percent of our population—the highest percentage that Jews have ever held.

Interestingly, the number of Jews in America today is still around 5 million, down to 1.5% of our population. Beneath the surface of this racial preservation and this concern about the changing mix was the Jewish immigration of Eastern Europe, the biggest bloc of immigrants in the early 1900s.

Does this remind you of Egypt when the Egyptians became concerned that their Israelite population was growing too fast? To our shame, anti-Semitism was also present in the U.S. in the early years of the twentieth century. In the public halls of Congress, Jews were labeled in hurtful, unflattering terms: "We need to limit the number of *undesirable aliens.*" Others thought of them as "*feeble-minded.*" It may be hard to see it this way, but in that timeframe, there was a widespread belief that, from an intellectual standpoint, Negroes and Semites were not as capable as white Anglo-Saxons from the United Kingdom. Today, the phrase would be "*mentally challenged.*" There was a belief that we would be diluting the overall intelligence of our nation if we allowed these kinds of immigrants into our nation.

In the minds of many, they were also "unclean, disease-ridden, did not wash, were lazy... slackers." While not specifically applied to Jews, the idea was that we might also allow criminal immigrants into the country. When immigrants came from a country that had a repressive-oppressive government, like Bolshevik Russia or Mussolini's Italy, there was the fear that the immigrants might want to overthrow our way of government.

Get Ready to Crash!

So what do these restrictions have to do with the stock market crash of 1929? Fair question.

The Emergency Quota Act of 1921 was the turning point of American immigration policy. Basing on a 1910 census figure, it reduced the total immigration to a maximum of 368,000 per year. This act was passed on May 19, 1921. This measure, drastic as it was, was intended as a temporary emergency measure, set to exist for a single year. What happened when that year expired? In 1922, the House asked to extend it another year to 1923; the Senate wanted to extend this provision for two years to 1924, to give time to draft a more comprehensive bill. The Senate version passed the House and was signed into law on April 15, 1922, but it was still a temporary, two-year measure.

The National Immigration Act became law in 1924. This was far more extensive, a fuller agreement with many provisions. Among other things, it further reduced the quota by half to 165,000. Even more significantly, the quota was based on the census from 1890. This was a massive blow to the Eastern European Jews because they hardly had any representation in the United States in 1890. Therefore, if you base your quota—how many immigrants you are going to allow in, based on a census of how many have already come in—and you move that census date back to 1890, hardly any Jews would be allowed in at all. That is exactly what happened. The peak of immigration for European Jewry dropped from 400,000 a year to around 4,000 a year—a 99 percent decrease. Yet, as bad as that was for Jews, it was supposed to be just a temporary measure. It was only in place for three years until 1927, when additional quota provisions were to be determined and put in place permanently.

The 1927 plan called for creating permanent rules for these quotas, not only to reduce the quota again—now down to 150,000—but to limit immigration based on an immigrant's national origin. This was called the National Origins clause, and it became a topic of great debate across the country. There were complications in the passing of this law, and Congress ended up delaying its decision by one year to 1928. By that point, the National Origins clause was an even hotter topic: it had created great confusion across the country, and was breeding infighting between congressional representatives based on the racial makeup of their own districts.

1928 was an election year and, because of the confusion and controversy, both presidential candidates said they were against it. Congress did not dare pass it then, and delayed the decision by one more year. On March 22, 1929, newly elected President Hoover, even though he had opposed this clause in his campaign, was forced by law to proclaim it. He said that unless Congress voted the National Origins Act down, the law would become permanent on July 1, 1929.

On July 1, 1929, the measure did, indeed, become permanent. The United States permanently shut down the number of people immigrating to the United States to 150,000—a mere one-eighth of what it had previously been. Within that 150,000, preference was given to white Anglo-Saxons from the United Kingdom above all other races, especially above Eastern European Jews. The United States had made its decision.

I believe, at that point, God had seen enough. *The United States was founded to be a nation of hope, not an island unto itself.* This decision to shut down the ability of Jews to immigrate would greatly add to the loss of lives in the Holocaust ten years later, as the Germans began to forge their maniacal plans. They knew Jews were not wanted in other countries, that they were trapped within their own borders, a perfect recipe for mass murder (genocide). I believe God had seen enough.

The Genesis 12:3 Curse

The "emergency" contrived in 1921 was to stop the United States from becoming too Jewish and to ensure that the white Anglo-Saxon race would dominate the make-up of this country.

But remember God's clear warning:

> I will bless them that bless you, [the seed of Abraham] and the one who curses you I will curse.

Genesis 12:3

From the very beginning of this process in 1921, Congressman Albert Johnson, Senator William Dillingham, who promoted the 1921 bill, and Johnson and David Reed of the Senate, who co-authored the 1924 bill, knew exactly what they were doing. Even before 1921, Albert Johnson had introduced a bill to the House to shut down immigration entirely. After the 1921 passage, Johnson even became president of the Eugenics Research Institute in 1923 and made no secret of his anti-Semitism. These men tapped into the national worry about the influx of aliens and couched their efforts as simply to protect the United States. The people bought into it, and the bills passed easily. While not directly discriminating against Jews in this country, we had struck a massive blow to the heart of European Jewry. We just did not know it yet.

What happened? The law went into permanent effect on July 1, 1929. The market was reasonably stable in July, but on August 9, we had the largest drop in two months at 4 percent. On September 3, the market hit an all-time high. On September 18, we had a day of wild fluctuations that began to spook the market, but the stocks ended up where they started on that particular day, so the fluctuations do not show in statistics. Then, on October 28, came the biggest one-day drop in the history of the stock market and, even today, it is the second biggest percentage drop of all time (the largest being in 1987, many years later). Why do we highlight those particular dates? (See the chart next page.)

If you start counting days, you can see that the 4 percent drop

DAY	DATE 1929	COUNT	RESULT	
Monday	July 1	Day 1	Dow 335	
Friday	Aug 9	Day 40	4% Drop	Largest Drop in 2 Months
Tuesday	Sep 3	Day 65	Dow 381.17	All time high
Wednesday	Sep 18	Day 80	Wild Fluxuations	But ends up where it started
Black Monday	Oct 28	Day 120	13% Drop	Biggest One Day Drop

occurred on the 40ᵗʰ day after the law became permanent. The wild fluctuations occurred on the 80th day of the law's passing. And Black Monday, the largest drop, occurred on the 120th day. This is not coincidence! This is a pattern. This connects the market drop to a Genesis 12:3 curse.

The idea that the Great Depression came as a Genesis 12:3 curse from God for treatment of Jews is certainly not the standard answer to the mysterious causes of the Great Depression. But it is *my* answer. The thesis of this entire book is that if you want to understand God's purposes for history and the future, you need to examine *Israel FIRST!*

Lessons from 1929

We must learn to see history through the lens of Israel and the Jewish People. The best chance we will ever have of answering the big "why" questions of history is to learn to examine the data in the context of the Jewish People overall. In that context, we have always considered the importance of how we treat Jews within our own borders. But the facts of 1929 reveal to us that the United States was being judged for its treatment of Jews *outside* its borders.

The Jewish People are the "apple of God's eye." We can see this in Zechariah 2:8:

> For thus says the Lord of hosts, "After glory He has sent me against the nations which plunder you, for he who touches you, touches the apple of His eye."

Jewish teaching explains that the *apple of the eye* is the pupil, the most sensitive part of the eye. In fact, it is the most sensitive part of the whole human body. When we act against Israel or Jews, we are touching something that is very, very sensitive to the Lord.

God does not have to wait for a certain season to act. If we come against Israel or the Jews as a nation, *God does not have to wait for a seventh (Shemitah) year to act.* This is exactly what seems to have happened in the 1920s. The crash did not wait for the next available Shemitah year. That is not to say that we were not also being judged for other failures within our country and that things could and did get worse in the 1931 Shemitah year that followed. However, I believe the beginning of the process was a result of our treatment against Jews.

God was reluctant to bring a curse upon us. He gave us plenty of time to rethink our approach to immigration from 1921 to 1929. Year after year, the House and the Senate would hear testimony from those who opposed the approach, who said it was lunacy to base immigration quotas on racial or national origin. Many of those speakers were Jews. Would we be so selfish? Would we listen to the cries coming from Eastern Europe? Would we listen to Jewish citizens of the United States who were eager to help their relatives immigrate and integrate into gainful employment in the United States? Would we hear their pleas to change our minds?

When this decision was made permanent, God moved very quickly. When He sees that hearts are truly hardened, judgment from a Genesis 12:3 curse comes swiftly.

Financial peaks set up a God story. The market's all-time high was after the enactment of the National Origins clause, not before. Why are peaks so important? It is because they are remembered. The drop from that highest peak in September was even more precipitous and noticeable than if the market had been stable for 120 days following July 1.

The Moses Effect, a period of probation

I think God's moves on Day 40 and Day 80, in advance of moving on Day 120, were hints. I believe God gives hints to those who look closely. I am calling the events of Day 40, Day 80, and Day 120 the "Moses effect" in honor of the three forty-year sections of Moses' life.

Why would God move in 40-day increments like this? A Root Source student suggested an insight from E.W. Bullinger, famous for his insights on chronology and numbers. Bullinger says that 120, 3 x 40, applied to time, signifies a divinely appointed period of probation.

Then the Lord said, "My Spirit shall not strive with man

forever, because he also is flesh; nevertheless his days shall be one hundred and twenty years."

Genesis 6:3

But applied to *persons*, it points to a divinely appointed number during a period of waiting. (See Acts 1:15.)

Now, let me show you something that I think is amazing.

I went back and looked at all of these laws being passed, all of these extensions and proclamations, and captured their dates. I asked myself a question: What had happened *in* 1929 on the anniversary of those dates? In other words, what would be the result in the Dow Jones if the loss/gain figures on the anniversary dates of those events in 1929 were totaled? I was curious. Guess what I found?

The Moses Effect!

DAY	DATE 1929	COUNT	RESULT	
Monday	July 1	Day 1	Dow 335	
Friday	Aug 9	Day 40	4% Drop	Largest Drop in 2 Months
Tuesday	Sep 3	Day 65	Dow 381.17	All time high
Wednesday	Sep 18	Day 80	Wild Fluxuations	But ends up where it started
Black Monday	Oct 28	Day 120	13% Drop	Biggest One Day Drop

Why Does God Move in 40 Day Increments?

Six major events–six stock market drops! The market, as you know, goes up one day and down another. Now the probability of having drops on all six of these events on the anniversary dates of 1929 is 1/64. But for these drops to be some of the serious drops that occurred during that first half of the year is even less likely.

Even in the first half of 1929, God dropped some hints for those with eyes to see. Certainly hints for those of us who may want to look back in time and try to determine if God is attempting to teach us His ways through history.

In addition, do you know what happens if you add up all of those drops in the last column? You get 13 percent; the very same 13 percent drop that occurred all in one day, on Black Monday. (Both percentages rounded up slightly.)

Interestingly, thirteen (13) is the number of rebellion, as defined in Genesis 14:4:

> "Twelve years they had served Chedorlaomer, but the thirteenth year they rebelled."

DATE	Law Passed	RESULT on that Same Date in 1929
May 19, 1921	1921 Emergency Quota Act	2.7% Drop
April 15, 1922	Extended Law 2 More Years	0.7% Drop
May 26, 1924	1924 Immigration Act	3.6% Drop
March 4 1927	Extended Law 1 More Year	1.6% Drop
March 31, 1928	Extended Law 1 More Year	2.7% Drop
March 22, 1928	Proclamation by Hoover	1.4% Drop
	TOTAL	13%*

13% on Black Monday!

Curses Can Be Lifted

So how did the United States ever make amends for its sins and come out from underneath this curse? We had to repent of our previous actions.

In 1941, we joined World War II, which reversed the course of our island mentality. From that point on, we were a world power, like it or not! Next, we used our strength and influence to sponsor a Jewish homeland in 1947 and 1948, the single most righteous act that ever occurred on American soil. The U.S. was the first country to recognize the State of Israel!

Once Israel was a sovereign state, Jews were able to migrate directly there, a better destination than the United States, releasing us from our history of closing our doors to Jews. Our "closed door" had become irrelevant, replaced by an open door to the real Promised Land, and we gained favor by not opposing that open door! God's plan for Jews was for them to immigrate to Israel, not anywhere else. The time of the United States service as a way-station was coming to an end.

Starting in 1948, our economy started growing again at the fastest rate in our nation's history, up to 10 percent per year. By 1954, the stock market had broken the all-time high set back in 1929, *twenty-five years later*. God is gracious to forgive, but recovery from bad decisions can take many years.

The *Promises to Israel*—or if you prefer, the *Genesis 12:3 Effect*—is another kind of principle that affects our past, present, and future. Just like the Blood Moons and the Shemitah years, it can be for us a positive factor (a blessing) or a negative factor (a curse).

In the next chapter, we will take a closer look at blessings and curses. We will even attempt to define the two major mistakes the United States must avoid so that we never again trigger another Genesis 12:3 curse.

Psalm 133:1 encourages: "How good and how pleasant it is for brothers to dwell in unity." And indeed, how much better and more pleasant it is to bless the seed of Abraham than it is to find ourselves once again reeling from the effects of poking our finger in the "apple of God's eye." ✡

CHAPTER 18

Blessings and "God Forbid"

Words are powerful. We see this from the very beginning of Scripture. All of creation was brought into existence with words, when God "said":

> Then God **said**, "Let there be light."
> Genesis 1:3

Words are also very important as shown in Proverbs 18:21:

> "Death and life are in the power of the tongue,
> and those who love it will eat its fruit."

God gives us an amazing opportunity to use our words to bring about change in the world. One such opportunity to do so is to bless.

Jewish Background on Blessing

When I call Gidon on the telephone, he answers and we ask each other, "How are you doing?" His response may be "I'm fine" or "Doing well," but he almost always includes the words "*Baruch Hashem*," literally, "Blessed is the Name." Gidon is not unique in this—it is a common part of greeting and conversation for religious Jews in Israel, and is not limited to religious Jews. For instance, Menachem Begin, the former Prime Minister of Israel—although he never wore a kippah (yarmulke-head covering)—would often work into his speeches such phrases as "Thank God," "Praise God," and "God forbid," (in Hebrew, of course).

Let us take a look at *Baruch Hashem*. Gidon explains that one of the best English translations of this phrase is: "God is blessed." The word *Baruch* comes from the Hebrew and has a three-letter root: *Bet-Resh-Kaph*.

בָּרֶךְ

The sequence of those three letters and their numerical meanings are significant. Every Hebrew letter has a defined, numerical value (this is called "gematria"). *Bet* equals 2, *Resh* is 200, and *Kaph* is 20. First, notice the sequence from 2 to 200. Does that remind

Bet "2" בּ
Resh "200" ר
Kaph "20" ך

you of a hundred-fold increase? Isaac received a hundred-fold increase in his crops in one year. (See Gen. 26:12) Second, notice that every letter has a 2 included in its numeric value. With all those 2's, the idea of a "doubling" also comes to mind.

Bending the Knee Doubles the Leg

The word *Barekh* actually means "knee." This also is related to doubling. The fruitfulness of the blessing is seen graphically when we look at somebody bending at the knee.

In Judaism, the idea of blessing is well known at the Bar Mitzvah (the coming of age ceremony at age 13). But what is not as commonly known is that Jewish fathers speak a blessing over each one of their children every Friday evening, as part of the festive Shabbat (Sabbath) dinner. You won't find pictures of this because cameras are not used by observant Jews on Shabbat. The father puts his hands on his child's head. Then he will lean forward and whisper a blessing over the child so that only the child can hear. Imagine what that would be like–to have a blessing spoken over you every week, 52 weeks a year, for as many years as you are under your father's roof? Wow! I think, as Christians, we have really missed out on a lot of opportunities to step into the idea of blessing.

Blessing by Christians

The New Testament has many references to blessing, but we'll take a look at only one of these verses:

> But I say to you who hear, love your enemies, do good to those who hate you, **bless** those who **curse** you, pray for those who mistreat you.
>
> Luke 6:27–28

Not only are we given the opportunity to bless other people, we are even asked to bless specifically and particularly those who might curse us. In the Christian community, in recent years, there has been an increase of blessing children in their early teen years. I myself formally blessed my daughters when they were growing up. We had some friends and family members over, and we each spoke blessings over them.

Blessings, though, can happen at any age. It is never too late.

About ten years ago, I asked my dad if he would allow me to stand in for his father and bless him, something my father had not received growing up. When my dad was in his 70s, I wrote out a blessing for him and, in a quiet place, while on a trip together, I blessed him in the presence of my wife. My dad seemed touched at the time, but the impact later was even more profound. Weeks after that event, he told me that my blessing had removed the last hindrances he felt over his walk. "I feel like nothing can stop me now!" he said. Indeed, my dad has become one of those people who is able to talk to anyone, and always brings the Lord into conversation, often praying for people on the spot. He has been a real blessing to so many.

Do not assume that if you are older, you are beyond receiving a fatherly blessing from someone! Do not assume if your children are well past their teen years, they would reject the idea of receiving a formal blessing from you! And finally, given that we as Christians are all adopted as sons, do not assume that you have to be related to the person you bless.

Background on Curses

Of course, there is another side of the story. In Luke 6, the downside is:

> But I say to you who hear, love your enemies, do good to those who hate you, **bless** those who **curse** you, pray for those who mistreat you.
>
> Luke 6:27-28

Many people have had someone "curse" them at one time or another. A verse in Proverbs brings comfort:

> Like a sparrow in its flitting, like a swallow in its flying, so a curse without cause does not alight.
>
> Proverbs 26:2

If someone has spoken unkind and negative words to you—and they are not true and are without merit—you can be sure that such a curse has no hold over you. However, we sometimes make a mistake and unintentionally receive a curse. For instance, if you are in traffic, and you accidentally cut somebody off—and they curse you with gestures or with words—your response should be to go to the Lord (after apologizing, if you can). We ask the Lord's forgiveness and bless the person who cursed us. By doing this, we don't allow a foothold for their curses to touch us in any way.

Even more importantly, we should be careful with our own words. Because words are so powerful, it is better to simply delete certain words and phrases from our vocabulary. One of the things that we hear sometimes is a comment like: "Who's to say that…"

Let me give you an example. A woman was considering a trip to Israel for the first time, and the issue of her safety in Israel was raised. Her response was a positive one of faith, but it included a negative ending. She ended with: "And *who's to say* that if I stayed home, I wouldn't get into a car accident here?" That woman was hit by another vehicle the day *before* she was scheduled to leave for Israel, and ended up missing her whole trip. Note that I am stopping short of making a direct connection between her statement "Who's to say that…" and her accident. I'm simply saying that there is no reason to seed or empower the enemy's desires for harm in the slightest way by speaking forth damaging possibilities. Should you catch yourself doing that, immediately renounce it and ask God's forgiveness.

Another example of the power of words is the way we may fight in a marriage. My wife and I took the advice of our premarital counselor and decided to remove the "D-word" from our marriage. We agreed never to verbalize that word especially in a fight! We now recommend that to other married couples. Speaking a word empowers it.

But what if the situation requires us to deal with negative eventualities? For instance, assume you are examining an insurance policy and what it covers. How might you ask questions about coverage for fire and tornadoes without using those words? Wouldn't that be empowering the negative?

Jews have a wonderful way of dealing with such things. It is to insert the phrase *God forbid*. For instance, I might ask: "If, *God forbid*, a fire breaks out, how much coverage would we have?" That protects from the negativity while discussing it, and even inserts an acknowledgment of the Almighty into the conversation.

But the examples above do not cover one very important area. Most of us, at one time or another, have spoken things over ourselves or others which are not true.

Words spoken over yourself:

I am always… (something negative).

I am not… (something positive).

I wish that I was…

I will never…

We can also hear and absorb words (or curses) spoken over us by others. Someone may have said over you:

Words spoken over you by others:

You are... (negative).

You are not... (positive).

I wish that you had never been...

You will never...

Since words have power, such things can come upon us and even mark or label us incorrectly—if we receive them. All of these things can be broken off. You can be free today from things that have been spoken to you even decades ago by just stepping into the promises you have from Scripture.

National Blessing and Cursing

Having covered the background briefly, let us now move on to blessings—and God forbid, curses—on a much larger scale: God's promises to Israel through Abraham in Genesis 12:3, the foundational Scripture:

> Those who bless you I will bless,
> and the one who curses you I will curse.

Most readers of this book already have the general idea and belief that if the nation in which we live were to turn against Israel, then Almighty God would, God forbid, turn against our nation. We have that general sense, but there are some specific questions that need more examination. Take another look at this Scripture, with the emphasis added:

> **Those** who bless you I will bless,
> and the **one** who curses you I will curse.

What's going on here? Have you ever noticed this before? My Christian interpretation would say: This looks like God's blessings are more inclusive than His curses. Do you remember the graph of the incredible growth of the United States stock market after May 14, 1948, averaging 7 percent per year? That blessing went to *all Americans*. It signified growth, jobs, and opportunity. While not all Americans supported the establishment of Jewish homeland, yet all Americans got the benefit!

A Jewish perspective on this Scripture goes even deeper. Gidon offers the following insights:

> I agree with Bob's analysis, and I would add a quote from the Talmud, where it is said multiple times that "God's trait of goodness is bigger than the phenomenon of hardship." Next, I would say that, ultimately, any group that attempts to focus on something negative (such as cursing Israel) will disintegrate, because even if they achieve that which they desire, they will turn against each other. So there is really no such thing as a group that curses Israel; it is always only a ragtag, ad hoc bunch of individuals. Regarding the blessing, even if someone starts out being in the minority of blessing Israel, even alone, he is "counted" by the One who counts as being part of the army of Abraham. So, the one who blesses is never alone.

Those are wonderful points!

Here is another question that the Genesis 12:3 text directs us to ask. Our President has certain authority and ability, especially when it comes to the matter of how our nation interacts with other nations. President Obama has had a strained relationship with Israel almost since he came into office. What if, God forbid, our President were to curse Israel? Could he have already done that? It raises a question. Would just he be cursed in return, according to the Scripture? I cannot say for sure.

Let us try to argue it both ways and see what you think.

A presidential curse WOULD affect the entire nation. Our president was elected by a majority of Americans twice, so in that sense we can say that we have witnessed and confirmed our choice. In that sense, all Americans are "with Obama" in what he does.

A presidential curse WOULD NOT affect our entire nation. We see many stories in the Bible where the king or leader is judged, and only his family is punished, rather than the entire nation. (One counter-example is God's decision to bring a plague on Israel as punishment for David's decision to count his own army.) Yet God is slow to anger. God cares for the people and looks with favor upon those Americans who love and support Israel.

So how do we resolve this? If, God forbid, our president were to curse Israel, we should acknowledge that God is just, and that He has a right to bring curses upon our nation, if deserved. But we should also ask for His mercy, and remind Him of the millions of Americans who love and support Israel.

There is another aspect to a negative decision our President might make. We are a nation of separated powers. There is the executive branch–the president–and there is Congress. While the president's dislike of Israel has been well noted, the Congress' appreciation of Israel has also been well noted, setting aside the few Congressmen who decided not to attend Netanyahu's speech in March 2015. Overall, Congress has been overwhelmingly favorable toward Israel. So we could rule this a tie.

However, we are a nation of three separated powers, not two. We also have the judicial branch–the Supreme Court and other federal courts. How would we judge the Supreme Court in its support of Israel?

The Supreme Court had an opportunity to weigh in on Israel in June 2015. Isn't God amazing how He directs the affairs of men in such a way that He brings rulings that force people to declare how they stand? The case hinged on a Jewish-American boy, born in Jerusalem. Would his passport recognize him as born in Jerusalem, Israel? Congress said yes. The President said no. The case was brought before the Supreme Court to decide whether Jerusalem is part of Israel, or not. The Court ruled in favor of the President. The boy's passport says Jerusalem, but not Israel.

In thinking about this case, I think of Zechariah 12:3–a verse parallel to Genesis 12:3:

> It will come about in that day that I will make Jerusalem a heavy stone for all the peoples; all who lift it will be severely injured.
>
> Zechariah 12:3

Curses on Israel?

What, God forbid, would actually qualify as a curse against Israel? In the current environment of the United States, the most likely cause would come from the office of the President. It would, therefore, require an action that is within his authority. What are some actions that the President has taken that would qualify as curses?

America negotiated with Iran about their nuclear program for nine months before it informed Israel. That was certainly not respectful. When the Prime Minister of Israel, Benjamin Netanyahu, visited Washington, D.C. to address Congress, President Obama was in town, in the White House, but refused to attend the event.

That was a definite snub and quite revealing. On July 14, 2015, under full direction of the president, the United States joined with China, Russia, France, Germany and the United Kingdom in reaching an agreement on a nuclear deal with Iran. That was incredibly unwise. Yet, I *do not* consider these things curses—at least, not at the national level. What, then, would define, God forbid, a curse against Israel?

First, such an action from the President must be perfectly clear as something that unequivocally produces significant hardship upon the nation of Israel. Secondly, it must be something of unquestioned historical importance—not a mere refusal to take a phone call or walking out of a meeting. Third, it must be something that all people would understand to be extremely negative. A great example, meeting all of three of these criteria, was the expulsion of the Jews from Spain in 1492. This decision clearly harmed the Jews; it was of unquestioned importance; and it was of historic proportions—the largest scale expulsion ever. It was something that people throughout Europe fully understood as an aggressive act against the Jewish people.

Curses on America?

Regarding curses on the United States and what might qualify, I would like to propose two ideas:

First, what if, God forbid, the United States stopped selling weapons to Israel? John Bolton, a noted expert on the Middle East, was asked about six months ago: "*What is your biggest fear regarding Israel's security?*" His answer to this question addressed this very issue: The worst thing the United States could do, from his standpoint, would be to stop selling weapons to Israel.

The United States in the run-up to the signing of the Iran agreement was using additional weapons as a bargaining chip to convince Israel to accept the Iran deal. Israel apparently rejected this idea and called off further defense weapons talks. Why? The United States may have begun to ask for assurances from Israel not to take any action against the Iran nuclear programs, in exchange for certain weapons sales. It seems Israel would not agree to this. A general negotiation strategy states that when you have an existing agreement in place but are in a negotiation that is heading toward a negative outcome, one of your best alternatives is to withdraw, to retain the status quo. The real question is: How would the United States respond to an attack by Israel against Iranian nuclear facilities? Would the U.S. punish Israel by stopping weapons sales?

Should, God forbid, the President order that all weapons sales to Israel be halted, those sales could be easily restored by the next President. In such a case, God in His mercy might delay judgment against our nation until that next President determined whether to continue the weapons sales embargo or lift it.

What if, God forbid, a U.S. President formally recognized a Palestinian State? This action by the President would be even worse, and almost impossible to reverse. The United States has consistently used its veto power to block such a proposal in the United Nations General Assembly. But this is under the control of the President. There have been rumors that the President has been rethinking his position on the issue for the Fall 2015 UN sessions. This is extremely disturbing. If, God forbid, the United States were to switch sides on this issue, we would have flipped from being the nation that was most supportive of Israel to the nation leading the charge against Israel. It would, God forbid, eliminate Israel's ability to ever negotiate with the Palestinians from strength again.

One of the most troubling developments along these lines came on May 13, 2015, when the Vatican announced its intention to recognize a Palestinian State, followed by a signed treaty with Fatah on June 26. That was eerily the same day that the Gay Marriage ruling was announced. Some saw this coming from the Vatican. For instance, in 2014, when the Pope visited Israel and spoke in Bethlehem, he was said to have changed his speech as written—"My Fatah *friends*"—and, instead, spoke out verbally: "My Fatah *brothers*."

If the U.S. President follows the lead of the Catholic Church and recognizes the Palestinian State, it might, in his mind, God forbid, offer him an opportunity for a legacy. Why? If Palestinian statehood were ever approved by the United Nations, it would be nearly impossible for any presidential successor ever to undo it. He can stop it from being voted on, but once voted on and passed, it would be all but impossible for the UN to reverse its position.

God forbid that we would ever turn away from Israel!

Final Thought from Bob

If, God forbid, the United States were ever to turn away from Israel, how would we pray? We should pray: "Yes, God, you are just and righteous, and we deserve your judgment, yet we ask for mercy to be upon us all for the sake of those who love Israel and continue to seek blessing for her."

And if, God forbid, that dreadful day were ever to come and we were asked on that day "How are you?" we should answer as Gidon does: "*Baruch Hashem*! God is blessed. Blessed be the Name of the Lord."

Final Thought from Gidon

Gidon leaves us with a parting thought on Genesis 12:3:

> *Those who bless you I will bless,*
> *and the one who curses you I will curse.*

It has to do with the words used for *bless* and *curse*. The Hebrew word *baruch* for "bless" is used twice in the first line. But the Hebrew words for *curse*, used in the second line, are two different words. Both mean *curse*, but they are not the same word.

By using the same word for "blessing" twice, God doubles the blessing and increases the *strength* of what is being spoken. It is the same as a rope made of a two-ply cord.

In the case of the curses, however, it is like two single cords rather than a double cord. This gives us hope. It gives us hope that even if a nation were to curse Israel, God forbid, there is hope to undo the curse, to unwind it. There is hope of repentance and returning to the way of blessing.

Amen. ✿

Section FOUR:

JUBILEE

CHAPTER 19

The Jewish Background of the Jubilee

This chapter is written by Gidon Ariel, an Orthodox Jew, from a fully Jewish perspective.

The obvious parallel to Shemitah is the Jubilee. To me, Gidon, it makes sense that if one observes the first, one is equally obligated to observe the second. From the Torah itself, as we shall see, there is no indication whatsoever that Shemitah could be diligently and properly observed while the Jubilee is all but ignored. But such is the case, and as far as we know, has been the case for over 2,500 years. Of course, for most of that time, Shemitah was also ignored, but at least it has enjoyed a partial comeback in recent years. Such is not the case with the Jubilee. It remains every bit as ignored and as forgotten as it has been since the destruction of the Second Temple.

Even observant Jews, that vanguard of preservers of ancient Jewish wisdom and tradition, have virtually dropped the Jubilee from their quite vast repertoire of Jewish knowledge. It comes up in an annual Torah reading, and everybody is familiar with it from there. It pops up in the Talmud every once in a while. But on the whole, it is about as obscure a subject as the Dead Sea Scrolls—a field that observant Jews have, for the most part, managed to avoid as if they were never discovered. With the scrolls, it is understandable. These were scrolls that nobody had ever heard of, and they emerged out of nowhere into a religion that had been rolling along for 2000 years without them. But with the Jubilee, we have a subject that is right smack in the Torah and seemingly right smack in the Jewish calendar. How did it get lost along the way?

To explore this question and several others, we are again going to use the "who, what, when, where, why, how" format. It seemed to work fine with Shemitah, so why not try it again with the Jubilee? As with Shemitah, there are plenty of verses in the Torah to work with, so there is no shortage of source material. But also like Shemitah, there is virtually no evidence from the rest of the Bible concerning how Jubilee was actually observed in biblical times. Let's work with what we have.

What Is the Jubilee?

What is the Jubilee? The word itself has very clear origins in biblical Hebrew. It is the Greek/Latin transliteration of the Hebrew word *Yovel*. The *y* became a *j*, the *o* became a *u*, the *v* became a *b*, and a double-e was tacked on at the end. It's a lot of changes, but it isn't all that difficult to see how *yovel* morphed into *Jubilee*. What does *yovel* mean? It has something to do with a shofar, the ram's horn that is blown on special occasions in the Bible and is still blown in synagogues on Rosh Hashanah and few other times throughout the year. *Yovel* seems to be an alternate word for *shofar*. There may be certain technical differences between the two, but for our purposes, we can safely ignore them.

The word *yovel* appears several times in the Torah, but by far the most frequent use is in the verses we want to examine. Those verses are found in Leviticus, immediately following the main verses of Shemitah. Here are the most relevant of those verses (original translation throughout this chapter from the biblical Hebrew by the author):

> You shall count seven Sabbatical years—seven years seven times—until the seven Sabbatical years come to 49 years. And you shall pass [likely meaning blow] the sound of a shofar on the tenth day of the seventh month, on Yom Kippur you shall blow the shofar in all your land. And you shall sanctify the fiftieth year and proclaim freedom in the land for all its residents—it shall be a Jubilee (yovel) for you, each man will return to his ancestral property, and each man will return to his family. This fiftieth year will be a Jubilee year for you—you shall not plant and you shall not harvest what grows, and you shall not harvest the vines. For it is a Jubilee, it will be holy to you—from the field you shall eat the produce. During the Jubilee each man will return to his ancestral property.
>
> Leviticus 25:8-13

This passage is followed by a few dozen other verses dealing with the technicalities of releasing slaves, returning ancestral property, and how to reckon the cost of land purchases when the land will automatically return to the original owners. The verses quoted above are really the foundations of the Jubilee year. They explain how it is counted, what is done to introduce the year, and the main commandments associated with the year.

Essentially, the "what" of the Jubilee is that it is the fiftieth year of the Shemitah cycle. In fact, it isn't really correct to call it the Shemitah cycle to begin with. It is really the Jubilee cycle, which is made of seven Shemitah cycles. The Jubilee year is culmination of this 49-year cycle.

It is a year-long commemoration of the completion of the old and the commencement of the new. The event that sets off the Jubilee is the blowing of the shofar on Yom Kippur. This, more than anything else, distinguishes the Jubilee from the rest of the years of the cycle. It is a very public and very national proclamation of a restart of society: slaves are freed, property is restored to its original owners, and the calendar is set back to zero.

How is the Jubilee Observed?

How is the Jubilee observed? The answer is in the details of the four activities associated with the Jubilee, mentioned in the Torah. These are:

- Blowing the shofar on Yom Kippur
- Freeing slaves
- Restoring landed property to its original owner
- Observing the agricultural restrictions as in a Shemitah year

Going through these one by one:

The shofar blowing likely resembled the ceremony that is still observed today on *Rosh Hashanah*. The *Mishnah*, the oldest recorded document of the Jewish oral tradition concerning Jewish law, states explicitly that the two are the same. The current custom of blowing the shofar on Rosh Hashanah has been expanded over the centuries because of doubt as to which is the correct sound to be made. Thus, in all likelihood, the shofar ceremony on the Jubilee was considerably shorter than the one used today since there is no reason to assume that this doubt existed back in biblical times.

The freeing of slaves is exactly as it sounds. Specifically, this referred to Jewish slaves, who entered into slavery for one of several reasons. Slaves could have been either male or female. They could be freed in various ways over the course of their term of servitude, but were all automatically freed when the shofar was blown on the Jubilee year. Thankfully, slavery is an aspect of biblical Judaism that was not continued beyond the biblical period, as far as we know. Consequently, this aspect of the Jubilee would probably be irrelevant, even if the commemoration of the year would somehow be reinstituted in modern times.

The restoring of property applies only to real estate. The land of Canaan was divided up between the various families according to the twelve tribes of Israel. Each family owned a specific plot that was considered to be their ancestral land forever. Even if some or all of that land was sold or ownership transferred in some other way (for instance, donation to the Temple), the land would be restored to the descendants of the original owner when the Jubilee year came around. Most of the details in both the Torah and the Mishnah regarding the Jubilee concern this particular aspect.

The calculations of land values, and which land it applies to and which it doesn't, are fairly complex. Like the commandment of freeing of slaves, this commandment also would be difficult if not impossible to observe if the Jubilee was somehow reinstituted. We currently do not have an exact method of knowing the borders of each tribe and, of course, are clueless as to the borders of family plots. In addition, barring a prophetic dictate, it would be nearly impossible for anybody to prove which tribe or family they descended from.

The agricultural restrictions are identical to those of the Shemitah year. Based on a simple reading of the Torah, this implies that there are two years in a row of restricted agricultural activity–the seventh Shemitah year and the Jubilee year which follows it. While this sounds like an impossibility by any standard of common sense, it does seem to be what the Torah is saying, and Jewish tradition knows no other interpretation. Presumably, the promise of a bountiful sixth year to cover for the Shemitah year would double prior to the Shemitah-Jubilee combination. But this matter is really related to how exactly the Jubilee fits into the Shemitah cycle, the subject of our next topic.

When is the Jubilee Year?

When is the Jubilee year? This is a surprisingly complex question that takes us into the intricacies of rabbinic Judaism. Despite what appears to be a rather simple method of calculation in the Bible itself, there are actually two rabbinic opinions as to how the Shemitah-Jubilee calendar runs. The first opinion, which appears to fit better into the words of the Torah, is known as that of the "Rabbis" (meaning the majority opinion). This opinion maintains that there were seven complete seven-year Shemitah cycles and the year following the 49th year was the Jubilee year. Thus, the Jubilee was the fiftieth year of the cycle, as the Torah clearly states. The next year, the 51st year, started the next Shemitah-Jubilee cycle. Thus, in every century, there were exactly two Jubilees with no extra years. This makes calculations of the Jubilee considerably easier.

The second opinion is that of Rabbi Yehuda, a well-known second century rabbi. He maintained that there were only 49 years in the cycle, with the "fiftieth year" coinciding with the first year of the next Shemitah-Jubilee cycle. According to this method, the first Shemitah cycle of a given Jubilee cycle had only five years of agriculture since the first year was a Jubilee year. It is not clear from the Torah what compelled Rabbi Yehuda to propose this system, but it is likely that he wanted the entire cycle to be only 49 years. He didn't want a single year to be "outside" of the rest of the cycle. The only way that he saw to do this was to overlap the Jubilee year with one of the years of the Shemitah cycle. Since the Jubilee had to be a "fiftieth year," it couldn't be the seventh Shemitah year, i.e. the forty-ninth year. Hence, he is forced to make it the first year of the next cycle.

Jewish tradition generally sides with the opinion of the "Rabbis," the majority. However, the story does not end there. This question has another aspect that gets us into Jewish history and subsequent rabbinic opinions. The primary authority of post-Talmudic rabbinic law is Maimonides, the twelfth-century philosopher/scholar whose main work covered the entire gamut of Jewish law, even those areas that were no longer being practiced. Among these "obsolete" sections is the Jubilee. Maimonides quotes a Talmudic opinion that the Jubilee ceased to be observed when some of the original twelve tribes were exiled from their land. According to this opinion, all the tribes had to be living in their proper locations for the Jubilee to officially "count." The first exile events took place sometime around 700 BCE. These were the two-and-one-half tribes that lived on the eastern side of the Jordan River. The rest of the "ten lost tribes" were exiled a decade or so later. The Jubilee was still counted after these exiles, but the commandments were no longer observed. There is somewhat vague scriptural evidence (see Jeremiah 34: 8-11) that at least one of the Jubilee commandments (freeing of slaves) was done at least a century after that first exile. There is also a rabbinic tradition based on a verse toward the end of the book of Ezekiel (40:1) that has a Jubilee occurring in the 25th year of the Babylonian exile of the Judeans.

Despite these indications, Maimonides maintains that the Shemitah-Jubilee count ceased with the advent of the Babylonian exile. The count restarted with the return of the exiles under Ezra in the Jewish year 3416, as we stated in the chapter on Shemitah. Even though the commandments of the Jubilee year were not observed during the period of the Second Temple, the count of the Jubilee was continued in order to retain the proper calendar cycle. Maimonides clearly goes with the opinion of the "Rabbis," that the Jubilee year followed the 49 years of the seven Shemitah cycles and stood alone, followed by the first year of the next cycle and not identical to it. He also maintains that this count continued after the destruction of the Second Temple until his time. Based on this calendar, he calculates a certain year of his own time as a Shemitah year.

But the story does not end here, either. Maimonides then brings a contrary opinion that only the Shemitah years were counted following the destruction of the First Temple. The count remained this way through the Second Temple period and the centuries following its destruction. He goes so far as to grant this opinion Talmudic support. He then states that the tradition among the "authorities and residents of Israel" follows this latter opinion and that Jewish custom follows this count. According to this system, he writes that the year that he had calculated to be a Shemitah year would instead be the first year of the Shemitah cycle.

Thus, Jewish custom now maintains a 49-year system consisting of seven Shemitah cycles and no Jubilee year. This is the way that most Jews understand things at present. It must be stated, however, that there is another view. That Talmudic support that Maimonides found for the opinion followed in Israel has its own elaborate rabbinic commentary. The main commentator, Rabbi Shlomo Itzhaki, the eleventh-century French rabbi, commonly known by the acronym of his name Rashi, writes that the Talmudic statement goes according to the opinion of Rabbi Yehuda, who insisted on a 49-year cycle including the Jubilee year. Therefore, the current system does not simply ignore the Jubilee; rather, it follows the Rabbi Yehuda system and continues to count the Jubilee in the calendar. The Jubilee count did not cease with the destruction of the Second Temple, nor did it cease with the destruction of the First Temple. It merely switched to a different system of counting, according to which Jubilees are calculated using a hybrid of both opinions, and only counted as a stand-alone "fiftieth year" (that is, outside the 49-year cycle) when the Jubilee is fully observed. Otherwise, the Jubilee year is included as the first year in the first Shemitah cycle.

It happens that there is some evidence concerning the Jubilee calendar that comes from non-conventional Jewish sources. One of the lesser known of the Dead Sea Scrolls actually describes a calendar that apparently was in use during the Second Temple period. There is little question that it used a 49-year cycle that probably worked along the lines of the system of Rabbi Yehuda. A second source is the slightly better-known apocryphal work of the Second Temple period aptly named the Book of Jubilees. This fascinating work, which essentially serves as an alternative recounting of the stories of Genesis and the beginning of Exodus, counts the years according to a Jubilee calendar. The years of the various events are always listed according to where they fall in a given Jubilee cycle. Many such years are listed but there is no case of a "fiftieth year." While this is certainly not conclusive evidence, it may lend further support to the 49-year system.

Based on this somewhat complicated reasoning, we can say that the Jubilee count is still rolling along in high gear according to the system of Rabbi Yehuda. Just as we can know which year is a Shemitah year, we can also know which year is a Jubilee year. It turns out that in the twentieth century, the two Jubilee years (every century will have at least two Jubilees, and in rare events, three) were 1917-1918 (the Jewish year goes from Rosh Hashanah to Rosh Hashanah, basically September to September) and 1966-1967. The first Jubilee of the twenty-first century will be 2015-2016, which started on the first day of the Jewish year, Sunday, September 13, 2015. All three of these Jewish (September-to-September) years follow a Shemitah year and represent the first year of the first Shemitah cycle of the next 49-year period.

Where Is the Jubilee Year Observed?

Where is the Jubilee year observed? The boundary includes the land east of the Jordan River that was inhabited by two-and-one-half tribes. Whether the agricultural restrictions also applied to this area is unclear.

Who Observes the Jubilee Year?

Who observes the Jubilee year? The commandments were incumbent upon all Jews living within the areas of biblical Israel. Currently, since the land is not divided according to tribal affiliation, the commandments do not apply. One other restriction to the applicability of the Jubilee year, according to Maimonides, is that all of the Jews must be living in the Land in their appropriate tribal locations. Simply speaking, at the very least, this means that all Jews must be living in Israel in order for observance of the Jubilee year to be restored.

Some recent rabbinic opinions claim that it is only necessary for a majority of Jews to live in Israel. It just happens that the Jewish population of Israel is rising to the degree that Israel will be home to the majority of Jews in the world within about a decade. Exactly what the ramifications of this will be for Judaism remains a (fascinating!) topic for the future.

Why Is the Jubilee Observed?

Why is the Jubilee observed? The simple

reason is Torah's explicit statement of "proclaim freedom in the land for all its residents." This famous proclamation, of course, is enshrined on the Liberty Bell with the words: *"Proclaim liberty throughout the land unto all the inhabitants thereof."*

Among Americans, it ranks among the most treasured quotes from the Bible and represents all the striving for freedom and liberty that the United States was built upon. The forms that freedom took in biblical times may have been considerably different from the way it manifests in modern times, but the basic idea is the same. Slaves were freed regardless of the reason or term of their slavery. Land purchases were all temporary–the land really belonged to God. The land itself was freed from its task of producing food.

Nowadays, we may look to different forms that freedom may take. We might emphasize freedom of speech or religion or some other human endeavor. We may see it as a quest of individual freedoms over the power of the government. It may take the form of freedom from oppression or hatred or control. But whatever form freedom takes, it is arguably the state of human society that is treasured above all others. That the biblical calendar celebrates freedom through the restarting of the Jubilee cycle is only fitting. The Bible brought a great measure of freedom to the world through its wisdom, its insight into human nature, and its great revelation of one God who creates, sustains, and guides the universe. Is there any better way to usher in the next great cycle in the calendar than to "proclaim liberty throughout the land"?

Can we bring this half-century celebration of freedom back into our lives? This is not really a question for the Jews alone as much as for all those who treasure the Bible and look to it for spiritual sustenance. Some–perhaps most–observant Jews may not feel that Jubilee has any practical place in their lives, owing to the current circumstances in Israel, Jewish law, and modern society.

In spite of that attitude, the Jubilee may have been silently riding along with the Jewish calendar throughout centuries and millennia. It may not have been noted as a special year, and it may not have separated one Shemitah cycle and another, but it was always there. Perhaps the time has come to revive this long-forgotten observance. Maybe those Jubilee years, coming as rarely as they do, signify something more than a few technical laws from the Old Testament. Maybe they represent something greater than that, something whose significance will only be understood as the decades and centuries and Jubilees role by. Only God knows–and only the future will tell. ✿

CHAPTER 20

A Promised Jubilee for a Promised Land

Now that you know the background of the Jubilee, it is time to look specifically at the reasons why Fall 2015 through Fall 2016 might qualify as a Jubilee year, and make some predictions about what God might do during this time period.

Before we begin, we want to once again thank Jonathan Cahn for including the Jubilee in the epilogue of *The Mystery of the Shemitah*. We think that he has made a strong case for the Jubilee that began in Fall 2015. In this chapter, we will explain our reasons for agreeing, and add specific predictions of our own.

Let us begin again with the foundational Scripture in Leviticus. After speaking about the Shemitah year, that chapter goes on to speak about the Jubilee:

> You are to count off seven Sabbaths of years for yourself, seven time seven years, so that you have the time [literally: days] of the seven Sabbaths of years, namely **forty-nine** years.
>
> You shall then sound a ram's horn [literally: Jubilee] abroad on the tenth day of the seventh month; on the day of atonement you shall sound a horn all through your land.
>
> You shall thus consecrate the **fiftieth** year and proclaim release through the land to all its inhabitants. It shall be a Jubilee for you, and each of you shall return to his own property, and each of you shall return to his family.
>
> Leviticus 25:8–10

We see in these foundational Scriptures that the terms *forty-nine years* and *fiftieth year* are used. To recap: the Shemitah cycle is a seven-year cycle that begins with Tishri 1, the first day of the year. For many years, a controversial question has raged: Is the Jubilee cycle 49 years or 50 years?

Forty-nine and Counting

Let us take a look at the difference in terms of how those might work. If the cycle is 49 years, that means that the 50th year, the year of Jubilee, is shared with the next seven Shemitah cycles. On the other hand, with the 50 years calculation, the 50th year stands on its own, and the next 49 year cycle starts the year afterward, so you actually count 50 years between cycles.

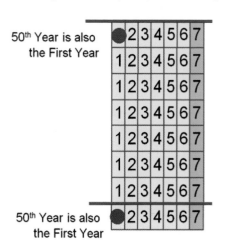

49 Years between Jubilees

The 50-year calculation on the other hand visually looks like this:

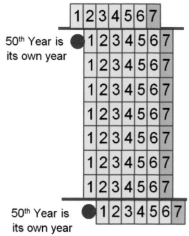

50 Years between Jubilees

After finishing a 49-year cycle, the next year—the 50th year—is a year on its own, the Jubilee year. Once that year is completed, then we start over again, counting 1 through 49. That makes it easier to count between Jubilees from a mathematical perspective; adding 50 to something is easier than adding 49. But, as you can see here, it does create a complication. Notice that the 7th year of the Shemitah cycle, when counting by 7, becomes the 6th year in the next 50-year cycle and then becomes the 5th. In other words, in a 50-year cycle, the exact year of the Jubilee must be known and agreed on by everyone, or even the celebration of Sabbath rest years will not be synchronized.

Why Forty-nine Is Better

The previous chapter explained the various discussions between Jewish rabbis; Christians have argued over this very point as well. Which of these methods is right?

I, Bob, would like to suggest the first method, the method of 49-year cycles, is much better and is much more likely to be correct. I will suggest a few reasons for that.

First, the pattern of the days of the week. In the same way that we look for the first occurrence of a word in Scripture, we need to look at the first occurrence of a cycle of seven. The model for all of these cycles of seven is the original pattern of the days of the week.

1	Sun-day
2	Moon-day
3	Mars-day
4	Mercury-day
5	Jupiter (Thors)-day
6	Venus-day
7	Saturn-day

Days of the Week

In the Jewish calendar, as well as in the Bible, the days are not named. The idea of naming the first day of the week after the sun and the second day of the week after the moon and so on is absolutely a pagan tradition, and so we marked through those names in the shown chart. God named the days of the week simply by their numbers, "the first day of the week" through "the seventh day of the week." So when we come to the idea of the Jubilee year being inserted as its own special year in the cycle, the foundational question is: When has a holiday ever created a new day of the week? Has it ever happened? Of course not. Even the Resurrection of Christ didn't create its own new day of the week! Thus, from the model standpoint, the idea of inserting another year does not fit the pattern of the days of the week.

Second, the Jews have never actually celebrated the Jubilee, as far as we know. The question of not celebrating Jubilee in the 50th year raises a problem. If it didn't get celebrated, then how could it have ever been counted? The Jews have actually been tracking cycles of Shemitah years for over a thousand years without inserting Jubilee cycles, and using that repeating pattern without Jubilee years inserted still shows an 80 percent correlation to financial downturns. With a 49-year cycle, that is exactly what we would expect to see. We can begin to celebrate Jubilee at any time without changing the cycle. But if Jubilees are supposed to be celebrated every 50 years, then God would seem to be changing His Shemitah calendar to match ours, simply because we have forgotten to keep the Jubilee, and He must then change the pattern once we start to celebrate the Jubilee again. This seems unnecessarily confusing.

Third, a comment by Jesus. The third reason is from the New

Testament, where Jesus specifically called out a period of 490. Jesus told Peter how many times to forgive:

> Jesus said to him, "I do not say to you up to seven times,
> but up to seventy times seven."
>
> Matthew 18:22

His choice of 490 has often been interpreted as that of completeness or wholeness, a topic to which Shemitah and Jubilee very much relate. His choice for completeness and wholeness leaves no room for Jubilee to be included in its own year.

Fourth, the historical fit. The fourth reason why 49 years between Jubilees seems to work better is because of some historical facts that better fit the 49-year pattern. Let us take a look at recent Shemitah years and see when potential Jubilee years might occur.

The Search for God's Jubilee Year Assuming a 49-Year Pattern

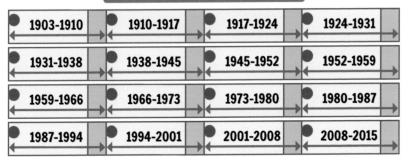

We have included over 100 years of Shemitah cycles in the figure above. Everyone agrees that a Jubilee must occur after a Shemitah year, even if they do not agree on the length of the cycle. Therefore, assuming a 49-year pattern, two or three of these blue dots need to be a Jubilee, the first year after a Sabbath rest.

Searching for the Jubilee

Is God giving us some help, some breadcrumbs, to lead us to the truth? Remember we discussed this idea earlier with the Blood Moons, pondering whether God might have *formed* the Blood Moons as hints in the sky to lead us back to understand His covenant purposes, and for later generations to be able to witness His covenant love over time for the Jews. The question about the Jubilee is: Would God give us a pattern in this case? Would He give us something to help us understand how the earth should celebrate the Jubilee?

Birth of Israel. Let us look at the "blue dot years" of the last century and see if we can discover what might be a Jubilee year. Here's an idea. Suppose we take the year that Israel was reborn as a nation, 1948. That qualifies as a *hugely* important event. Could it be a Jubilee?

When we compare 1948 to the end of the Shemitah year, which ended between fall of 1944 and fall of 1945, we see right away that the following year, the potential Jubilee year, does not encompass

the rebirth of the Nation of Israel. Nice try, but it just does not fit. What else might we try?

The reunification of Jerusalem in 1967. That was a pretty important event.

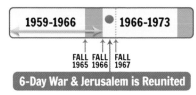

It fits! This particular event, the reunification of Jerusalem during the Six-Day War, occurred in the first year after a Shemitah cycle. That looks extremely interesting and extremely important. Now let us go back 49 years to see what might have happened then and if that pattern continues.

Going back 49 years takes us to **Balfour Declaration,** which was also in the first year after the Shemitah cycle and General Allenby entering Jerusalem. Let us take a look at those two events in more detail.

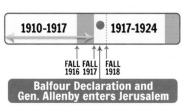

The Balfour Declaration stated that the United Kingdom would use its best efforts to create a homeland for the Jews in Palestine; that was in November 1917.

About a month and a week later, General Allenby liberated Jerusalem from Ottoman rule and,

Lord Balfour and the Balfour Declaration

General Allenby Enters Jerusalem in 1917

very humbly, he decided to walk into the city rather than to ride in on horseback. These facts were highlighted in Jonathan Cahn's book.

Let's take his pattern and push it a little bit further. If we go back another 49 years, before 1917, do we find anything interesting?

Other Possible Jubilee Years

Two pretty interesting things happened in the period of 1868 and 1869. The country of Germany was in the process of bringing equality to its Jewish citizens, and it completed the process on December 3, 1868, when Saxony was the last state to grant equality to all the Jews. Actually, Prussia then created a confederation with Germany later in that Jubilee year that created even more widespread equality for Jews on July 3, 1869. (For more information on those events see the Wikipedia articles: History of the Jews in Germany and Jewish Emancipation.)

Another Possible Jubilee Year in 1868-1869

While unrelated to the Jews, it is interesting that the United States *pardoned* the last of the Confederate rebels on December 25 of that Jubilee year. The Confederate soldiers had been pardoned in phases over the preceding years, but the job was finally completed in this Jubilee year, which, of course, is the year granting *release*—allowing people to return to their homes. That is exactly what happened in the case of the Southern soldiers.

What about the freeing of the slaves? The Shemitah year of 1867 to 1868 was the year in which the 14th Amendment was ratified! The 14th Amendment granted equality and due process to the slaves, a positive example of Shemitah year legislation.

So if there is a clear pattern of coincidences every 49 years after the Shemitah cycle's end, we have a compelling case for God answering our question.

1. The Jubilee occurs every 49 years.
2. It is remembered by God even if it is forgotten by mankind.

The Coming Jubilee

Using this pattern, when would the next Jubilee year occur? Counting 49 years from 1966-1967, we reach the Fall of 2015 to Fall of 2016. Pretty exciting, isn't it?

The Next Jubilee Year

What might another Jubilee mean for Israel? Let us go back to the Scriptures:

> You shall then sound a ram's horn abroad on the tenth day of the seventh month; on the day of atonement you shall sound a horn all through your land.
>
> You shall thus consecrate the fiftieth year and proclaim a release through the land to all its inhabitants. It shall be a Jubilee for you, and each of you shall **return to his own property**, and each of you shall **return to his family**.
>
> **Leviticus 25:9–10**

08	09	10	11	12	13	14	15
09	10	11	12	13	14	15	16

September 14 (Fall 2015) Tishri 1   Elul 29 (Fall 2016) October 2

What does it mean to return to family? That is explained better in another verse associated with the Jubilee:

> If a countryman of yours becomes so poor with regard to you that he sells himself to you, you shall not subject him to a slave's service.
>
> He shall be with you as a hired man, as if he were a sojourner; he shall serve with you until the year of jubilee.
>
> He shall then go out from you, he and his sons with him, and **shall go back to his family**, that he may **return to the property of his forefathers**.

Leviticus 25:39-41

What we have in the Jubilee is a combination of people and their property. Put another way, it is the property *returning* to the people who originally owned it.

When we look at the Jubilee year starting in fall of 2015 to 2016, what property associated with the Jews or Israel might return to its rightful owners? This begs the question: What property has been sold or *given away* by Jews in the last 49 years?

What Israeli Property Should Be Returned?

The Temple Mount. Israeli soldiers captured the Temple Mount in 1967 and raised flags there. Chief Rabbi Shlomo Goren sounded his shofar. However, the soldiers were immediately asked to take down the flags. Moshe Dayan, the Defense Minister, made a decision to turn over the administration of the Temple Mount to the Jordanians, and told them he would give them and their Supreme Muslim Council

Moshe Dayan Gives Away Control of the Temple Mount from "Jerusalem, City Without a Wall" by Uzi Benziman
Photo courtesy of Schocken Books © all rights reserved

the right to administer it. This meant the Jews could visit there, but were not allowed to pray. From Moshe Dayan's standpoint, there was no issue with that. He considered that the Temple Mount was primarily a historical site, whereas the Western Wall is a holy site. So he considered that Jews did not need to be praying on the Temple Mount, but simply visit.

I, Bob, have personally walked on the Temple Mount plaza on Jerusalem Day 2014 and watched Israeli soldiers command a dozen Jews to "Continue moving forward. Do not stop. Keep walking. And stop moving your lips while you walk!" Our visitation time on the entire plaza was limited to several minutes only.

Rabbi Yehudah Glick, one of our Root Source teachers, is leading a movement to persuade the Israeli government to uphold the human right of prayer for everyone – Muslims, Christians, and Jews – to pray on the Temple Mount. Gidon will say more about Yehudah in the next chapter.

Judea and Samaria – The West Bank. In 1993, the Oslo Accords between Israel and the PLO (Palestinian Liberation Organization) were signed. Even though the PLO failed to meet most of the provisions of the agreement, Israel implemented many of the aspects that were laid out there, in the hope that such acts of good faith might bring peace to the land. That whole process was halted in its tracks by the Second Intifada that began in September, 2000. What the Oslo Accords stated was that there would be three kinds of areas in the West Bank (Judea and Samaria).

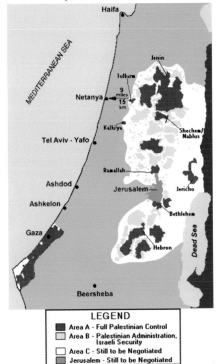

Area A, shown here in brown, is under full Palestinian control where they run their own administration, police, and security. Cities in Area A include: Bethlehem, Hebron, Shechem (Nablus), and Jericho.

Area B, shown in yellow, is comprised of areas that tend to be more rural. Those areas are administered by the Palestinians, but security is provided by Israeli forces.

Area C, shown in white, comprises all other areas in the West Bank where Israel has full and sole responsibility for administration and security.

LEGEND
Area A - Full Palestinian Control
Area B - Palestinian Administration, Israeli Security
Area C - Still to be Negotiated
Jerusalem - Still to be Negotiated

Oslo Accords - Areas A, B and C –
Map courtesy of www.iris.org.il

All Jewish settlements are located in Area C and they constitute a fraction of its geographical area.

What would it mean for that land to return to Israel? It is hard to say for sure, but it could involve Israel taking over complete administration of the Temple Mount, allowing access once again to Joseph's Tomb in Shechem (Nablus), and undivided access to the Cave of the Patriarchs in Hebron. The Oslo Accords even allowed for complete access to these sites by Jews, but Israel has not enforced it. Will it happen? We do not know. Yet, is the idea of that happening consistent with the principles of Jubilee? In our opinion, yes.

The Palestine Liberation Organization (PLO), now the Palestinian National Authority, has had these lands in its possession since the late 1990s. The principle of the Jubilee is that no matter when you start to take possession of an area of Israel, it reverts back to the original owners in the Jubilee Year. The Temple Mount was handed over in the Jubilee year of 1967, so that has been out of Israeli control for the full 49 years. The areas in brown in the West Bank (Area A) were released by Israel in the 1990s, less than 20 years ago.

How might this retaking of those lands possibly come about? One likely way might be as a *response* to something that the United States might do. For instance, as we discussed in Chapter 18, what if, God forbid, the USA recognizes a Palestinian State like the Vatican did on June 26, 2015? What could we possibly say about that?

Here is what I suspect Jesus would have to say about it—the very same thing He has said previously:

> "Woe to the world because of its stumbling blocks! For it is inevitable that stumbling blocks come; but woe to that man through whom the stumbling blocks come."
>
> Matthew 18:7

It could be this very kind of action that might force the hand of Israel to make this kind of change.

Jubilee and Christians Worldwide

Let us now turn to a much more positive subject. How might Christians participate in the Jubilee? We have discussed the Jubilee in the context of Israel only. Is it solely an Israeli event? We don't think so! Here are some practical ideas of how we Christians can participate in the coming Jubilee:

1. **We can pray** that God's will regarding Israel and the restoration of its land be accomplished in this coming Jubilee Year. That is a wonderful prayer to pray! It is safe, and yet it acknowledges that God can do something in this particular year. It is coming alongside God and saying, "You do what you want to do, Lord."

2. **We can help** Jews return to the Land of Israel. Remember that the Jubilee is about people—people moving back to the land of their forefathers. There are many Jews who are interested in making Aliyah. We as Christians can support that effort financially, in prayer, and in many practical ways. For example, I have heard that some Christians in the United Kingdom are making their homes way-stations for Jews to escape quickly out of mainland Europe on their way to preparing for Aliyah to Israel. What a wonderful way for Christians in the United Kingdom to redeem Britain's past record of failing to live up to the promises of the Balfour Declaration.

3. **We can proclaim freedom throughout our own land.** Whenever God does something in Israel or for the Jewish People, the benefits spill over to the rest of the world. We can celebrate the Jubilee not only with the Jews and their Land; we can celebrate that God wants to proclaim freedom throughout *our* land. What form will that freedom take? Will there be massive repentance, praise God? Will there be major revival, will there be miracles, the likes of which have never been seen before? We should proclaim freedom and see what God does during that proclamation. Yes, waiting to see what God will do is an act of faith, but it is also an act of coming alongside God and His proclamation to the Earth. This may never happen again in our lifetime! Remember the exhortation in James 4: You have not because you ask not! We must be bold in our asking, and see how God responds!

4. **We can let something rest.** If God so moves you, then you may choose to let something "rest" as a way to honor God. Let us look at this "Rest" idea in more detail.

The "Rest" Principle

Why would we suggest letting something rest? Again, what does God's Word say?

> You shall have the fiftieth year as a Jubilee; you shall not sow, nor reap its aftergrowth, nor gather in from its untrimmed vines.
>
> For it is a Jubilee; it shall be holy to you. You shall eat its crops out of the field.
>
> Leviticus 25:11-12

These are the same rules that apply to the Shemitah year! What did you think when you read in Chapter 13 about letting your investments rest in the Shemitah year? Did you feel left out because the Shemitah year was over by the time you read about this idea? I have good news for you. There is another rest year coming. The Jubilee Year! And the Jubilee was intended as another Shemitah year.

In Chapter 13, I said that I had sold stock positions and moved into a cash position, just to let the money rest. Who knows? Now after preparing this chapter, I might keep those investments at rest for much longer. I might even keep them at rest through the entire Jubilee year, perhaps.

Other readers of this chapter are not invested in the stock market at all. Their income matches their expenditures at best; maybe they have a few thousand dollars in the bank. To those people I would say that essentially your investments are already at rest. So if you want to let something rest, in the Jubilee year, you will need to find another area than finances.

Still other readers of this chapter not only have no investments, but are in debt. To such people, I say: You can still let something rest. What might that be? You have been investing in promises to repay. Your promise was made in exchange for that debt. So you might respond to this rest idea by taking a rest from making any new such promises in the next year! That might be a way to honor God in the Jubilee year.

With regard to the Jews in Israel and the Jubilee year, Gidon does not expect the Jews to let their land rest for another year because no accepted rabbinical authority rules that Fall 2015-Fall 2016 is actually a Jubilee year with regard to any commandments, and there is no way for Jewish law to be updated and changed so fast. The Jewish system is very deliberate!

But while Jews cannot adapt so fast—we can! As Christians, we can. We have the advantage of being able to make relatively quick decisions individually, for ourselves, in prayer before God, listening to the direction of the Holy Spirit. We can each make a decision before God about whether we will let something rest during the Jubilee year, and if so, what.

Most of us are not going to live to see another Jubilee Year. The next Jubilee Year, should the Messiah tarry, will not be until 2064.

I am asking the Lord about Jubilee, and I am trying to determine what would be honoring to God. You have the same freedom. It may not be money that you are letting rest; it may be something else.

But whatever you decide to do or not do in the Jubilee Year, we strongly suggest one thing:

Make it count! ✡

Section FIVE:

THE CAPSTONE

The How-To Guide to Blessing Israel

You are holding in your hands a miracle.

Not in the magical, against-nature, never-before-and-never-again kind of miracle, but a surprise culmination kind of miracle. Something like the birth of a baby: Nothing throughout the process is unnatural, but when the baby arrives, everyone knows that it is from God.

That is the nature of the ideas and concepts presented in this book, and no less the story of how this book came to be–not only the personal journeys of the book's contributors, but the direction in which history was moving for thousands of years, when overnight, it seemed, everything turned around.

I, Gidon, am speaking of the dynamic between Christians and Jews. I believe that this relationship and related phenomena are the focus of God in His activities operating in the world, especially bringing about His end-time objectives.

Instead of writing a full history, I will share my own personal story with you, and how God has intersected my life in some unusual ways to accomplish His purposes.

A Nice Jewish Boy

I was born in Queens, New York, to a traditional but not strictly observant Jewish family. In the '60s and the '70s, this was not out of the ordinary.

I attended a private Orthodox Jewish day school called a *yeshiva* until fifth grade, when my parents decided to pull me out and enroll me in a local public school; I assume this was for financial reasons. Even though the majority of kids in that school were Jewish, as could be expected in New York, I felt the Jewish focus was missing. To paraphrase Joni Mitchell, I "didn't know what I had 'till it was gone." During that year, I made a conscious decision to actively pursue and strengthen my Jewish identity.

Sure enough, my parents saw how miserable I was and put me back in the yeshiva for sixth grade. Thank God, a local youth group leader from Bnei Akiva, the world's largest religious Jewish Zionist youth movement, introduced himself that year, and I was hooked. The idea of attaching myself to timeless values of Jewish identity–the religion of Israel, the Nation of Israel, the State of Israel, the Land of Israel, and above all the God of Israel–was so vitally attractive to me, that although I was barely twelve years old, I knew I had found my life's calling.

For the next three or four years, I spent more time in the youth movement's club house than my own home. So much so, that when the time came in ninth grade for my parents to discuss where I would attend tenth grade–the high school I attended in ninth grade was not a very good one; it closed soon thereafter–my parents surprised me and asked, "Gidon, have you ever considered going to Israel for high school?" I jumped at the chance!

Studying in Israel

I landed in Israel a few days before the start of my tenth grade school year. Luckily, as was traditional in those years, Israel was having its annual teachers' strike to start off the school year. This gave me an opportunity to hang out with my newfound friends and learn Hebrew.

But beyond the Hebrew language, I was overjoyed to learn something else–the *Torah*. This multi-faceted word encompasses a number of things: first, the Pentateuch (five books of Moses, Genesis to Deuteronomy); second, the entire Old Testament (known as *Tanakh* in Jewish parlance), Tanakh being an acronym that stands for *Torah* [see above], *Nevi'im* [Prophets, including Joshua, Isaiah, and Zephaniah], and *Ketuvim* [Writings, including Psalms, Job, and Proverbs]); and third, the orally transmitted laws, stories, and ideas given to the Jewish People at Mount Sinai, together with the Written Torah; and any related idea that any student comes up with, from the time of Moses (some 3400 years ago) to the present day!

After finishing yeshiva high school in Jerusalem, I continued on to an advanced Jewish Studies academy, also conveniently, if not confusingly, called a yeshiva. This program was unique, in that it was a combined study-military program for soldiers in the Israel Defense Forces. Instead of spending three years in the army, participants in this program spend five years in the army, but only 1.5 years or so in active training and duty. The rest of the time, we sit and study Torah. By the way, that is what yeshiva means: "to sit and study."

"As Iron Sharpens Iron"

My experience in the high school yeshiva was wonderful, but this advanced yeshiva was literally out of this world. From dawn to midnight on the average, we would sit with a study partner, reading and explaining to each other a text, trying to understand it and, when appropriate, disagree with it. Respectful disagreement with sources and teachers is an inherent, substantial component of Torah study. As the Jewish Sages say in the *Chapters of the Fathers* (a classic compendium of Jewish teachings compiled around the third century): "The timid cannot learn, and the strict cannot teach."

Each day, I had a lineup of some dozen study partners, studying something different with each one. Over my six years at that yeshiva (I stayed an extra year; some people never leave), I must have spent time studying with over a hundred different people! This experience of pitting one's mind and personality against so many others' makes for especially sharp wits and sensitive personalities. As taught in Proverbs: "As *iron sharpens iron, so a friend sharpens a friend.*" (27:17, NLT)

The International Christian Embassy—A Phenomenon!

During a break one day from studying to run some errands in the city, I spotted a sign on an apartment building across the street. Now it was a hobby of mine to read the street signs in Jerusalem; did you know that you can get a degree in Jewish History just by reading Jerusalem's street signs? In any case, upon crossing the street and looking closer at that sign, it read: "ICEJ, The International Christian Embassy, Jerusalem."

Now *this* was a surprise. I mean, I am just a regular, garden-variety Jew. We are pretty keep-to-ourselves-in-a-friendly-to-others-sort-of-way kind of folks. I mean, over the past few thousand years, we've learned a lot, but mainly that most everyone who isn't a Jew is an anti-Semite. Present company excluded, of course. Seriously, Jewish history is pretty much a laundry list of horrors: prohibition of fundamental Jewish practices such as Shabbat, circumcision, kosher food, and learning Torah; blood libels; forced conversions; destruction of synagogues; burning of the Talmud; the Crusades; the Inquisition; pogroms; and the horror of horrors—the Holocaust. Today it is centered on anti-Israel sentiment. And this is just a general overview, pretty much from memory. For a longer (but by all means not exhaustive) list, search Wikipedia for "Timeline of

Anti-Semitism."

Yet here I was, facing a sign testifying to another kind of Christian. I walked inside.

After collecting some of the flyers, I started looking into this phenomenon of pro-Israel, philo-Semitic (Jew-loving) Christians. I walked around Jerusalem and surfed the Internet, discovering other pro-Israel Christian organizations–Bridges for Peace, Christian Friends of Israel, Friends of Israel, Christians for Israel, Christians United for Israel, International Fellowship of Christians and Jews–and soon I discovered the lynchpin: the Knesset Christian Allies Caucus. This official Knesset caucus has assembled the most comprehensive list of Christian leaders with a heart for Israel. Little by little, I began to make friends with many of these leaders. (The fact that I was a member of the central committee of the Likud Party didn't hurt.)

One of those leaders was Christine Darg. Christine is a mighty woman of God, who divides her time between the U.S.A., England, and Arab countries (where she evangelizes Muslims to Christianity), and Israel, where she shares her love for Israel with her Christian friends from all over the world and her Jewish-Israeli friends, among whom I am humbled to be counted. I frequently address the groups she brings to Israel through her organization "Exploits Ministries" and "The Jerusalem Channel," sharing this story of my own new and growing relationships with pro-Israel Christians, and introducing Jewish concepts, to the delight of my Christian audience.

Commanded to Teach

One brisk winter day in January, 2014, I decided to share with Christine's group an idea that had been forming in my mind: Since I enjoyed teaching Christians so much, and since so many of them seemed to enjoy learning from me, what if I teach–only using the platform of the Internet rather than a classroom? A Christian online yeshiva, if you will. A collective gasp went up from the group, followed by one word: *Hallelujah!* Afterward, many people came up to me to encourage me in this new endeavor, including one in particular, Bob O'Dell, who told me that he wanted to be the first to sign up for the venture.

As they say, the rest is history. Bob, an unassuming, ever-smiling, high-tech executive, had recently completed an "exit" (an Israeli word that means "the sale of a start-up to a big company for a lot of money") and after a few initial meetings with me, we created Root

Source, the first online platform of Israeli Jews teaching Christians about Israel, Jewish concepts, Torah, and the Jewish and Hebrew origins of their faith.

Now I had always believed that Jews teaching the world about the God of Israel is a prophetic commandment, as Isaiah 2:3 spoke, "For out of Zion shall come the Torah, and the word of God from Jerusalem." The Jewish people had been mandated thus in the Sinai Covenant: "You shall be for me a nation of priests." Israel's priests, the sons of Aaron, are commanded to teach the rest of the Jewish people: "For the Torah of Truth was in the Priest's mouth... and the people will ask to learn Torah from his mouth." (Malachi 2:6-7, author's paraphrase)

So the analogy is clear: if Aaron's sons are commanded as priests to teach their brothers the Jewish Torah, and the Jews are the priests among the nations, then the Jews are commanded to teach Torah to the nations, not to mention the explicit mandate that Abraham was given by God to spread the knowledge of Him throughout the world.

But we Jews had a slight handicap in executing this requirement for two thousand years or so. We were a bit preoccupied with surviving the attacks of the many nations that were trying to kill us. We must thank our friends, the Christians, for picking up our slack and spreading the good news of monotheism throughout much of the pagan world in our absence. And now that we Jews have come back to our homeland, thank God, we can and must once again pick up our job of teaching the world about the God of Abraham.

Blessing Israel: A Unique Perspective

Back to Root Source: Since I knew that there were many Christians who would appreciate such teaching, I thought that I could do my little part with a few blog posts and online videos. But Bob saw things quite differently. "This is a tremendous way for Christians to bless Israel!" he exclaimed. And in fact, Christians, like all nations of the world, are promised a reward of being blessed if they bless Abraham and his people. "By blessing the teachers of Root Source—prolific teachers who step out of their comfort zone to teach Christians—our students will be doubly blessed: empowered with new knowledge of God and His plans for the world, and biblically rewarded for observing this fundamental commandment!"

I was a bit surprised by this. Surely, blessing Israel today can take many forms: advocating for the besieged State of Israel in op-ed pages, campuses, and parliaments; supporting poor Jews in Israel and worldwide, especially Holocaust survivors; visiting Israel and strengthening the economy while enjoying the sights; and in general being a good person vis-a-vis the Jews. Sadly, this last item has not been so obvious over the past centuries. But Bob truly discovered a new facet to this Christian commandment: "Do not be arrogant toward the branches. If you are, remember it is not you who support the root, but the root that supports you." (Romans 11:18)

Most of the blessings listed above, and others like them, assume the Christian "blesser" has something that the Jewish "blessee" does not have. Think about that: There is a measure of arrogance in this position. But when Christians take their spot at the *feet* of their teacher–much as Mary did in Luke 10:39–they are assuming a position of humble student. Now, let me hasten to point out that my fellow teachers and I want anything but to be venerated. We just want to teach what we like to teach, to people who want to learn. No big deal. But it is clear from the **hundreds** of unsolicited comments and accolades we have received (in the past month alone!) that we have clearly struck a nerve.

Bob and I do not suggest that you refrain from other methods of blessing Israel. If there is one thing I have learned from my interactions and relationships with Christians, it is that there is no limit to the human spirit, to the Christian spirit. I sincerely believe that following your *yetzer hatov*–your good inclination, your conscience–is listening to the divine spark within. And everyone's "spark" is different, suited uniquely to them. Some people contribute money to the poor, some volunteer to teach English, some battle on Facebook. But we challenge you to challenge yourself! And browse our offerings at **www.root-source.com.**

Here are some of the channels being offered as of this writing:

Channels of Blessing
Women in the Bible

Dr. Rivkah Adler knows that the role of women in the religions of the world is very much in the news. Looking deeply into the stories told about women in the Bible can help us gain perspective on the changing roles of women today. We begin with Eve, the mother of all living souls. What really happened in the Garden of Eden and how does that impact all women until today? We will examine the lives, personalities, deeds, and marriages of the matriarchs of the Jewish people, the women of the Exodus from Egypt, the women in the books of Prophets all the way through to Queen Esther.

Even if you know these stories, our approach of augmenting Bible text with classic rabbinic commentary guarantees you will gain new insights into the lives of women you thought you knew. You will learn from the ancient Jewish sources, the names of women, such as the wife of Noah and the mothers of Samson and King David. And you'll meet for the first time many other women, like Serach Bat Asher, Elisheva, Tirtza, Jephthah's daughter and Abishag.

The Holy Temple

In the Holy Temple channel, Rabbi Yehudah Glick shares about all things concerning the Holy Temple, including its history and the scriptural basis for building a third temple.

In October, 2014, Rabbi Glick narrowly survived an assassination attempt by a Muslim terrorist. The attempt on his life stemmed from his public advocacy of human rights, including the right to pray, for *all* people—Muslims, Jews, Christians, and others—on Jerusalem's Temple Mount. As a result of Rabbi Glick's tireless efforts, in May 2015 he received the Moskowitz "Lion of Zion" award. This honor is conferred on outstanding Israeli men and women who act from a feeling of personal responsibility, vision, and national mission, often while sacrificing their personal welfare and even endangering their personal security.

This channel delves immediately into the topic of The Holy Temple, and were all recorded after the assassination attempt.

God: The Jewish Image

God needs no introduction, and most people either believe in God, or they do not. But in spite of God's all-or-nothing quality, He must be examined, imagined, and, to the best of our abilities, defined.

In this channel, Rabbi Gedalia Meyer reveals that Jews have a long and somewhat hidden history in exploring God, not so much as a bounded investigation, but as a collective journey. Join Rabbi Meyer and reflect on how that journey can impact your own journey today, even as it has deeply impacted his.

Jewish History—Jewish Future

The Root Source Jewish History channel will help you understand both the past and the future of the Jewish People. It is taught by one of the most experienced and admired Jewish teachers in all of Israel.

The channel opens with a Week One interview of Rabbi Ken Spiro in his own home. Then in Week Two, it shifts to uncover the divinely inspired context of Israel's history with an exciting, fast-paced, four-part series entitled "The Seven Wonders of Jewish History."

Next, the channel shifts to the future, with a four-week series called "The Edge of History," which explains the Jewish view of End-Time prophecy. The Jewish view of the End Times is one of the least understood, yet most interesting topics to many Christians.

Already a favorite among Israeli Jews, Ken makes his topics come alive with his naturally energetic style. Root Source is delighted to feature him with material he is now recording specifically for Christians.

Proverbially Speaking

Rabbi Aryeh Leifert believes that one of the biggest patches of common ground between Christians and Jews is the Wisdom of Solomon. An Israeli tour guide who is active and adventurous, Rabbi Leifert invites you to join him in "touring" one of his favorite books of the Bible: Proverbs.

After meeting Aryeh Leifert in a cafe in Jerusalem in Week One, join with him week-by-week in "Proverbially Speaking" and begin discovering the nuggets of wisdom that have changed his whole perspective on what it means to live life in modern Israel.

Come see how approachable, upbeat, and interesting Rabbi Aryeh Leifert can be!

Deceptions of Islam

Avi Lipkin, a pioneer in Jewish-Christian relations, and now a household name, was one of the few voices in the 1990s to warn about a coming terrorist attack on the United States.

This channel tells you where Islam is headed, explaining it like nobody else can. Avi makes a clear distinction between "loving Muslims," which he does, and "the trap of Islam," where he holds back nothing. The channel opens with "The Five Deceptions of Islam," where Avi explains how to contrast your Christian faith with Islam, and then continues with other materials to help you pray and prepare for the difficult, dangerous road that lies ahead for all of Western Civilization.

Think you have already "heard it all" about Islam? Think again! We guarantee this channel will tell you things you have NEVER HEARD before.

Biblical Hebrew

Instant Biblical Hebrew from Root Source is the perfect way for Christians to learn Hebrew, step by step, in the comfort of their own home. While Biblical Hebrew is almost the same as Modern Hebrew spoken in the land of Israel, a Biblical Hebrew course has the added advantage of working  from the Hebrew Scriptures directly, teaching the students the words that would be needed in their own biblical study, beginning with Genesis 1:1.

Seth Young is an Israeli Jew living in Jerusalem and is one of the world's leading Hebrew teachers, as well as being well-versed in Torah study, which makes him uniquely qualified to teach this topic.

Seth did not learn Hebrew until he was an adult, and so he knows how it feels to approach the language without previous experience. His Hebrew teaching system was born out of these struggles, but he turned them into an advantage. He has now helped thousands of students learn Hebrew the way he wishes he had been taught.

Israel and the Nations

David Ha'ivri has a great love for the physical Land that God promised to Abraham. This is only matched by his love for people, and for the God of Abraham.

David brings these three streams together into one place and time, when he observes Jews and non-Jews working to become fully alive in their relationship to the Land, to each other, and to God as they restore the Land of Israel, piece by piece, meter by meter, to its former beauty and productivity.

In this channel, David gives Christians an inside look and perspective on the importance of the various places in Eretz Yisrael (the Land of Israel). He reveals these places in the context of history and the present, as well as the context of the Jews and the surrounding nations.

Chapters of the Fathers—Pirkei Avot

"Chapters of the Fathers," the classic Hebrew text *Pirkei Avot*, is often referred to in Jewish life by its other name, "Ethics of The Fathers."

Capturing the most famous sayings passed down from the time of Moses, this is one of the best-known Jewish texts worldwide. It reveals how the early Jewish fathers applied the newly written Torah to their lives, advice that Jews still widely use today.

Wonder how Jewish family life still thrives in the twenty-first century? Look no further. Wonder how Jews first learned how to reason from their Hebrew Scriptures? Look no further. Simply put, this course will teach you more than just how to "think like a Jew," it will teach you how to "think like a Jew in your own home." That's the difference between academic knowledge and practical wisdom.

Experience Rabbi Elan Adler's winsome, compelling style firsthand as he introduces himself and then introduces to you this foundational text of Jewish life, and you'll find yourself eagerly anticipating the arrival of each week's surprisingly refreshing lesson.

Pray Like a Jew

What better way for us to dedicate the launching of Root Source to the Almighty God than by turning to Him in prayer in the very first class recorded on Root Source, as taught by the CEO, Gidon Ariel.

In this foundational channel, you will have the opportunity to deepen your relationship with God by learning to pray alongside Jews who turn to Him in prayer each morning. Gidon will teach you every word he prays, and give you his insights to the meaning and beauty behind it all. Let's join Gidon and learn what it means to Pray Like a Jew!

Moses: Profile of a Leader

The prototypical leader of the Old Testament, second only to God himself, is undoubtedly Moses, or *Moshe* in the original Hebrew.

But who was this man? What were his personality traits, his leadership qualities, and his characteristics that we can learn from and apply to our own lives?

Join Gidon Ariel as we delve into the Jewish Sages' traditions about Moses and discover what it takes to be a God-inspired leader in our lives today.

In the year since we launched Root Source I, Bob, have often pondered on the "why" question: Why are Christians interested in learning their Jewish roots by interacting directly with Israeli-Jewish teachers? I have come up with four main reasons:

- **Context**–Jewish context allows Christians to understand the Bible more deeply, because it was and is a Jewish book, and it is Jewish practices and Jewish knowledge that create that context.

- **Deeper insight**–Many Christians are amazed to discover the insights of great Jewish scholars of the past two thousand years, who make valuable observations in Jewish writings such as the Talmud, the Midrash, and commentaries–writings that have been completely overlooked in Christian history.

- **Relationship**–Many Christians, even though they do not have Jewish heritage, find within themselves a longing to connect with Jews, especially to those in Israel. There is something mysteriously drawing them to the Land and to the People.

- **To be a blessing**–An increasing number of Christians want to help repair the sins of the past by showing modern-day Jews honor, respect, and friendship without an agenda. They realize that being willing to sit and learn and ask meaningful questions is exactly the way to be a tangible blessing to Israel, to walk differently from their Christian forefathers, who often approached Jews with arrogance and a sense of superiority.

I believe that these four things speak to something much larger than Root Source. They speak to Christians and Jews coming together respectfully in new ways in the years to come. Root Source is not an end in itself. Root Source is just a *parable* for what could happen when Christians and Jews "interact around our common Root Source–the Hebrew Scriptures." (Thanks to our friend, Dr. Marvin Wilson, for this fitting quote.)

Nobody knows where this larger view of interaction may go in the years ahead, but I have a hunch that it will be hastened by world affairs. When nations turn against Israel, Christians within those nations will stand with Israel and bless her.

What might that standing, that blessing, look like? I will offer you an answer within my area of my expertise: business. I see Christians partnering with Jewish and Israeli Jewish businesses more than ever before. I see Christians seeking out employment in businesses that bless Israel or the Jews. I see Christians starting new businesses together with Jews. I see Christians working in sales, marketing, and distribution for Israeli companies. I see Christians providing Israelis with services of artistic and linguistic expertise. I see Christians mentoring Israeli businesses, helping them through the bureaucratic mazes of their countries. The opportunities for Christians and Jews to work together are virtually unlimited. All these things are already happening in isolated cases, which mean that enormous opportunities still exist for those who want to explore them.

Imagine a future when a Jewish CEO in an Israeli company is talking to her Jewish marketing officer in Israel, discussing how to expand into Country A. Today, that conversation might first focus on: "What Jews do we know in Country A that can help us?" But imagine a future conversation where those two people ask each other: "What *Christians* do we know in Country A that can help us?" Such Christians would be the first to be considered for consulting positions and employment opportunities. As the first Israeli companies begin to be successful in Country A, other Israeli companies will follow, and other Christians in country A will see the benefit of engaging in Jewish business opportunities.

Blessing Israel is not just for the benefit of Israel. It is God's will and good pleasure that many will be blessed when Israel is blessed. How much more can Christians bless Israel when they have developed relationships with Jews in Israel! Be creative. Be bold. Be persistent. And don't stop until you have made useful connections with Jews and can find a way to be a blessing to them in your own country.

Baruch Hashem! May God be blessed, and may He bless us all to find a way to help each other in the years ahead. ✿

CHAPTER 22

Putting the Pieces Together

God is on the move.

Even as the world turns away from God, refusing to acknowledge that He exists and that He is an active participant in world affairs, God in turn is determined to act more openly, more overtly, to get our attention. His desire is not for judgment but for repentance. And even His judgments are measured over time because of His mercy, giving us the opportunity to wake up, acknowledge Him, and return to Him.

God's primary witness in world affairs is the nation of Israel: the People, the Land, and the State of Israel.

We have seen Israel as witness in the **Blood Moons**. Time after time through history, the Blood Moons witnessed His everlasting covenant to the Jewish People, marking their physical migrations—like a mini-Exodus—from a place of great trouble to a place of safety. The Blood Moons are a witness to His commitment to bring the Jews back to their Promised Land. And in the process, the world benefits, because every time one of these periods elapses, a new spiritual treasure is released into the world. The giving of the Torah itself on Mount Sinai, the Psalms of David, the writing down of the Oral Law, the Jewish prayer book, the invention of the printing press (enabling the Bible to reach the ends of the earth), the Dead Sea Scrolls, the Founding of the State of Israel—each of these is a treasure to all mankind.

We have seen Israel as witness in the **Shemitah**—a seven-year cycle inserted by God into the history of man, initiated soon after the Israelites entered the Promised Land. This cycle has been active, way before Israel was reborn in 1948, and today its impact permeates the Western nations and the entire world. It is the cycle by which God restores wholeness to the earth, and His means to bring a reckoning and a repayment of debts owed. It is an opportunity to bring social restoration, even as the enemy defiles those key moments to advance institutionalized godlessness. And most excitingly, the Shemitah need not be a mystery, as it is clearly spelled out as a 28-year cycle in Leviticus 26.

We have seen Israel as witness in the **Promises to Israel** of Genesis 12:3, "*Those who bless you I will bless, and the one who curses you I will curse.*" This is shown throughout history: nations that bless the Jewish people are rewarded, while nations that curse them decline. We showed how the United States suffered a Genesis 12:3 curse in the Crash of 1929 and the Great Depression, due to its decision to turn away from God's intention for it to be a place of refuge for Jews, taking on an "island mentality." The United States openly declared its desire to prevent changing its national ethnicity, but the primary concern was to prevent large numbers of Jews from emigrating from Europe, thereby indirectly increasing the magnitude of the Holocaust a dozen years later. Then the United States reversed that curse by joining World War II, and by sponsoring the rebirth of a Jewish State in 1948. We warn against actions that, God forbid, could usher in another Genesis 12:3 curse: the refusal to sell weapons to Israel or the formal recognition of a Palestinian State.

We have seen Israel as witness in the **Jubilee year**. God has moved precisely in time, in 49-year increments. In 1917, through the United Kingdom, He freed Jerusalem from the Ottoman Empire and prompted the Balfour Declaration. Then in 1967, through the Israel Defense Forces (IDF), He reunified Jerusalem as the eternal capital of Israel and liberated the heartland of Israel, Judea and Samaria. In 2015-16, what might God restore? We confidently assert that God's moves in Israel will reap spiritual blessings for the whole world, and we challenge and exhort Christians everywhere to not only pray for Israel during this time, but to proclaim freedom in all lands wherein they live.

In each of these four areas, we have made many individual predictions, which are summarized in Appendix B. We will be keeping a scorecard of our predictions at **www.root-source.com,** honestly assessing what was correct and what was not, and trying to understand what we missed and why.

How do all four puzzle pieces come together?

Two of these four—the Shemitah and the Jubilee—are both fixed in time. As the Shemitah year ended in September 2015, we look for

God's Shemitah responses as outlined in Chapter 16.

Regarding Jubilee, we will watch Israel carefully from Fall 2015 to Fall 2016.

The impact of the Blood Moons spans many, many years, and we are already seeing it in full force: the amazing rise of Israel and the peaking of the Western nations that had previously held full power over the Jews in their lands. But a massive migration of Western Jews, including residents of the U.S., to Israel has not happened yet, and we suspect it will happen in earnest only when Jews no longer feel welcome in their current countries of residence, and when Israel is considered safe. Blood Moons seem to be a sign of both: they show how peaking empires turn against their Jewish populations, and they show Israel as a place of safety from external attack, once the second of the four Blood Moons has passed.

But the most difficult prediction is the Genesis 12:3 curse against the United States. We hope never to see another one, but what would happen if we did? It would be the most dramatic of all, and could happen anytime! The year 1929 saw a Genesis 12:3 curse, followed by a Shemitah year in 1931. What if they occurred in reverse order this time? What if we incur a judgment from the Shemitah in Fall 2015– a judgment not as economically focused like the one we incurred in 2008, but one that begins with the beasts of the field being let loose as described in Chapter 16? And then what if our nation were to additionally curse Israel in the next seven years, bringing upon ourselves a double judgment in the same seven-year Shemitah cycle? And finally, if such a curse were attempted against Israel before the end of the Jubilee year in Fall 2016, would it not be utterly poetic for God to transform that attempted curse into the next great restoration of land to the Jews, and a mighty coming together of Jews and Christians worldwide?

Israel FIRST! makes many predictions about the moves of God, but the overall message of this book is not just to *know* that God is on the move upon Israel first and then to the rest of the world, but to find ways to *get involved* with that move. The opportunity to *bless Israel* is a commandment for nations, churches, families, and even individuals. Every individual who blesses Israel joins with the God of Abraham.

There is something new here. Jews reaching out to Christians is new. Christians responding humbly to that outreach is equally new. This call to come together is a divine call, issued by the Almighty. It is God's call, not ours. For sure the work God does will be multifaceted and beautiful, and much larger than anything we at Root Source might ever accomplish alone.

How all this will play out is up to God, but we can be sure that Almighty God, *Hashem*, is on the move and that He will eventually receive all the glory due His name! *Baruch Hashem!*

We encourage you, dear reader, to ponder how God wants you to participate in His plans for Israel. Then, whatever God tells you–and your friends together with you–go and do! ✡

A Summary of *Israel FIRST!* Views

*I*srael FIRST! has added to the discussions!

The left column is not the view of any particular author or person; rather, it is our perception of what interested Christians have come to believe about them. Christians read from multiple sources—often reading between the lines—and draw their own conclusions from their personal belief systems about the End Times. The left column is our attempt to capture what we think is generally believed.

The right column contains our response to those perceived beliefs and where to read more.

After each comparison table is a list of new ideas that we have added for consideration in this book. Naturally, not every item we list as new is new to every reader, but feedback from Christians who took our Root Source courses in 2015 cause us to perceive them as generally new.

Blood Moons	
Commonly Held Christian View	*Israel FIRST! View*
Blood Moons are causing Christians to pay more attention to the Jewish Calendar and Israel.	Strongly agree. In fact it is an indication that Christians in general need to pay more attention, and be more respectful of Israel.
Blood Moons indicate that judgment is coming to the U.S.	Yes, judgment is coming to the U.S., but not as a direct result of the Blood Moons. Rather, Blood Moons indicate that the U.S. is peaking in power over the long term. It is the Shemitah and Genesis 12:3 passages that indicate the U.S. is about to be judged. (See Chapters 9, 12, and 17.)
Primary scripture is Joel 2:31: The sun will turn into darkness and the moon into blood before the great and awesome day of the LORD comes.	This Scripture does not fit well, because Blood Moons occur after periods of trouble, not before. Instead, we use the book of Exodus as a model for God bringing Israel from a difficult situation to a new situation. (See Chapters 5 and 6.)

Blood Moons

Commonly Held Christian View	Israel FIRST! View
The main Blood Moons of historical interest are 1967-1968, 1949-1950, and 1493-1494	We have discovered that all of the Blood Moons are historically important and show a pattern of a mini-Exodus, even the ones that occurred before the common era (BCE). We used all these in the development of our theory, not just the recent Blood Moons. (See Chapter 6.)
The Blood Moon on Sept 28, 2015, visible in Israel, is an omen of war for Israel.	We take the opposite view. We see the Blood Moons as a positive gift to the Jews, a witness to God's faithfulness to bring the Jews into the Promised Land. Wars, when they occur, are between the first and second Blood Moons. We are past that timeframe, so Israel is in a period of celebration and safety. We predict that there will be no war on Israel soil in the next few years and that Israel is a good long-term investment. (See Chapters 6 and 10.)
Blood Moons indicate the Messiah's return is near.	Messiah's return is not directly predicted by the Blood Moons. Instead, they are a witness to God's eternal covenant with the Jewish people. The re-establishment of the Jewish homeland is a sign of the nearness of the Messiah. (See Chapter 7.)

New Blood Moon Ideas in *Israel FIRST!*

• The solar eclipse on March 20, 2015 was rarer than the Blood Moons because it touched the North Pole on the first day of Spring, the first day of the Hebrew month Nissan. (See Chapter 2.)

• We issued a call to prayer of Isaiah 11:9 for the two minutes of this total solar eclipse. (See Chapter 2.)

• A theory cannot be separated from its own backstory and the story of the person who discovered it. (See Chapter 3.)

• At the exact same time the Jews were preparing to be expelled from Spain, a solar and lunar eclipse were marking North and South America as a future homeland for the Jews. (See Chapter 4.)

• Facts are accurate enough when you allow them to challenge the weaknesses of your own arguments. Otherwise, you aren't teaching, you're selling. (See Chapter 5.)

- All world history needs to be viewed through the lens of Israel and the Jews if we ever want to understand world history from God's point of view. (See Chapter 5.)

- Bigger theories require more Scripture than smaller ones. (See Chapter 6.)

- We put forth a new theory of the Blood Moons that seems to solve problems from earlier theories, and fits all of the Blood Moon Tetrads. (See Chapters 5 and 6.)

- The Blood Moons may well be signaling a new era of positive, productive relationship between Christians and Jews. (See Chapter 7.)

- Christians need to expect a very large Exodus of Jews from Europe and the U.S. to Israel. (See Chapter 7.)

- We issued a joint call to prayer with Mark Biltz to pray Psalm 122 for the Peace of Jerusalem during the 4 minutes 44 seconds Blood Moon on April 4, 2015. (See Chapter 8.)

- The Blood Moons are primarily intended by God to be a gift to the Jews. (See Chapter 8.)

- Each wave of Blood Moons comes with spiritual treasure given by Jews to the world. (See Chapter 8.)

- A Blood Moon Tetrad may have occurred during the original Exodus out of Egypt. (See Chapter 8.)

Shemitah

Commonly Held Christian View	Israel FIRST! View
For reasons not fully understood, the U.S. has exhibited a 7-year pattern that correlates to the Shemitah cycle.	Strongly agree. (See Chapter 12.)
The stock market is an excellent way to see the Shemitah's impact.	Strongly agree. (See Chapters 12 and 13.)
Shemitah impacts the U.S. because the U.S. was founded on biblical principles.	No. Shemitah was designed to impact the entire world from its inauguration. We think the current view is too U.S.-centric. (See Chapter 12.)
Shemitah has a cycle of 28 years, such as 1917 to 1945, and 1945 to 1973. It is seen through the building of "towers," such as the Empire State Building and the Twin Towers, and correlates to these cycles.	Strongly agree. But we also believe we are halfway through another one of those 28-year cycles. (See Chapter 16.)
The impact of Shemitah has grown stronger since 2001, with stock market drops in 2001 and 2008, coming specifically on Elul 29.	Strongly agree. (See Chapter 16.)

Shemitah

Commonly Held Christian View	Israel FIRST! View
The Shemitah tells us when God might act, but not what He will do.	We believe God has forecasted His planned actions in advance. (See Chapter 16.)

New Shemitah Ideas in Israel FIRST!

- We explain for Christians the traditional Jewish perspective on the Shemitah. (See Chapter 11.)

- The Shemitah is the central cycle for all world economies. (See Chapter 12.)

- Christians should consider the possibility of putting something (such as investments) "to rest" during the Shemitah year to honor God and participate in the Sabbath rest. (See Chapter 13.)

- The story of Joseph is an excellent way to look behind the curtain of how God works in seven-year cycles. It not only tells us about God, but what He expects from us, which is to be able to bless others. (See Chapter 14.)

- The seventh year of the Shemitah cycle is designed by God for social restoration. The enemy knows this and attempts to defile that very year with social degradation. (See Chapter 15.)

- We offer a brand-new scriptural model using Leviticus 26 to explain exactly where we are in the cycle of judgment for the U.S. Following that model, we predict how God will respond in the next Shemitah cycle (2015-2022) and in the cycle after that (2022-2029). We refrain at this time from commentary about what might happen after 2029 if we do not repent, even though the model predicts it. (See Chapter 16.)

Promises to Israel in Genesis 12:3

Commonly Held Christian View	Israel FIRST! View
Christians are generally familiar with the application of Genesis 12:3 "Those who bless you I will bless, and the one who curses you I will curse." to the nation of Israel, that blessing Israel is a good thing and can bring benefits.	Agree. (See Chapter 18.)
Christians are not always familiar with how Israel can be blessed in practical ways.	Agree. (See Chapter 21 for some new ideas.)
If a nation ever turns away from Israel, then God will turn away from that nation.	Strongly agree. But we provide more details for what a Genesis 12:3 curse might look like. (See Chapters 17 and 18.)

Promises to Israel in Genesis 12:3

Commonly Held Christian View	Israel FIRST! View
The U.S. has historically only been a blessing to the Jews.	No. We cursed Israel in 1929 by closing our doors to the Jews of Europe. (See Chapter 17.)

New Promises to Israel Ideas in Israel FIRST!

- The U.S. was blessed greatly because of its blessing Israel through helping to establish a homeland for the Jews. (See Chapters 9, 10 and 17.)

- We offer for Christians some Jewish commentary on Genesis 12:3. (See Chapter 18.)

- While Shemitah explains many financial downturns, it does not explain the biggest one of all—the Crash of 1929 and the Great Depression. We present new evidence that the 1929 Crash and the Great Depression were part of a Genesis 12:3 Curse on America. (See Chapter 18.)

- We explain two decisions that the President of the United States has the power to make, which would bring a Genesis 12:3 Curse on the US once again. (See Chapter 18.)

The Coming Jubilee

Commonly Held Christian View	Israel FIRST! View
Confusion abounds about whether Jubilees ought to occur every 49 years or every 50 years.	Agree about the confusion. Both sides of the Jewish debate on that topic are described in detail. (See Chapter 19.)
Jonathan Cahn and others believe they occur every 49 years.	We agree. (See Chapter 20.)
The actual year of the most recent Jubilee is a matter of speculation. It can never be known for sure.	No. We agree with the case as proposed in The Mystery of the Shemitah, Epilogue Part 2, suggesting Fall 1917-18, Fall 1966-67, and Fall 2015-16. (See Chapter 20.)
What happens on Jubilee is something of a mystery.	God wants Jubilee to be fully understood and to be restored to its rightful position in His calendar.
The Jubilee as written in the Torah is a matter pertaining to Israel alone.	While Israel was commanded to observe Jubilee, its impact is felt worldwide. (See Chapters 19 and 20.)

New Jubilee Ideas in *Israel FIRST!*

- Jubilees have never been observed in Jewish history. (See Chapter 19.)

- Jewish religious practices evolve slowly, so it could take many years for agreement to be reached on how to observe the Jubilee. (See Chapter 19.)

- We suggest that God will use the 2015-16 Jubilee year to restore parts of the Promised Land back to its legal owners. (See Chapter 20.)

- Jubilee is an opportunity for Christians to pray for Israel and to receive blessings in their own nations. (See Chapter 20.)

- Christians can honor the Jubilee by helping Jews return to Israel. (See Chapter 20.)

- Jubilee will have a very positive spillover effect on the Christian world. (See Chapter 20.)

- Jubilee, like the Shemitah, is an opportunity for Christians to decide to put something to "rest" to honor God. (See Chapter 20.)

New Concluding Ideas in *Israel FIRST!*

- Being willing to learn from Israeli Jews is a way to bless Israel. (See Chapter 21.)

- Christians need to learn how to be a blessing to Israel personally, even if their own nation is turning against Israel. (See Chapter 21.)

- One of the best ways to bless Israel is to help Israeli businesses grow. This includes seeking employment opportunities from them, starting new businesses, or helping them expand into your own area. (See Chapter 21.)

- We are beginning a great new era of cooperation between Christians and Jews. Finding a way to participate in this great move is one of the most important opportunities before us. (See Chapter 22.)

List of Predictions

These are the predictions made in this book, listed by chapter. Consult each chapter for context and more details.

Please go to our website **www.root-source.com** to see how we score ourselves for accuracy over time.

Chapter 7. A New Story Begins

- The tetrads of 1949, 1967 and 2014 might represent three phases of one big move of God.

- What might the 2014 tetrad, the third tetrad in the cluster, signify? The Temple Mount!

- The 2015 Blood Moon phenomenon is perhaps actually a message from God to the Jewish people, to recognize that this outreaching in friendship by Christians is a sign for us to recognize the sincerity of that overture and to work together to bring about the expansion of the knowledge of God amongst Jews, Christians, and all people worldwide.

- The coming together of Jews and Christians is a work God wants to take to a whole new level.

- The United States is peaking.

- The last eight Blood Moons—the four in 1967/1968, as well as the most recent four in 2014/2015—may be a sign that American Jews will move back to Israel in much greater numbers than ever before.

- This is not the beginning of the end for Israel; rather, it's the end of the beginning.

Chapter 9. The Peaking of the United States

- We could possibly be looking at the peak of all of Western Civilization as we know it?

- The three tetrads in 1949, 1967 and 2014 indicate:

    o 1949/50 The Moral Peak of the United States
    o 1967/68 The Political Peak of the United States
    o 2014/15 The Economic Peak of the United States

- The days of mourning [like Tisha Be'av] will turn into days of joy for the Jews. This is possibly a positive harbinger of the future. (Explicit Biblical prophecy, Zechariah 8:19)

- God considers the lives of some of His saints very precious and preserves their lives in trying times, ending their lives before trouble comes. Isaiah 57:1-2. This may well have been fulfilled in part by the passing of Lance Lambert.

- Lance Lambert's prophetic word:

> Everything in Israel will change, upside down and inside out. Nothing will be where it used to be. They will seek to destroy Israel, but they will see that they are destroying themselves. Bibi Netanyahu has been faithful. Everything will change, and the only certainty is this: "I am The Lord. Do not fear, I will defend Israel and I will save her. You will suffer, and suffer greatly, because I will turn everything upside down and inside out. I will not fail you and I will not fail Israel. Take note when you see these things. I am in the battle and I have won. Keep your eyes on My power and you will be safe."
>
> We have to know the Lord and the power of His resurrection. It's not enough to be a dead Christian. If The Lord says it's going to be unparalleled, then it is going to be unparalleled. It's worth it all–knowing Him and trusting in Him.
>
> "Watch Russia, for she is up to no good. Watch her carefully," says the Lord. "With your own eyes, you shall see My triumph over darkness and evil. Trust Me," says the Lord.

Chapter 10. The New Ancient Israel

- The United States is a nation that is peaking, and has reached its economic climax.

- Israel is a nation that is presently being seeded.

- What we are seeing regarding Israel's growth is *nothing*

compared to the sprouting we might see in the next few years. Even as other parts of the world deteriorate, Israel will advance at an accelerated rate in these momentous times.

- Caution: Israel is an emerging economy, considered to be quite small overall, and easily influenced by world events. Israel should be considered as a long-term investment only.

- When considering investing in Israel, there is another top concern—the ever-present possibility of war. In Chapter 6 we showed that the pattern of the Blood Moons does not indicate major wars immediately *after* the Blood Moons are completed. That this observation contradicts what some others are predicting about the meaning of the Blood Moons. Based on the historical pattern, I am not expecting a war against Israel in the near future.

- Investing in Israel now seems like investing in the United States in 1948, with the strong probability of increasing your investment 183 times over 67 years – an excellent long-term investment. I personally believe there is no better long-term investment than the country of Israel.

Chapter 12. How Powerful is the Shemitah?

- A fundamental shift in the understanding of what is the center of gravity of economic activity around the world will become evident. The Hebrew Calendar is at the center of all nations, including the United States.

- Wise business people will make key business and investing decisions using the seven-year cycle, aligned with the Hebrew calendar.

- Ultimately, I do not believe we will ever find a field of endeavor where God is present or wants to be present in every field of endeavor. He wants a witness of Himself made known to everyone. Man may choose to ignore it or may deny it, but every person will be without excuse.

- Shemitah will be an increasing source of frustration for nations that do not acknowledge God.

- Shemitah will also give Israel a new opportunity to be used by God. God will showcase His principles in the Nation of Israel to the whole world.

Chapter 14. Joseph: Feast and Famine

- We are entering a transition during the next seven years. We must prepare for a surprise: God's plan for judgment that will be more complex, more extensive, and more pervasive than imagined.

- **God's plans for redemption are good beyond anything we can see, a plan for good, a plan to give us a future and a hope.**

- We do not fully understand God's purposes for the next seven years. We do not understand what He is fully trying to accomplish. But if we press into Him, we will know. It should not be too long. Give us a year or two, into 2016 or 2017 at most, and we should be able to see God's larger plan. We will understand where our view is too small, and we will behold God's "bigger picture." We will see God's heart and embrace His greater purposes as we begin to understand.

- God will do a new thing soon, He will launch something important within a two-year span.

- There will be a physical movement of His Jewish people in a more profound way than we have ever seen; for instance, large numbers of American Jews making Aliyah to the Land of Israel.

- One great benefit of a famine—or any disaster—is that many people will awaken out of their stupor, humble themselves, and admit they need help.

- Famine brings opportunities for the godly. That is our job too— *tikkun olam*—to help repair the world and provide in times of trouble. Famines do bring opportunities for those who love God.

- In times of difficulty, people move toward drugs, alcohol, and other forms of addiction. Some will move even further down that path to escape the difficulties surrounding them. In future days, there will be a segment of our society that will go into slavery. Maybe they are slaves to sin now, but it will get even worse. They will be in more debt. They will endure even worse forms of addiction that will take hold of them. Let us pray that many will be saved out of that deep abyss through God's mercy.

Chapter 15. Shemitah and Society

- Gay marriage is like a hydrogen bomb.

- Because God is slow to anger and abounding in lovingkindness, He may give us a few years to come to our collective senses and reverse this specific Gay Marriage interpretation.

- Because of the massive, dominant sexual sin culture that has taken hold in our Western nations, God has every right to judge us severely, and that response is ripe to begin immediately.

- Regarding gay marriage specifically, we should begin looking for what may be a "new" kind of response from God. He may choose to unleash confusion on false marriage covenants, just as he did with the Tower of Babel.

- If the secularists have their way, we Christians could be placed in virtual cultural exile, attacking us with legal ramifications and challenges, if not outright imprisonment. But we must take heart that even exile is not the end. In fact, God performed more miracles for the Jewish people during their Babylonian exile than He had for many years before that. He is able to work in exile. We also believe that where sin abounds, grace abounds even more. I believe in the coming days, we will see greater miracles taking place to restore and heal battered individuals from sexual sin.

- Christians might lose the right to refer to our homeland as a Christian nation, but even if that happens, we will never lose our deeper identity in God.

Chapter 16. Shemitah: God's Seven-Year Forecast

- We might now reaching the halfway point of a new 28-year cycle—a 28-year cycle that is going to decide the outcome of our nation.

- The following items define the primary method of God's [Shemitah] judgment upon us in the years 2015-2022:
  1. *I will let loose among you the beasts of the field,*
  2. *which will bereave you of your children*
  3. *and destroy your cattle*
  4. *and reduce your number*
  5. *so that your roads lie deserted.*
  6. *And if by these things you are not turned to Me,*
  7. *but act with hostility against Me...*

- The following items define the primary method of God's [Shemitah] judgment upon us in the years 2022-2029:

  1. *I will also bring upon you a sword which will execute vengeance for the covenant;*

  2. *and when you gather together into your cities, I will send pestilence among you,*

  3. *so that you shall be delivered into enemy hands.*

  4. *When I break off your staff of bread, ten women will bake your bread in one oven and they will bring back your bread in rationed amounts,*

  5. *so that you will eat and not be satisfied.*

  6. *Yet if in spite of this you do not obey Me,*

  7. *but act with hostility against Me...*

- We don't know if the model will ultimately be shown to be correct or not, but we will know a great deal more by 2018.

Chapter 17. When God Reluctantly Cursed America

- If we come against Israel or the Jews as a nation, *God does not have to wait for a seventh (Shemitah) year to act.* This is exactly what seems to have happened in the 1920s.

Chapter 18. Blessings and "God Forbid"

- A Genesis 12:3 curse may descend upon America if, God forbid, the United States stopped selling weapons to Israel, or if a US president formally recognizes a Palestinian State.

- Even if a nation were to curse Israel, God forbid, there is hope to undo the curse, to unwind it. There is hope of repentance and returning to the way of blessing.

Chapter 19. The Jewish Background of the Jubilee

- Perhaps the long-forgotten observance of the Jubilee years will be revived, representing something whose significance will only be understood as the decades and centuries and Jubilees unfold.

Chapter 20. A Promised Jubilee for a Promised Land

- We make the case in this chapter that God will use the 2015-16 Jubilee year to restore parts of the Promised Land back to its legal owners.

- The principle of the Jubilee is that no matter when you start to take possession of an area of Israel, it reverts back to the original owners in the Jubilee Year. The Temple Mount was handed over in the Jubilee year of 1967, so that has been out of Israeli control for the full 49 years. Area A of the West Bank was released by Israel in the 1990s, less than 20 years ago.

- How might this retaking of those lands possibly come about? One likely way might be as a *response* to something that the United States might do. For instance, as we discussed in Chapter 18, God forbid, the USA recognizing a Palestinian State.

- Whenever God does something in Israel or for the Jewish People, the benefits spill over to the rest of the world. We can celebrate the Jubilee not only with the Jews and their Land; we can celebrate that God wants to proclaim freedom throughout *our* land. In what form will that freedom take? Will there be massive repentance, praise God? Will there be major revival, will there be miracles, the likes of which have never been seen before? We should proclaim freedom and see what God does during that proclamation. Yes, waiting to see what God will do is an act of faith, but it is also an act of coming alongside God and His proclamation to the Earth. This may never happen again in our lifetime! We must be bold in our asking, and see how God responds!

Chapter 21. The How-To Guide to Blessing Israel

- I see Christians partnering with Jewish and Israeli Jewish businesses more than ever before. I see Christians seeking out employment in businesses that bless Israel or the Jews. I see Christians starting new businesses together with Jews. I see Christians working in sales, marketing, and distribution for Israeli companies. I see Christians providing Israelis with services of artistic and linguistic expertise. I see Christians mentoring Israeli businesses, helping them through the bureaucratic mazes of their countries. The opportunities for the ways in which Christians and Jews can work together are virtually unlimited.

Chapter 22. Putting the Pieces Together

- Blood Moons are a sign of two things simultaneously: they show how peaking empires turn against their Jewish populations, and they show Israel as a place of safety from external attack, once the second of the four Blood Moons has passed.

- The most difficult prediction is the Genesis 12:3 curse against Israel. It could happen anytime. The year 1929 saw a Genesis 12:3 curse, followed by a Shemitah cycle in 1931. They may appear in reverse order this time. We may, God forbid, incur a judgment from the Shemitah in Fall 2015—a judgment not as economically focused like the one we incurred in 2008, but one that begins with the beasts of the field being let loose as described in Chapter 16. And, if our nation were to additionally curse Israel in the next seven years, we would bring upon ourselves a *double judgment* in the same seven-year Shemitah cycle. And finally, if such a curse were attempted against Israel before the end of the Jubilee year in Fall 2016, God might transform that attempted curse into the next great restoration of land to the Jews, and a mighty coming together of Jews and Christians worldwide. ✡

Index

Shalom friend,

This book, *Israel FIRST!*, has been a labor of love for us. We hope that you have enjoyed reading this book as much as we have enjoyed creating it for you.

If you have any comments, please post them on
www.root-source.com/blog/israel-first,
we will be happy to connect with you there.

SPECIAL OFFER

We are happy to offer you your entire purchase price
of *Israel FIRST!* back as a rebate!

Simply go to **www.root-source.com/secret-refund**
(password: book) and sign up for Root Source.
Make sure to include your book/kindle/audio book purchase
details (what you bought, where you bought it, price you paid,
receipt number)

If you select an annual subscription, you will get a discount of your
purchase price above and beyond the 17% discount!

If you select the monthly payment, you will get a refund of your
purchase price after 6 months of membership!

Thank you, and looking forward to learning with you,

~ Gidon and Bob

P.S. Make sure you sign up there for our free e-newsletter too!

www.root-source.com/secret-refund